years with

CAR AND DRIVER

First published in the United States of America by
Filipacchi Publishing
1633 Broadway
New York, NY 10019

ISBN 1-933231-00-9

Printed in China

Design by Keith D'Mello
Editing and proofreading by Jennifer Ditsler-Ladonne

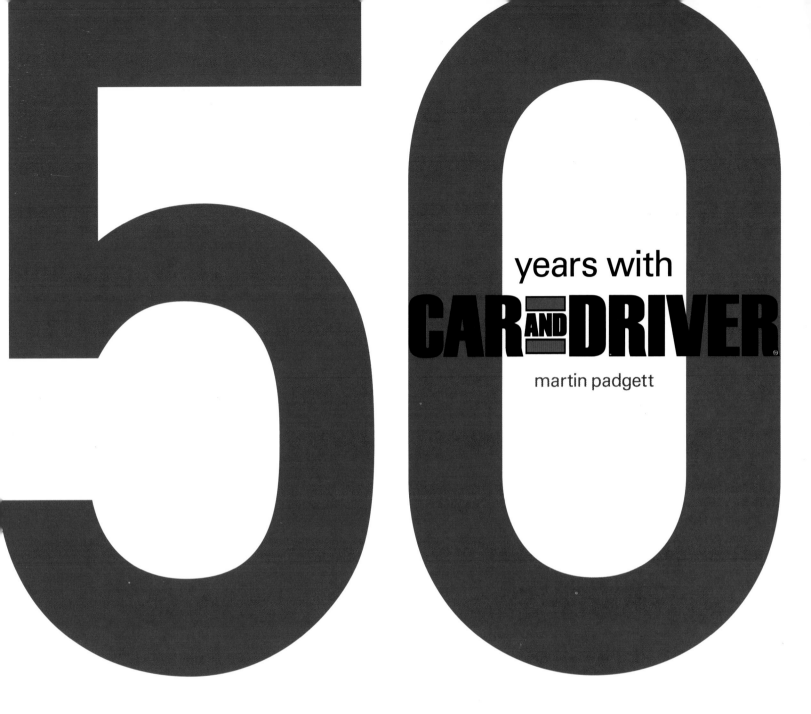

50

years with

CAR AND DRIVER

martin padgett

filipacchi publishing

Contents

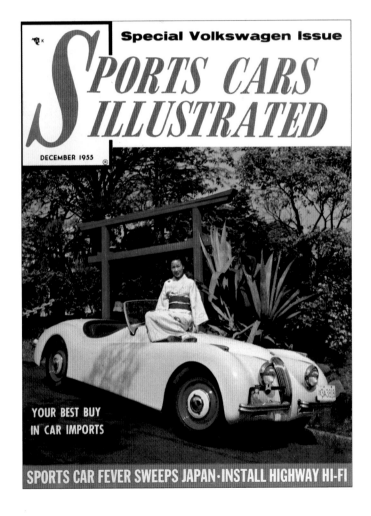

5

Foreword

Everybody claims to have passion these days. Whether selling water-softener salt at Wal-Mart or designing a new cup holder for the latest sport-utility vehicle, every employee is purportedly passionate about his or her job—until he or she moves on to a new position—working for a different company in a completely unrelated business.

Here at *Car and Driver*, however, there has always been a deep and committed dedication to cars and the joys of driving them. Not only have there been several core writers who have been with the magazine for 10, 20, and even 30 years, but almost every key staff member who has hooked up with *Car and Driver* has also had an abiding love of automobiles and the experiences related to them.

Karl Ludvigsen, for example, who was the editor when the magazine's name changed from *Sports Cars Illustrated* to *Car and Driver* almost 40 years ago, has spent his entire career at the product-intensive tip of the automotive business. After his tenure as a magazine journalist, Ludvigsen went on to a successful career in the auto industry, rising to a vice-presidency at Ford before founding an automotive consulting business and writing more than three dozen books about cars and the auto industry.

David E. Davis Jr. has served two tours of duty as editor and publisher of *Car and Driver*. When he wasn't so occupied, however, he was selling ads for *Road & Track* magazine, writing advertising copy for Chevrolet, and starting another car magazine from scratch. If automobiles weren't involved in a job, Davis wasn't interested.

Same goes for Brock Yates, who has been with *Car and Driver* continually since 1964. Patrick Bedard was a Chrysler engineer before he joined the magazine in 1967. I designed engines for Ford before joining up in 1980. Over the years, numerous staff writers have devoted a decade or more of their careers to *Car and Driver*.

The attraction has always been simple to those of us fascinated with four-wheeled machinery. That's because being on the staff of *Car and Driver* meant a seat at the leading edge of automotive culture. In fact, as members of the staff, we not only had a ringside seat watching the latest developments in our favorite pastime, but we could also influence the evolution and direction of automotive development.

When the auto industry was laid low by the twin burdens of high fuel prices and strict exhaust emissions controls in the '70s, the editors at *Car and Driver* responded with project cars that were created to enhance the performance of the anemic production offerings.

During that time the editors also took to the racetracks in search of excitement, technical innovation, and the shear fun of competition. Some of the competition took place on public roads as Brock Yates organized several Cannonball runs, which were outlaw races from New York to Los Angeles. Even during the dark times, our editors have had no trouble enjoying cars and driving.

During the '80s, as cars gradually regained some of their lost muscle and acquired handling and braking to support their sheer speed, we stepped up our racing efforts and competed in dozens of production-based events, as well as other races where we could snag rides.

During my tenure, I've competed in the Press On Regardless SCCA Pro Rally and the Baja 1000, and at Bonneville and countless road races in various cars at major tracks. The object of the exercise was always to produce an interesting story for *Car and Driver* magazine. But the reward was the experience of pushing a car to its limits in a competitive environment.

Patrick Bedard's competitive fires burned even hotter. He parlayed his driving talent and magazine connections into two drives in the Indianapolis 500,

producing several fascinating first-person accounts along the way.

In the search for interesting stories, various writers explored other machines, such as jet fighters, nuclear submarines, house-sized earthmovers, various armored vehicles, and anything else that moved under its own power.

When not engaged in such motorized adventures, we've spent our time driving the latest and greatest products that the world's car manufacturers produce year after year, while picking the brains of their top executives and engineers to better understand the inner workings of these vehicles.

In short, we love our subject, which is why most of the dominant members of *Car and Driver*'s staff have, throughout its history, remained connected with the auto industry, even when they weren't associated with the magazine.

My 25 years with *Car and Driver* have been tremendously rewarding, and I believe every staff member who has been a part of our large family would express a similar sentiment. For 50 years, we've collectively worked to bring to life in the pages of the magazine the joy we've found in motoring. And we have every intention of continuing to do so for the next 50.

Csaba Csere, Editor-in-Chief

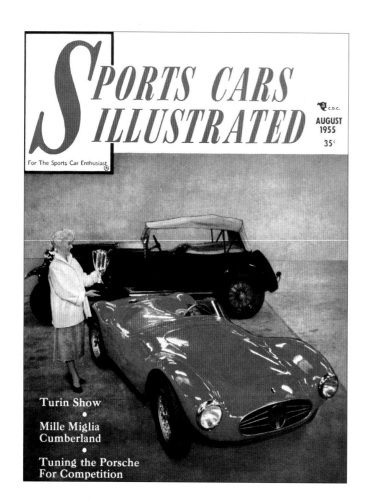

Sports Cars Illustrated — August 1955, 35¢
For The Sports Car Enthusiast

Turin Show
•
Mille Miglia
Cumberland
•
Tuning the Porsche
For Competition

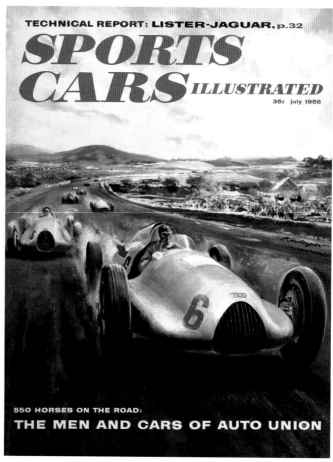

TECHNICAL REPORT: LISTER-JAGUAR, p.32

Sports Cars Illustrated — 35¢ july 1958

550 HORSES ON THE ROAD:
THE MEN AND CARS OF AUTO UNION

CAR and DRIVER
DECEMBER 1964 • 50 CENTS
WE ROAD TEST THE MGB AND THE CHEVY 409
16-PAGE ACCESSORY SECTION—GIFTS GALORE!

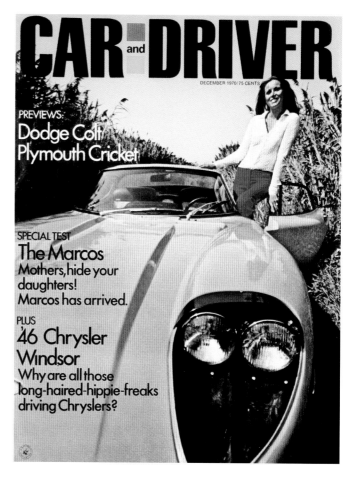

CAR and DRIVER
DECEMBER 1970/75 CENTS

PREVIEWS:
Dodge Colt
Plymouth Cricket

SPECIAL TEST
The Marcos
Mothers, hide your
daughters!
Marcos has arrived.

PLUS
46 Chrysler
Windsor
Why are all those
long-haired-hippie-freaks
driving Chryslers?

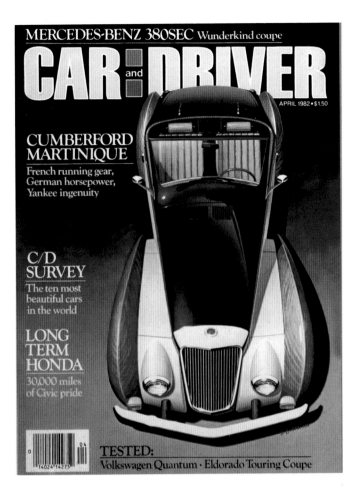

MERCEDES-BENZ 380SEC Wunderkind coupe

CAR and DRIVER

APRIL 1982 • $1.50

CUMBERFORD MARTINIQUE

French running gear,
German horsepower,
Yankee ingenuity

C/D SURVEY

The ten most
beautiful cars
in the world

LONG TERM HONDA

30,000 miles
of Civic pride

TESTED:
Volkswagen Quantum · Eldorado Touring Coupe

TESTS: 380-HP MERCEDES, PONTIAC GRAND AM

CAR AND DRIVER

JANUARY 1992 • CANADA $3.95 UK £1.95 $2.95

TEN BEST CARS

Most of them you can even afford.
See page 35.

Plus: Things That Need Inventing. Roadhouses.
Insanely Kustomized Kars. Winners and Losers.
The Toyota Previa after 30,000 hard miles.

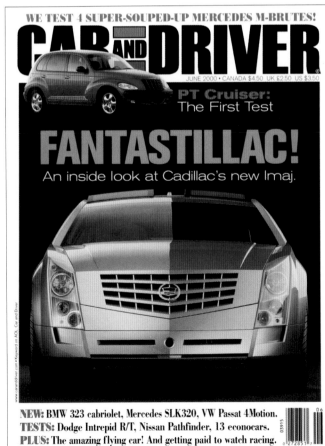

WE TEST 4 SUPER-SOUPED-UP MERCEDES M-BRUTES!

CAR AND DRIVER

JUNE 2000 • CANADA $4.50 UK £2.50 US $3.50

PT Cruiser:
The First Test

FANTASTILLAC!

An inside look at Cadillac's new Imaj.

NEW: BMW 323 cabriolet, Mercedes SLK320, VW Passat 4Motion.
TESTS: Dodge Intrepid R/T, Nissan Pathfinder, 13 econocars.
PLUS: The amazing flying car! And getting paid to watch racing.

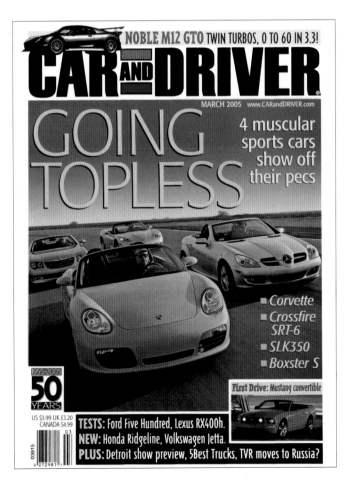

NOBLE M12 GTO TWIN TURBOS, 0 TO 60 IN 3.3!

CAR AND DRIVER

MARCH 2005 www.CARandDRIVER.com

GOING TOPLESS

4 muscular
sports cars
show off
their pecs

- Corvette
- Crossfire SRT-6
- SLK350
- Boxster S

First Drive: Mustang convertible

1955-2005
50 YEARS

US $3.99 UK £3.20
CANADA $4.99

TESTS: Ford Five Hundred, Lexus RX400h.
NEW: Honda Ridgeline, Volkswagen Jetta.
PLUS: Detroit show preview, 5Best Trucks, TVR moves to Russia?

1955

1962

From *Sports Cars Illustrated* to *Car and Driver*

"Bill Haley's *Rock Around the Clock* was the year's number one pop tune, the Chevy 265 V-8 was putting everything else on the trailer, and Senator Joe McCarthy was a dying drunk, probably more nearly forgotten then than now." So recalled editor David E. Davis, Jr. of the earliest days of what would become an institution in automotive journalism, not to mention a staple of study halls and dentists' offices everywhere. What began life as *Sports Cars Illustrated* opened its pages to readers in the middle of the 1950s, but within a few years it would be transformed into the largest automotive magazine in the world: *Car and Driver.*

1955

Tennessee Williams wins the Pulitzer Prize for "Cat on a Hot Tin Roof"

Winston Churchill resigns as British Prime Minister

Albert Einstein dies

>

But long before it became the Bible of midlife crises and 0-to-60 trivia buffs everywhere, *Car and Driver* would sputter before it ran smoothly. Fortunate to spring to life in the midst of a postwar economic boom, what became *Car and Driver* rode the transformation of American society into a prosperity machine never imagined before its day.

The origins of *Car and Driver* magazine lay in the ashes of World War II and the earliest years of the Cold War. In the late 1940s, President Truman steered the country and its economy back into civilian mode. As the war victor with the least devastating losses, America had a natural economic advantage in pulling out of the war's pall. Combat never destroyed America's factories, as it had in the European and Japanese theaters. And though casualties were heavy, America didn't lose entire generations of young men in turning back the Axis powers, as did England and France. Waves of young soldiers returned home to build families, homes, careers and dreams—and the nation's businesses were ready.

The automotive industry was among the first to revive. Their workforce returned and their factories relieved of wartime production, the automakers faced an unprecedented pent-up demand wrought by a nearly four-year drought of new vehicles. By 1947, American manufacturers were just, as *Car and Driver* columnist Warren Weith wrote in 1973, "getting the olive drab flushed out of the spray guns." For a while, everyone did well: even small brands like Studebaker, left moribund during the war years, staged sales comebacks.

Cars weren't the only winners: a housing boom mushroomed from low-interest G.I. Bill loans, as more and more Americans joined the home-owning middle class. They brought with them better jobs as well: prior to the war, America's progress from a farming society to an industrial one had been completed, and the transition to a new era where white-collar workers outnumbered blue-collar workers had already begun. The end of the war threw fuel on that trend. In a few short years, America built thousands of housing developments, hundreds of shopping malls and new factories, even an interstate highway system—and in the process, a new society based on the consumer economy.

As historian David Halberstam put it in his landmark history, *The Fifties*, "In the years following the traumatic experiences of the Depression and World War II, the American Dream was to exercise personal freedom not in social and political terms, but rather in economic ones. Eager to be part of the burgeoning middle class, young men and women opted for material well-being, particularly if it came with some form of guaranteed employment For the young, eager veteran just out of college, (which he had attended courtesy of the G.I. Bill), security meant finding a good white-collar job with a large, benevolent company, getting married, having children, and buying a house in the suburbs."

15

| The Warsaw Pact links the Soviet Union and its satellite states in Eastern Europe | The Brooklyn Dodgers beat the New York Yankees 4-3 in the World Series | James Dean dies in a head-on collision in the California desert | Rosa Parks defies Montgomery. Alabama's. bus segregation laws | **1956** |

With the return of soldiers crating up European sports cars and Jeeps alike and bringing them to America, and the boom in new car sales, the relatively new American car hobby was ripe for a boom itself. And it wasn't long before a rash of enthusiast magazines gunned for those Americans newly infatuated with their vehicles.

Car and Driver, and before it, *Sports Cars Illustrated*, has its roots in the slew of auto publications launched in the late 1940s, which included rivals like *Motor Trend* and *Road & Track*. The concept wasn't new: In Britain, particularly, the horseless carriage had spawned a newsstand full of weekly magazines. Including *Autocar and Motor*, which would eventually be merged after nearly a century in operation, Britain's automotive magazines can be traced to the turn of the 20th century.

In 1947, what would become *Car and Driver* arose from the offices of a small East Coast publisher. The distant ancestor of *Car and Driver* was a publication called *Speed Age*, started up in Hyattsville, Maryland, by a group of racing enthusiasts who were focused on writing a single magazine that could bridge a gulf in the speed crowd. According to contemporary accounts, in the postwar era, enthusiasts were either fans of European machinery or American-made iron, and usually not both: "Much of the trouble stemmed from the giant rift that had developed between the two worlds of enthusiasm—the hot rodders and the sports car set. It was a totally parochial world. Neither hot rodder nor sports car addict recognized the other—the oval track racers were separatists too, with stock car racing in its infancy and no one to challenge—or even paid a lot of attention

to Indianapolis," a 1969 retelling of magazine history put it. "This brand of automotive separatism was particularly virulent in Southern California, where most of the advertising support for automotive magazines was coming from at the time...this schism between the two camps of enthusiasts was fierce in the 1950s, and very few interchanges took place between their representative magazines...."

In short order, *Speed Age* began to sink and was rescued from the brink by a New York publisher named Harry Scharf. It would later peter out completely, but its subject so captured Scharf's attention that he created two other magazines: 1954's *Car Life*, which was later sold to the publishers of *Road & Track*, and *Sports Cars Illustrated*.

Scharf's timing was keen, but his business acumen wasn't necessarily as finely tuned. In 1956 he sold *Sports Cars Illustrated* to the Ziff-Davis group, which invested the energy of a major publisher into the magazine. They searched for editorial talent and came up with Ken Purdy, an acclaimed journalist and former editor of *True*, and John Christy, of *Honk*. Purdy, who would go on to win several *Playboy* writing awards, would be editorial chairman; Christy was the first editor of the magazine.

The earliest days of *Sports Cars Illustrated* were as muddled and revelatory as any new undertaking could be, as the magazine looked for inspiration and its own tone. Racing coverage featured prominently; American cars were nearly ignored. The magazine reached out to women drivers with reportage from women writers and undercut its own efforts with pieces recommending

16

Egypt and Israel battle over the Sinai Peninsula

Elvis Presley's "Heartbreak Hotel" hits the charts

>

Soviet troops crush uprising in Hungary

Dwight Eisenhower is reelected president with 457 electoral votes to Adlai Stevenson's 73.

SPORTS CARS ILLUSTRATED

C.D.C.

JULY 1955

35¢

For The Sports Car Enthusiast

Tuning the MG For Competition

Chuck Wallace Reports On the New Jag 140

A Day With the Lotus At the Sebring Race

18

sportswear for women waiting trackside for their racing paramours. Brilliant profiles, like those of the racer Portago, often anchored whole issues as Christy and Purdy put the pieces of what would become *Car and Driver* into order.

The format of the magazine hadn't yet crystallized but the mission had. *Car and Driver* would provide a lifestyle companion for those who raced or drove for pleasure. "If you were reading this magazine 30 years ago, you were reading *Sports Cars Illustrated*; that was our name then, a clear reflection of the motoring enthusiasms of the day," Patrick Bedard wrote in 1989. "Sports cars were more than just two-seaters. They were a way of life, with social protocol, weekend competitions, heroic tales of roadside repair, and animated nattering about the marque you owned and the one you hoped to own next—just as soon as you got the money together. Sports cars were much more than cars; they were the nucleus of a movement, a reason to get out of bed on Saturday morning."

The rabid enthusiasts that would define the magazine's readership weren't confined to them, though. As often happened at the magazine, writers came into the fold as readers of the magazine. Even in its earliest days as *Sports Cars Illustrated,* it had its fans, and among them were other writers.

"I knew I was going to work for the magazine as soon as I saw the first issue," recalled Warren Weith. "That was July of 1955. The first issue contained articles like 'With the Lotus at Sebring,' 'Tuning the MG,' and 'The Lead Foot Lady,' and even more esoteric information. I must admit that the contents fitted in, more or less, with the publication's promise of devotion 'to the owners and drivers in the sport.'"

Weith came to the magazine as an editor, and recalled how the magazine functioned as an extension of its young male stewardship. It was in 1957, "back when I had a crew cut and Eisenhower was president. Christy hired me. Possibly because I had worked for *Speed Age*, *Hot Rod Illustrated*, *Foreign Cars Illustrated*, and a few others that I'd rather not remember. I was young, the father of a newborn son, and knew everything. One thing I didn't know was just how much the magazine I was about to go to work for was going to become a part of my life.

"Most months were sort of three weeks long. It took about two weeks to put the magazine together. Ergo: let's work two weeks a month. Looking back now, God, how dumb we were. Most of us wanted the time to fool around with cars or be with people who fooled around with cars. And that's what we did, or what we thought we did. Worked two weeks each month. The rest of the time we went to races, auto cocktail parties, and parties for someone who had just come back from an auto show in Europe, or was about to leave for one. It was all cars, cars, cars seven days a week. And that's why we could slap out a passable—for its time—car magazine in two weeks flat. And even during those 14 days we still managed to find some time for fun and nonsense…. When I was young and brash I was involved in the day-to-day business of putting together this magazine. And that's just the way it came out—young and brash."

While Christy managed the daily operation of the magazine, Purdy's role came from his talent, not administration, Weith said. "Ken W. Purdy was the first

19

Alaska and Hawaii
become the 49th and
50th states

1960

Soviets shoot down U-2
spy plane piloted by
Francis Gary Powers

John F. Kennedy
is elected by a
narrow margin over
Richard M. Nixon

<

1956 Lancia D50, the year Ferrari
acquired the Lancia team, which came
to be known as a Lancia-Ferrari.

man in the United States to bring a command of the language to bear on all those terrible cars that were running up and down Main Street. He told us early on that they didn't have to be terrible and, as a matter of fact, as in England they could even be fun," Weith wrote in a 1973 issue of *Car and Driver*.

"Of course, I have to put this into perspective for all of you. The hot setup in the U.S., at that time at least, if your mother had to run the thing to the various stores (this was even before shopping centers) was something like a salesman's coupe, with a flat-head, six-cylinder engine. We, meaning my sainted mother and my all too knowledgeable father, had a Plymouth coupe, only because it was lighter than the other two. There wasn't much choice in those days. He and I thought it was great, particularly after we put a thinner head gasket into it, hot dog. And then Mr. Purdy came along in *True* magazine and spoiled everything. You just couldn't take the corners in that Plymouth, 'faster and faster.'"

The magazine had a decently firm footing when Christy and Purdy gave way, at least on the masthead, to another of the founding fathers of the magazine, Karl Ludvigsen. Ludvigsen was the editor of the magazine as it hit its stride as *Sports Cars Illustrated*. Editor from 1959 to 1961, Ludvigsen helmed the magazine as it changed its identity from *Sports Cars Illustrated* to *Car and Driver*. A technical editor under John Christy and then a European correspondent during his time in the army, Ludvigsen came back to the United States in the summer of 1959 and assumed the editor's chair.

"My tenure started with a bang: the Mercedes-Benz 300SL gullwing coupe," he recalled in *Car and Driver* in the 1990s. "Electrifying by any standards, it was the McLaren F1 of its day, outpacing the ordinary cars of the era. At the rock bottom of the 300SL market, I bought one in Germany in 1959, then sold it in Detroit in 1963. What a car. Of course, the 1955 automobile I really craved was the Lancia D50 Formula 1 car. We featured this brilliant design by Vittorio Jano on the September 1957 cover to announce the first installment of my two-part story on the machine. It was the first F1 car to make effective use of an unblown V-8—a layout that has won a few races since—and the first to use the engine itself as a major structural element of a tubular spaceframe. Modified by Ferrari, the D50 was Fangio's championship mount in 1956.

'A French car made similarly big news in 1955: the Citroën DS19. How modern could a car be? Hydraulic assist for everything, including steering, brakes, clutch, and gearshift, it offered front disc brakes, self-leveling hydropneumatic suspension, a "spokeless" steering wheel, single-nut wheel attachment, and a fiberglass roof. Moreover, the DS19's aerodynamics made other contemporary cars look as if they were standing still. Technologically they were.

"In America, we had our own winner that year: the 1955 Chevrolet Bel Air V-8. Compared with Chevy's ruthlessly simplified and purified engine, all other V-8s looked decades old. The car looked great too, with its Ferrari-like grille. Even before the 1950s concluded, we were modifying these V-8s to power race-winning cars like Scarabs and Listers. The Mouse motor keeps powering fast Chevrolets today. Just sneaking in under my timeline with a launch in late 1959, was the Ford Falcon. Contrasting it with the Corvair, we said: 'Ford has taken

21

22

the opposite tack from its major competitor and produced an absolutely normal compact car and in so doing has come up with something quite new.' The Falcon was, in fact, the breath of fresh air the industry needed after the suffocating excesses of the late 1950s. General Motors immediately copied the Falcon, building the Chevy II, later the Nova. Without those new platforms, there would have been no Mustang, Cougar, Camaro, or Firebird. By celebrating simplicity, the Falcon set new standards. It's a lesson some could relearn today."

Ludvigsen's success was in transforming the magazine into an enthusiastic journal matched with engineering rigor. Decrying the lack of a compensating spring in the Corvair's rear suspension, for example, Ludvigsen set the tone for the magazine's obsession with the technology of cars: "*Sports Cars Illustrated* shows this month as always its complete familiarity with the technics of the automobile—and, we hope, has given these bits of machinery some significance in your eyes."

And yet, as the first issues of *Car and Driver* were reaching newsstands, Ludvigsen left. "I've greatly enjoyed the years since Watkins Glen, 1951. I've seen the great cars race at Elkhart Lake, Riverside, Reims, Cumberland, Monza, Indianapolis, Niirburgring, Westover, Sebring, Spa, Bridgehampton, Harewood, Lime Rock, Thompson, and Monaco. I've seen them made at Porsche, Maserati, OSCA, Meyer-Drake, Ferrari, Bugatti, Abarth, BMW, and Mercedes-Benz. A nut about cars (which I am and seem doomed to remain) can't ask for much more than that," he wrote in the January 1962 issue.

"This is the last issue of *Car and Driver* that will be prepared under my direction, as I've recently joined General Motor's public relations staff. With the help of a wonderful staff

we've put together two years' worth and had a ball doing it. *Car and Driver*, of course, will carry on as usual, and I'll be reading it every month, along with you."

But to the magazine's great fortune, it didn't fail completely when ill-advised changes were taken after his departure. "When [Ludvigsen] resigned as editor a couple of years later, his successor lost it editorially at the fast turn, went deep into the woods at about a hundred ill-advised miles per hour, and destroyed everything Ludvigsen and Christy had worked so hard to build," wrote the man that would right the editorial ship. "Combined with readers' confusion regarding the name change, this short burst of malfeasance almost proved terminal. At that point I was hired to be the light at the end of the tunnel. It was a great opportunity for me, but it was a grim time for *Car and Driver* ."

That man was David E. Davis, Jr. After Ludvigsen's departure and the short tenure of Bill Pain, Ziff-Davis turned to Davis to steer the magazine back on track. Davis had served as the advertising manager of *Road & Track*, and knew the road-to-car-magazine success came from taut writing and love of its subject, as Purdy and Christy and Ludvigsen had shown. To that mix Davis would add candor and chutzpah, not an easy task for a Kentucky native with a fondness for good whisky.

But Davis's predecessors had laid the right pavement. And in its earliest days, from *Sports Cars Illustrated* to *Car and Driver*, the magazine had grown and had been shaped to fit the new sensibility of American drivers. At the dawn of the 1960s, vast changes were about to shift society and the automotive world from one extreme to the other, from the Edsel to the Beetle. And *Car and Driver* would be there to document it in a hair-raising, hard-charging, paradigm-changing way.

Baseball legend Ty Cobb dies	The Bay of Pigs invasion of Cuba is crushed	**1962**	Country singer Patsy Cline dies in a plane crash	**Marilyn Monroe dies of a suspected drug overdose**
				>

KARMANN-GHIA VOLKSWAGEN *Road Research Report*

CAR and DRIVER

JANUARY 1962 • 50 CENTS

*New
G. P. Engines
from Porsche,
B.R.M. and
Climax!*

23

Driving the Booming Sports Talbot-Lago

| John Glenn becomes the first American to orbit the earth | The Cuban Missile Crisis ends when the Soviet Union withdraws missiles from Cuba | Eleanor Roosevelt and William Faulkner die | Johnny Carson takes the helm at NBC's "Tonight Show" |

August 1957
Portago

By Ken W. Purdy

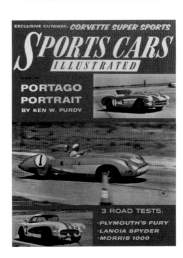

Don Alfonso Cabeza de Vaca y Leighton, Carvajal y Are, Conde de la Mejorada, Marquis de Portago, was 28 when he died at Guidizzolo, a few miles from Brescia and the end of the Mille Miglia, on the 12th of last May. Portago had been a flier, a jai alai player, a poloist, a steeplechase rider (the world's leading amateur in 1951 and 1952), an Olympic bobsledder and record holder, a remarkable swimmer, and he was at his death one of the dozen best racing drivers in the world.

He had never sat in a racing car until 1954, but he believed he would be champion of the world before 1960, and most of the men he ran against every week thought he very well might be—if he lived. Certainly, Portago was uniquely gifted. An athlete all his life, he was not a big man, not heavily muscled, but he had unusual strength, great endurance, abnormally sharp eyesight, and a quickness of reaction that was legendary among his friends. He was highly intelligent, courteous, and very much aware of the world around him.

Gregor Grant, editor of the British weekly *Autosport*, said just before the Mille Miglia, "A man like Portago appears only once in a generation, and it would probably be more accurate to say only once in a lifetime. The fellow does everything fabulously well. Never mind the driving, the steeplechasing, the bobsledding, the athletic side of things, never mind being fluent in four languages. There are so many other aspects to the man. For example, I think he could be the best bridge player in the world if he cared to try, he could certainly be a great soldier, and I suspect he could be a fine writer."

Portago's death, I suppose, proved out again two well-worn British aphorisms:

"Motor racing is a sport at which you get better and better until you get killed," and the other, less optimistic one, "There are two kinds of racing drivers: Those who get killed before they get good, and those who get killed afterward." But whether they will die at the wheel sooner or later or not at all, most men have to serve years of apprentice time before they make the big league: the racing team of one of the major factories. They drive sports cars, stock and not-so-stock, in rallies and dreary airport events; they cadge rides in scruffy hand-me-down racing cars, hoping to attract a wealthy sponsor's eye.

When and if they are invited to Italy or Germany or France or England to sign a racing contract, they have behind them thousands of miles of competition driven in dozens of makes of cars. This is standard, this is usual, and, as with most of the other rules, Portago broke it. Driving relief in his first race—the 1,000 kilometers for sports cars at Buenos Aires in 1954—he did three laps so badly that he dropped the car from second place to fifth, because he had never learned how to shift gears! To the day he died, he had driven few makes of competition automobiles: Maserati, Osca, Ferrari. He never drove the usual sports cars—MGs, Jaguars, and so on. For personal use, before he began to compete, he usually drove American cars: Fords and something else that may have been a

DeSoto, he wasn't sure. Explaining this the last time I talked with him, he said, "Automobiles bore me, I know next to nothing about them, and I care less. I have no sentimental attachment for a car," he said. "I can hardly tell one from another. Sometimes I make a little scratch on a car, in an inconspicuous place, so I can recognize it the next time I'm in it, so I can remember its defects. I'm not interested in cars. To me they're a means of transportation from point A to point B—that, or a machine for racing. When I have a racing car that I'm going to drive, I walk up to it and I look at it and I think, 'Now, is this son of a bitch going to hold together for the next 500 kilometers?' That's the only interest I have in it. And as soon as the race is over I couldn't care less what happens to it. I think some drivers are not only indifferent to their cars, but hostile to them. They look at the car before a race, and they think, 'Now, what is this thing going to do to me today? How is it going to let me down, or make me lose the race—or perhaps even kill me?'"

Portago's forthright disclaimer of interest in the machines on which his career was based was typical. To the outermost limits which custom and law allowed, the 12th Marquis de Portago said precisely what he pleased and did exactly what he liked. When he saw a girlfriend in the crowd lining the streets at the Rome checkpoint in his last race, he stood on the brakes, locked everything up, waited for her, kissed her, and held her in his arms until an official furiously waved him on. The girl, of course, was actress Linda Christian, and Portago was probably the only man in the race who would have allowed himself such a gesture. He would have done it at the risk of his life. Portago was an avowed romantic, and he had remarked that in another age he would have been

a crusader or a knight-errant. He often dressed in black. His hair was black and curly, usually long over his neck and ears, clinging to his head like a skull-cap.

He moved quickly and rarely smiled. He sometimes looked like a juvenile delinquent or a hired killer, but more often like what he was, a Spanish grandee.

The remark that he had been born three or four centuries too late was a cliché among his friends.

"Every time I look at Fon," one of them said, "I see him in a long black cape, a sword sticking out of it, a floppy black hat on his head, riding like a fiend across some castle drawbridge."

When he began to drive, Portago was not among the best-loved figures on the international circuit, nor was he when he died, if it comes to that. Lacking the technical skill to balance his bitterly competitive instinct, he was dangerous in his first races, and to most people he seemed arrogant and supercilious. He was reputed to be enormously wealthy, he was a great lady-killer, and if he was not pugnacious, still he was quick to fight. Most of the other drivers preferred to leave him alone. Nobody expected him to be around for very long in any case. Many thought he was just another aristocrat dilettante who would quickly lose interest in racing cars, but the few who knew his lineage were not so sure.

His mother, an Englishwoman who brought a great fortune to his father, is a firm-minded woman; and a determined lust for adventure, plus an inclination for government run through the Portago line. Spanish history is studded with the name—in the 16th century, one of Portago's forebears, Cabeza de Vaca, was shipwrecked off the Florida coast. He walked to Mexico City, recruiting an army as he

went. Another conquered the Canary Islands, another was a leader in the fight to drive the Moors out of Spain. Portago's grandfather was governor of Madrid, his father was Spain's best golfer, polo player, and yachtsman. He was also a fabulous gambler—said to have once won two million dollars at Monte Carlo—a soldier, and a movie actor. He died of a heart attack on the polo field, while playing against his doctor's orders. The last King of Spain, Alfonso XIII, was Portago's godfather and namesake.

Naturally enough, in the light of his background and his own propensity for high-risk sports, Portago was constantly accused of fearlessness, of clinging to a death wish, and what not. We talked at length about that the last time I saw Portago. We sat in my room in the Kenilworth in Sebring; Portago had been very punctual and had apologized for being unable to keep his promise that there would be no interruptions—he had placed a phone call to Caracas, and he asked if he might tell the operator to put it on my wire when it came through. I wanted to record the interview, and I asked him if he would object to a Minifon recorder. He said he would not, and he told me about an interview recording he was making for Riverside Records, a house specializing in sports-car material. We talked generalities for half an hour and then I turned the machine on. I mentioned a newspaper article that had said something to the effect that he "lived on fear."

"A lot of nonsense," Portago said. "I'm often frightened. I can get frightened crossing the street in heavy traffic. And I know I'm a moral coward. I can't even go into a shop to look around and walk out without buying something. As for enjoying fear, I don't think anybody enjoys fear, at least in my definition, which is a mental awareness of a danger to your body. You can enjoy courage—the performance of an act which frightens you—but not fear. I know my first ride in a racing car frightened me. That was the Mexican Road Race in 1953. I had been riding horses in competition for a long time, at least twice a week for two years, but I had to give it up because I put on some weight I couldn't get rid of. I couldn't get by no matter what I tried, and I tried most things: weighing in with papier-mâché boots and saddle, made to look like leather and weighing nothing, or hiding a five-pound weight on the scale so that the whole standard of weight for all the riders would go up! I met Harry Schell and

27

Luigi Chinetti at the Paris auto show in 1953, and Chinetti asked me to be his codriver in the Pan-American race. All he really wanted me for, of course, was ballast. I didn't drive a foot, not even from the garage to the starting line. I just sat there, white with fear, holding on to anything I thought looked sturdy enough. I knew Chinetti was a very good driver, a specialist in long-distance races who was known to be conservative and careful, but the first time you're in a racing car, you can't tell if the driver is conservative or a wild man, and I didn't see how Chinetti could get away with half of what he was doing. We broke down the second day of the race, but I had decided by then that this was what I wanted to do more than anything else, so I bought a three-liter Ferrari.

"I was fortunate, of course, in being able to buy my own car. I think it might have taken me five or six years longer to make the Ferrari team if I had had to look around for a sponsor and all that. I was lucky having had enough money to buy my own car—even if I'm not enormously wealthy. In those years I was perpetually in debt." (Portago earned perhaps $40,000 a year as a driver; he had various trust funds, but his mother controlled the family fortune, which was of American origin and reputedly very high in the millions.) Harry Schell and Portago took the three-liter to the Argentine for the 1,000-kilometer sports car race.

"Harry was so frightened that I would break the car he wouldn't teach me how to change gears, so when after 70 laps (the race was 101) he was tired and it was my turn to drive, after three laps, during which I lost so much time that we dropped from second to fifth place, I saw Harry out in the middle of the track frantically waving a flag to make me come into the pits so that he could drive again. We eventually finished second overall and first in our class. I didn't learn to change gears properly until the chief mechanic of Maserati took me out and spent an afternoon teaching me."

Schell and Portago ran the three-liter at Sebring in 1954. The rear axle went after two hours. Portago sold it and bought a two-liter Maserati, the gear shifting lesson thrown in, and ran it in the 1954 Le Mans with Tomaso codriving.

They led the class until five in the morning, when the engine blew up. He won the Grand Prix of Metz with the Maserati but, according to Portago, "there were no good drivers in it," and ran with Chiron in the 12 Hours of Reims, Chiron blowing up the engine with 20 minutes to go while leading the class. He ran an Osca in the Grand Prix of Germany, and rolled it. "God protects the good, so I wasn't hurt."

In 1954, Portago broke down while leading the first lap of the Pan-American race in a three-liter Ferrari, and won a class, an overall, and a handicap race in Nassau. He bent an automobile occasionally, and he was often off the road but he was never hurt until the 1955 Silverstone, when he missed a gearshift and came out of the resulting crash with a double compound break in his left leg.

The crash had no effect on Portago's driving. He continued to run a little faster on the circuit and leave it less frequently. At Caracas in 1955, he climbed up on Fangio until he was only nine seconds behind him and finished second.

He was a member of the Ferrari team in 1956, an incredibly short time after he had begun to race. He won the Grand Prix of Portugal in 1956, a wild go-round in which the lap record was broken 17 times, the last time by Portago. He won the Tour of France, the Coupes du Salon in Paris, the Grand

December 1957
Sports Cars Illustrated Road Test:
The 1958 Corvette

"Like most manufacturers, Chevrolet is none too happy about some of the attempts made to bring 'boulevard' engines up to all-out F.I. specs [fuel injection?]." A standard Corvette of the year came with a 283-cubic-inch V-8, a single four-barrel Carter carburetor, a three-speed transmission and the choice of a hardtop or a folding one. Upgrades included a 290-hp fuel-injected engine, solid lifters, and an 8,000-rpm tach, a four-speed shifter, Positraction limited-slip differentials and a sport suspension and brake package.

Top speed: est. 125 mph
0-60 7.6 seconds
Fuel economy 18.5 mpg average driver;
15 mpg racing trim; est. 8 mpg competition form
250 hp/305 lb-ft (283 cid engine)
Price: $5,095

—Stephen F. Wilder

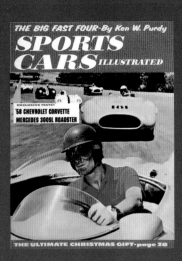

THE BIG FAST FOUR-By Ken W. Purdy
SPORTS CARS *ILLUSTRATED*

EXCLUSIVE TESTS!
'58 CHEVROLET CORVETTE
MERCEDES 300SL ROADSTER

THE ULTIMATE CHRISTMAS GIFT-page 28

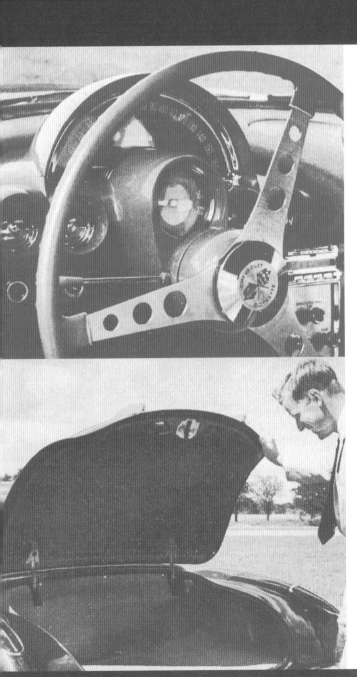

BELOW: Despite a lacerated arm, cut to the bone in a bobsled accident three weeks earlier, Portago nearly won GP of Cuba, holding off Fangio until a fuel line broke.
OPPOSITE: With Fangio. Portago had a keen sense not only of his own driving ability but of those competing with him.

Prix of Rome, and was leading Moss and Fangio at Caracas when a broken gas line put him out of the race. After Caracas that year, I asked Stirling Moss how he ranked Portago: "He's certainly among the ten best in the world today," Moss said, "and as far as I'm concerned, he's the one to watch out for."

In Cuba, just before Sebring this year, he was leading Fangio by a respectable margin when a gas line let go again. "I don't think anyone will be champion as long as Fangio competes," Portago told me. "If the absolute limit of adhesion of the car through a certain bend is 101.5 miles an hour, the old man will go through at 101, every time. I may go through at 99, or 102—in which case there will be an incident. Moss is of course better than I am, too. If I pass Moss, I wonder what's the matter with his car! But I'm learning still. I think I get a little better with every race. I hope so, anyway."

Portago ranked Collins, Behra, Schell, Musso, and himself after Moss as equals. He carefully repeated his estimate of Schell: "Harry is very, very fast," and then said that he considered Schell his closest friend. They spent much time together. Both appeared to be tense, or more accurately, taut, something that was not in any way allied to nervousness but was instead a peculiar expression of awareness. Like Portago, Schell walks rapidly, he turns his head constantly, he seems to be always trying to see something that is just out of sight, to hear something that is just out of earshot. I said as much.

"It sounds corny," Portago said, "but I think that because racing drivers are very near to death every Sunday in the season, they are more sensitive to life and appreciate it more. I take it that is what you meant by what you called 'awareness' when you saw Harry and me walking together. Speaking now

only for myself, I'm sure I love life more than the average man does. I want to get something out of every minute, I want no time wasted. You know, people say that racing drivers are daredevils who don't care whether they live or not, and you've seen stories about me and my flirting with death and all that. Nonsense, all nonsense. I want to live to be 105, and I mean to. I want to live to be a very old man. I'm enchanted with life. But no matter how long I live, I still won't have time for all the things I want to do, I won't hear all the music I want to hear, I won't be able to read all the books I want to read, I won't have all the women I want to have, I won't be able to do a 20th of the things I want to do. And besides just the doing, I insist on getting something out of what I do. For example, I wouldn't race unless I was sure I could be champion of the world."

31

"Can you imagine yourself driving when you're Fangio's age?" I asked him.

Portago smiled. His mouth was unusually small and straight-lined, and his smiles were brief, but warm enough.

"Never," he said. "Certainly not. In any case I'll stop when I'm 35, and if I'm champion of the world, sooner."

"And then?"

"Well, I'm very ambitious," Portago said. "I wouldn't be racing automobiles if I didn't think I could get something out of it, and not only the championship…"

The phone rang beside me. It was Portago's Caracas call, and I handed the instrument to him. I had passed the open switchboard in the lobby an hour before, when he had placed the call, and I had overheard the operator, so I knew to whom the call was going and I knew it would be personal.

"I'll take a walk," I told him. "Call me."

"Please," he said. "Don't go. Please. Anyway I'm going to speak Spanish."

As it turned out, the call was a report that the party in Caracas was unavailable.

"Forgive me," he said. "I didn't mean to be rude. I didn't mean to suggest that naturally you wouldn't speak Spanish. I'm sorry."

I told him that he was right, in any case. "We were talking about what you intend to get out of automobile racing," I said. "I had the impression you thought of it as preparation for something."

"I do," Portago said. "I haven't told this to a great many people. You see, Spain has had no new national hero for many years. That is what the championship of the world means to me. When I give up racing, I'm going to Spain and into politics."

Later, from Paris, Portago sent me a photograph of himself and Fangio and the pretender to the Spanish throne. But on it he had written, "With Fangio and Don Juan, the future King of Spain."

The rumor that Franco intends the restoration of the Spanish monarchy has been knocking around the world's chancelleries for several years. Portago seemed very sure. For all I know, he may have had superior information.

His frank statement of the purpose to which he intended to put the championship amused me. A few minutes before, he had been strongly critical of another driver who has some public business ventures:"He's commercialized himself so much," Portago said, rather disdainfully.

Still, one never expects consistency in anyone who gets his head above the ruck. Consistency is one of the marks of the drudge. Portago was of course a cynic, and I have no doubt he thought himself skilled in the management of other people—reporters included. If he did, it was a new idea for him, a product of the past two years, because he conceded he had been very shy during most of his life, highly introverted, and that he had occasionally covered it with actions that could be interpreted as rudeness. Certainly, he was enormously perceptive, and conversation with him was easy and pleasant. He obviously knew that real conversation can concern itself only with ideas, not things, and I think that, like all first-rate minds, his natural preference was for ideas; he knew that it was necessary to listen and he could be forthright, even in response to rough questions.

Portago was married in 1949 to the former Carroll McDaniel, a South Carolina girl. They have two children, Andrea, six, and Antonio, three. Two hours after he met

September 1959
Enzo Ferrari

Ferrari is a common surname in Italy. It adorns countless bars and shoe stores and occupies that thick section in Italian telephone books which in the United States features Brown or Jones. But within the past 20 years the world has come to know Ferrari as the name of an extraordinary Italian whose crest of a black horse rampant on a yellow field adorns the most successful racing cars in history. Enzo Ferrari's comparatively heavy and incredibly tough cars have been in the public eye since, as Ferrari describes it, "I picked up the torch laid down by Alfa Romeo in 1937." Ferrari himself has remained remote, content to have his laurels shipped to Modena and stepping forward only when pressured to do so. This insistence on privacy has had predictable results. Admirers and detractors have woven stories around him composed of rumor and hearsay. In real life Ferrari is essentially a plain person of monumental will and dignity who like his cars, is sturdy and powerful. Assisting the storyteller is the fact that Ferrari's life is full of paradoxes, of which the most striking is that despite a fervent desire to lead a simple life, he has found himself in constant complications. The red racing cars of Scuderia Ferrari have won more prize money than any other marque in history, yet Ferrari is not a rich man and the finances of his factory have often been shaky. Ferrari has immense pride and awareness of his position, yet has been forced to make a public appeal for support. He dislikes arguments and bickering yet he is involved in almost constant skirmishing with the Italian government and press, race organizers, suppliers, and customers. He is a former driver of considerable skill whose whole being is bound up tightly with his racing cars, yet for business and personal reasons he believes he should not be present when his cars are raced. He speaks earnestly of "equally valuable lessons learned in defeat and victory," yet the pressure to win which surrounds his equipe is almost overpowering. Ferrari is one of the few men to succeed financially by building competition cars, yet he believes himself hounded by disappointment and tragedy. There is an Italian proverb that runs: *Donne e Motori, Gioie e Dolori*, Women and Engines, Delight and Anguish. One of Ferrari's admirers once said that as far as the engine end is concerned, there is no man to whom this proverb better applies than Enzo Ferrari.

—Steve McNamara

Special Issue:
THE FABULOUS CARS OF ENZO FERRARI

SPORTS CARS ILLUSTRATED
50¢
September 1959
sports · economy · competition

Double Test:
FERRARI CALIFORNIA
FERRARI BERLINETTA

3 RACE REPORTS: TARGA · ZANDVOORT · NÜRBURGRING

McDaniel, Portago told her he intended to marry her. He had discovered even earlier in life that women respond to daring as to nothing else—to daring, to indifference, to arrogance and certainty and sensitivity—and in one sense, at least, women were more important in his life than anything else.

"The most important thing in our existence is a well-balanced sex life," he said to me. "Everybody knows this is true, but nobody will admit it—of himself, that is. But if you don't have a happy sex life, you don't have anything."

"It's the first thing historians suppress when they write the lives of great men," I said. "And it was often an astonishingly big factor in their lives."

"Of course," Portago said. "Look at Nelson, look at Napoleon."

"Well, look at George Bernard Shaw," I said, "who gave it up altogether, and married on condition his wife would never mention sex to him."

"A freak," Portago said. "A very atypical writer. Look at Maupassant. A prodigy, in more ways than one. Well, as for me, making love is the most important thing I do every day, and I don't care who knows it."

Portago was willing to maintain his opinions under most circumstances, whether by debate or a right cross. I had heard that he had once challenged a man to a duel, but he denied it. He fenced rarely, he said. He was taught boxing by Edmund Nelson, who died with him in the Mille Miglia. Nelson was a British ex-boxer who was just out of the merchant marine and working in New York's Plaza Hotel when Portago, still in his teens, resided there. It was Nelson who taught Portago bobsledding—the first time Portago went down the St. Moritz run, he went down steering, and he took

15 seconds off the time of the then champion of Switzerland—and it was Nelson who said, "I know Fon says he'll live forever, but I say he won't live to be 30."

It is not on record that Portago lost many fights. He was always in condition. He ordered milk at most of the world's best bars. He smoked constantly, but never inhaled. His reactions were freakishly fast, beyond normal to an extent that even he apparently didn't appreciate. He once remarked after a car had spun with him, "It went very slowly. There was lots of time to think." Another time, speaking of steeplechasing, he said, "When your horse falls after a jump, you look around for another horse to hide behind."

Recently, in Paris, Portago stepped off a curbstone as a Citroën went past, much too close, Portago felt, to the feet of the lady he was with. He flipped a cigarette at the driver so quickly and so accurately that he hit him in the face with it. The man got out, and Portago knocked him down twice. He handled his own defense in the consequent law proceedings and was thoroughly trounced by the plaintiff's attorney.

"I hate to fight," he told me. "I'll do anything honorable to get out of a fight, but I get into situations in which there is no way out. I was with some friends, they were in shipping transport, and a man called them 'a bunch of bloody pirates.' I'm afraid I hit him. Another time I suggested to a man on a dance floor that it might be nicer for everybody if he put his cigar away when he danced. He'd already burned a friend of mine with it. When I started to leave the place later, two of this cigar-lover's friends stood in my way and wouldn't move. What could I do once I'd asked them to please let me by? I lowered the boom on them."

34

We talked of a good many things that don't much matter now in the time we sat in that room. It had rained hard during the night, but the sun was steaming it off now, and outside we could hear cars slowing for the corner around the hotel that led to the circuit. Two team Maseratis came past, the mechanics who drove them blipping their engines incessantly.

"Genuine Italian-type sports cars," I said. "Suitable for summer touring."

Portago grinned. "This is an easy course in one way," he said. "There's only one genuine fast bend in it. But the flat corners, the way it ruins brakes. A race I don't like is the Mille Miglia. No matter how much you practice, you can't possibly come to know 1,000 miles of Italian roads as well as the Italians, and as Fangio says, if you have a conscience, you can't drive really fast anyway. There are hundreds of corners in the Mille Miglia where one little slip by a driver will kill 50 people. You can't keep the spectators from crowding into the road—you couldn't do it with an army. It's a race I hope I never run in.

"I have a quotation in a story, a piece of fiction that won't be published until this summer," I told Portago, "something that I thought at the time I wrote it you might have said: that of all sports, only bullfighting and mountain climbing and motor racing really tried a man, that all the rest are mere recreations. Would you have said that?"

"I couldn't agree with you more," Portago said. "You're quite right. I've thought of bullfighting, of course, but the trouble is that you must start when you're a child, otherwise you'll never really know the bulls. And the only trouble with mountain climbing for me is the lack of an audience! Like most drivers, I'm something of an exhibitionist."

Portago and I had promised ourselves a certain length of time. We had run an hour past it when he stood up and I shut off the wire recorder. We shook hands and said good-bye. I saw him three more times, very briefly, before the 1957 Sebring was over and everybody had dispersed. In April, he sent me a note from Paris to say he had won at Montlhéry, beating sports cars with a gran turismo car and breaking the lap record. He said he was going to run in the Mille Miglia and at Monte Carlo.

I did a draft of the story and sent a copy of it to him in Paris, as I had offered to do, but not before we talked. I'm not sure he ever saw it, because I heard from him next from Modena. Finally, the day before the race, a cable came from Brescia, asking if I could use his first-person account of the race. Obviously, he intended to live through the Mille Miglia now, although earlier he had written to Dorian Leigh—an internationally famous beauty with whom he had a close relationship—a note that had suggested premonition: "As you know, in the first place, I did not want to do the Mille Miglia. Then Ferrari said I must do it, at least in a gran turismo car. Then I was told I had to do it in a new 3800cc sports car. That means that my 'early death' may well come next Sunday."

He told a reporter he was intent only on finishing, that it was important to him to come back to Brescia "safe and sound," an obvious reference to the fact that someone was waiting for him. But when he got out on the road, Nelson hunched enigmatically beside him, Portago began to go, and he was fourth at the first checkpoint. When a broken half-shaft put Collins out at Parma, Portago began to try for second place, and he was straining for a sight of Von Trips's car, lying second to Taruffi, when a tire blew at something between 125 and 150 miles an hour on the straight at Guidizzolo. And the 3.8 Ferrari, a model he loathed, lifted its wheels off the road and left him helpless. The car killed him, it very nearly destroyed his body; it killed Edmund Nelson, too.

Except for the final seconds after he lost the car, seconds that must have seemed so long to him, Portago's last hours were happy ones. Once he had started running, he would have set aside all premonitory fears. He was doing what he wanted to do, and doing it far better than the form chart said he possibly could. He was surely thinking, as he screamed down the Valley of the Po toward Brescia and the finish, that he might conceivably win the race.

Most men die regretting the errors they have made in the multiple choices life forces upon us, and Portago knew, in the fraction of time in which he could think about it, that error was killing him. Motor racing, like every other human endeavor, rigidly reserves the ultimate reward for those who are talented, lucky, and totally devoted. Portago was enormously talented, he was luckier than most, but he did not have in the fullest measure the vital ability to concentrate obsessively on a single purpose. The gods, in which he did not believe, or fortune, or fate, or something else for which we as yet have no name, somehow guards those who do own this thing. Portago knew what it was, as many men do not, and he often spoke of it. "You must have the mental strength to concentrate absolutely," but he could not maintain it as rigidly as, say, Phil Walters used to do, or Stirling Moss does today. He did not want to run in the Mille Miglia. A wiser man might have stayed out, even if it required an illness of convenience. He had not made even one practice circuit of the course, but he tried to outdrive men who could not remember how many dozens of times they had run it. Perhaps saddest of all, he overruled the Ferrari depot at Florence when he was urged to take two new tires for the run to Brescia.

In a sense, though, none of these things was a mistake, because actually Portago had no choice. There was no caution in him. A refusal to count odds was the essence of his nature. Usually, he won, but he was intelligent and he knew that averages would almost certainly trip him ultimately. Knowing this, he still preferred to accept hazard. That was his nature, the core of his being, and he could do nothing to alter it. Had he been cautious, we would never have heard of him. Portago's determination to take what he wanted out of the world, on his own terms and no matter what the price, present or potential, made him what he was: the absolutely free spirit.

"If I die tomorrow," he told me the day before Sebring, "still I have had 28 wonderful years."

I cited to him a Spanish proverb: "In this life, take what you want—but pay for it."

"Of course," he said. "Of course, that's exactly it. You must pay. I remember someone who wrote about the British in the First World War, about the terrific mortality rate among young officers who had to lead bayonet charges against fixed machine guns, and most of them, or many of them, were aristocrats in those days. They had a life expectancy at the front of 30 days or something like that. And this man, he was a journalist, I can't remember his name, said, 'In war, the British aristocracy pays for the privileges they enjoy in peacetime.' You pay—you try to put it off, but you pay. I think, for my part at least, the game is worth the candle."

Mille Miglia 1957. Portago and Nelson
are ready to go off the ramp in the
3.8 Ferrari which was punched out to
4.0 liters. He hated this car and
maintained that the car hated him.
The truth is, he had no desire to run
in the Mille Miglia at all.

January 1960
Project Time Machine

By Griff Borgeson

As a child in the 1930s I was privileged to deposit my knuckles' hide on the metal of blown Mercedes-Benz, petite Bugattis, noble Hispanos, and Winfield-equipped Ford roadsters. I worked on and drove Duesenbergs, DuPonts, RCSes, and Crane-Simplexes. But the ultimate machine I could only glimpse from afar. It was the Miller 91.

The supercharged, 1500 cc Miller was exceedingly rare. About 35 were made, of which about a dozen used front-wheel drive. The conventionally-driven 91s carried a catalog price of $10,000 in the late 1920s and the FWD's cost exactly $5,000 more. They dominated thoroughbred racing in the U.S. and drew voluntary expressions of humility from Europe's best designers. Strictly because of their superlative excellence they destroyed the golden age of racing in America. Their incredible performance shamed that of the cast-iron merchants, who withdrew from racing precipitately because it had "become too specialized." Machinery "had become too perfect, too costly."

The honors of the Miller 91 are legion. Let's name a few:
1. Nearly all records on every big-time track in the U.S.
2. One-way of 171 mph on gasoline, turned by Frank Lockhart in a straightaway run in 1927. His two-way record through the AAA clocks was 164.85 mph. One car in the world was faster—a Daytona record machine with 30 times the 91's displacement.
3. In 1927 the world record for 250 miles was 116.37, set by Lockhart in a 91. That year Leon Duray averaged 124.7 mph for 250 miles on the 1¼-mile Culver City board track.
4. In 1928 Duray set the Indianapolis lap record at 124.018 mph. This was not exceeded until 1937—the longest the record has ever remained unbroken.

5. That same year Duray set the absolute world record for speed on a closed course, using the then-unfinished 2½ mile Packard Proving Ground track. His record of 148.17 mph stood for 26 years.

Duray's remarkable speeds were, admittedly, helped by his exceptional skill and courage as a driver and by his unusual ability as a practical engineer. He personally pioneered the use of methanol fuel, and the trademarks of Le Diable Noir were his black racing costume and the unique supercharger intercooler, which he had designed. In 1929 he changed his racing colors from black to violet and campaigned a team of three 91s under the name of Packard Cable Specials and the sponsorship of the Packard Electric Division of General Motors. The Indianapolis race that year marked the end of the 91-cubic-inch formula in the U.S. and the adoption of the 366 cubic inch so-called Junk Formula. Dural sold his rear-drive car and took his two remaining front-drives to Europe, where he hoped they could be disposed of at a better price than in the U.S. One of the greatest mechanic-engineers in American racing worked with Duray on these cars throughout in 1929: Jean Marcenac.

Duray's first essay on this European campaign was to attack the absolute closed-course record on the Montlhéry track. Although its circumference was only half that of the Packard track, in early August he was clocked officially at 143.169 mph.

Wrote G. Fraichard in *Paris Match*, "With a 1500 cc car or, to be more precise, with a car of 10 CV taxable horsepower, to achieve such speed proves clearly that the Americans are far in advance of us. We have no French cars of similar displacement capable of rivaling the speed of these Millers." Or of any displacement, he could have added. To Ettore Bugatti these were bitter words.

A month later, Duray and his spidery, violet cars competed in the Monza Grand Prix. Afterward he had set a new lap record at just under 120 mph. Duray's luck soured and both of his cars were eliminated from the race by minor mechanical failures. At this point Duray found a taker for his cars. Ettore Bugatti wanted them and got them in exchange for a sum of cash and three brand-new Bugatti 2.3 liter, supercharged Targa Florio models which Duray brought to Hollywood and sold. Bugatti immediately tore down and analyzed the Miller engines and adapted the Miller top-end design to his own purposes. All Bugatti engines from the Type 51 onward breathed more freely thanks to Miller-derived design. And the Packard Cable Specials passed into limbo.

In 1951, I made the acquaintance of Leon Duray, who had retired to the pleasant high-desert community of Twenty-Nine Palms, California. I asked him what had become of the old cars. He had no idea. Of those days Duray retained only a few photos, a French medal and a fine gold pocket chronograph on the back of which were engraved the date and speeds of his Packard test track records.

In 1954, the story of a visit to Molsheim appeared in *Bugantics*, the publication of the Bugatti Owners Club of England; included in the illustrations was a photo of the two ex-Duray machines covered with dust in the Bugatti factory.

I lost no time in writing the author of the article and the factory, to ask the former for general information and the latter (a) if the cars still were at the factory, (b) their condition, and (c) if they could be purchased.

Author J. D. Scheel of the Royal Danish Embassy in London sent photos of the cars that he had taken in 1953. He had been informed that the cars were the Cooper Specials that Earl Cooper and Pete Kreis had driven in the Grand Prix of Europe at Monza in 1927, in which Cooper finished third. Evidently the cars had been covered with a protective coating of grease or cosmoline and their Packard Cable identification was not visible.

M. Arnaud, secretary general of Automobiles Bugatti, replied that the cars still were on the premises, that they might eventually consider selling them to me, and that I should be fully aware of the missing-parts situation: the superchargers, mags and carbs were gone.

I wrote back saying, "Fine. Kindly quote me the price of *les deux voitures de course Miller.*"

Here communications bogged down. Bugatti was reluctant to quote and I hesitated to bid. After a couple of years of indecisive correspondence I asked American Bugattiste Bob Estes to look the cars over for me on his next trip to Europe. On his return he reported, "They look very rough. One car's engine is on the floor with its blocks off and with the rods and pistons sticking out of the case. But there should be enough parts to build one completely restored car."

"Good," I said. "I'd like to go ahead with the purchase. Please try to work out a price with them on your next trip to Molsheim." Estes, a far-gone collector himself, may have suffered the frustrated passion of Cyrano de Bergerac but he continued to negotiate on my behalf, and after a session with

December 1960
300SL at the Kremlin

At about 6:35 in the evening I parked my Mercedes-Benz 300SL near the spires of St. Basil's Cathedral, outside the Spasskaya Tower Gate of the Kremlin. I couldn't drive it inside, since only official cars are allowed in Red Square itself. Three years old and with nearly 70,000 miles on its odometer, the SL had been driven all the way there and would be driven back. While it was poised there I wanted to see how the Russians reacted to it. Laboring with an official Intourist guide along for the ride, David Douglas Duncan tried out Glasnost 30 years before it became official policy. On the road to Leningrad from Moscow, Duncan passes a Moskva sedan and sees the horror in his guide's face—"which immediately made me ask what was wrong." You passed him!" "Of course I passed him. This is a much faster, more powerful car, as you know, so what is strange about passing him?" "Yes, I know about your car, but he was doing the best he could...and you passed him!"
—*David Douglas Duncan*

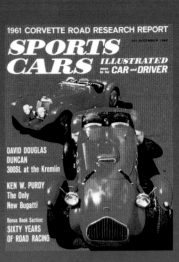

1961 CORVETTE ROAD RESEARCH REPORT

SPORTS CARS *ILLUSTRATED* soon to be CAR and DRIVER

DAVID DOUGLAS DUNCAN
300SL at the Kremlin

KEN W. PURDY
The Only
New Bugatti

Bonus Book Section:
SIXTY YEARS
OF ROAD RACING

director general Pierre Marco at the factory in October 1958, he came back with a firm price for the two cars. It was a fair price to both sides.

Then began the arrangement of final details, with liberal use of cablegrams and the transatlantic telephone. Jean Marcenac, who had served in the French Air Force in the First World War, had known Ernest Henri, had been Jean Chassagne's riding mechanic, and had come to the U.S. with the Ballot team immediately after the war, handled the conversations in well-remembered French punctuated with frequent OKs. The details took time, particularly the financial arrangements.

This is where *Sports Cars Illustrated* and the Ziff-Davis Publishing Co. entered the scene. To my amazement they offered substantial financial help for a project they immediately recognized as being significant to the history of the American automobile. It is because of this invaluable sponsorship, this very tangible respect for the glories of the past, that the ex-Duray, ex-Bugatti Millers have been renamed *Sports Cars Illustrated* Specials.

Because the cars were disassembled when Estes had examined them it seemed highly desirable that we have a knowledgeable representative supervise their packing in Molsheim; Bugatti recommended this independently. What they did not say was that they had put skilled mechanics to work on the cars, cleaning them and assembling all dismantled parts.

On a flying trip to Europe John Christy went through Molsheim to examine the cars. "You won't believe it when you see them," he reported. "They're in unbelievably good shape, except for the tires that naturally have decayed. You can I still smell the fuel in the tanks!"

Wrote Karl Ludvigsen from Europe in March: "The cars are ready to go as they stand. Considering the time and the trials these two cars have been through, their condition is literally staggering. The purple paint, the Packard Cable Special lettering, all is tatty but intact. It was a blinding glimpse into the past."

So we gave Bugatti the go-ahead, asked them to have the crating done by the most competent people possible, which, we found, in France translates as American Express. Weeks passed and I had visions of the cars sitting exposed on a dock at Le Havre but the worry was unnecessary.

Marcenac was keyed up like a young bride. "I'll give you any reasonable help, my son," he said. "If you can get the engines running, bring them here and I'll tune them for you on the Novi dyno. Don't expect that 280 hp that some people used to claim. But I can get you an easy 230."

Leo Goossen (he did the original engineering on the 91, chassis and all) of Meyer & Drake (says Lou Meyer, "Best engine we ever built was the 91") was excited too. "Bring your technical problems to me," he said. "And if you get the cars running then let's get together. I've got some ideas for improving the 91."

As the word spread that the cars were coming, help and offers of help began coming in. Bunny Phillips, who used to drive Millers and Bugattis on the Championship Trail, had preserved practically all of the original Miller 91 patterns and engineering drawings and made them available to the project. Gordon Schroeder, who had owned the Lockhart streamliner 91-based engine, contributed tools, including a tooling jig for milling all the surfaces on the 91 block. Ernie Olson contributed special Miller spanner wrenches that he'd had wrapped up for 30 years. From enthusiast John Cannon came replacements for the

May 1961
Jaguar's Sensational XKE

This is the most exciting sports car news of 1961. In late January, Jaguar Managing Director Sir William Lyons gave the go-ahead to plans to announce the XKE at Le Mans and road testing at England's MIRA proving ground. Jaguar is finally building a sports car directly descended from its competition experience. The 150-mph XKE will be available in closed or open form, both models powered by the 265 bhp, 3.8-liter XK six-cylinder engine. It will be no surprise to anyone if a team of XKE roadsters appears at Le Mans in June—in full race trim. How fast is the new Jag? The speedo reads to 160 mph and test driver Norman Dewis has lapped the banked MIRA track at 150. Under the right conditions it would seem that it wouldn't be too difficult to get the needle close to its 160-mph maximum. From the aerodynamic standpoint, in fact, the car should be capable of no less than 180 mph, with 265 bhp and the right gearing, which would pretty effectively make it the world's fastest series production car today, as the XK120 was in its time.

—Jesse Alexander

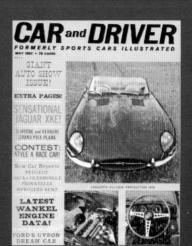

Leon Duray and the Miller 91 was
an overpowering combination at the
"Brickyard." FWD acceleration off
the corners at Indy was just too much
for the rear drive competition.

missing superchargers. Bill Kenz of Bonneville fame scoured
Denver and came up with more blower parts.

Companies helped: Brown & Sharpe, whose micrometers
are the world's best, offered to help with precision measuring
instruments. Proto Tool Company, anticipating unusual tool
problems, offered to help with these. Firestone Tire & Rubber
Co. managed to find eight of the last 20-inch Indytires (800 x
20's built for the Novis) in existence and made them available at
a sporting price. Goodyear Tire and Rubber Co. had an old
500 x 20 mold shipped from their Australian plant in which
new tires of vintage dimensions could be made. These are just
a few of the firms and individuals whose imaginations have
been fired by Project Time Machine. The project is far too
complex to be executed successfully by one person. It's a
labor of love that needs many helpers.

On July 30, the French Line's *MS Wyoming* docked in
Los Angeles. The local office of American Express relished its
participation in an off-beat, historic situation: the return to their
birthplace of what appear to be the last front-wheel drive Miller
91's in existence. The French Line people enjoyed it too, and
when American Express proposed a reception for the unloading
of the Millers, the French Line offered the hospitality of its ship.

Marcenac and Olson were there to catch the first glimpse
of the ancient machines with which they had helped create
racing history. So was driver Pete de Paolo, who had won the
National Championship in 1929 in a FWD 91. Bunny Phillips
arrived in a pristine Type 57 Bugatti convertible, along with other
racing personalities. The press was there in force, TV cameras
and NBC's *Monitor* taped the occasion. Seeing the crates
opened, catching the first sight of the cars on American soil in
three decades was unforgettable and very moving.

Following this ceremony we all retired to the festively
bedecked ship where we enjoyed hors d'oeuvres, fine
wines and vintage, bilingual bench racing. Big collector
and SCCA-USAC functionary Lindley Bothwell had one of
his trailaway trucks standing by. After the last cork was popped
we said good-bye to our French hosts and took the 91s to my
mountain retreat which, by the sheerest coincidence, happens to
be a stone's throw from Harry Miller's famous old Malibu ranch.

What happens now? Well, in spite of a crowded schedule,
the restoration project moves ahead. One car is being left
untouched for the present and the other is being torn down
to its frame. In time there should be a before-and-after exhibit
that will tell a remarkable story.

Restoring the cars to like-new appearance for public
exhibition will be relatively easy, and barring unforeseen acts of
God, will be accomplished with spectacular results. That is the
formal, stated goal of Project Time Machine.

But many of us, of course, want these cars to spring to life
once more. We want to hear the unique scream of almost dollar-
sized pistons pumping at 8,000 rpm, trains of spur-cut gears
howling and blower impellers winding out to 40,000 rpm. The
problems that may be encountered here are unpredictable and it
would be extravagant to promise that the cars will run again.
However, all stressed parts are being Magnafluxed or Zygloed
and the project proceeds on the assumption that they will run
again. Time will tell.

Meanwhile, we have a matchless opportunity to study
and analyze the design and construction of vehicles that are
widely recognized as the high point of American automotive
achievement. Our next report on the SCI Specials will contain
the factual and photographic results of this study.

44

April 1962
Fast Flight In a Sprite

1. At SCCA Pomona Race Ashley Shulter (163) spins and crashes into John Hooper's Sprite (95).
2. Impact of crash flips 95 and sends 163 into a fast, backward, opposite spin.
3. Car 95 begins sickening second flip with Hooper helplessly hanging from seat belt, his arm dangling.
4. Vaulting end over end, 95 leaves ground as Shulter's car skids backward on dirt.
5. Hooper's car comes to final stop, landing upside down.
6. As track attendant rushes for aid, John Hooper struggles to free himself.
7. Miraculously alive, Hooper is helped to his feet. Seat belt and roll bar limited injuries to broken arm and finger.

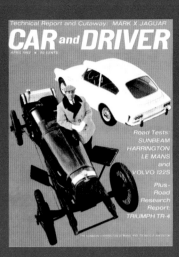

Technical Report and Cutaway: MARK X JAGUAR

CAR and DRIVER

APRIL 1962

Road Tests:
SUNBEAM
HARRINGTON
LE MANS
and
VOLVO 122S

Plus-
Road
Research
Report:
TRIUMPH TR-4

1963

1970

Heyday and Hellions

"It was nuts. For the last half of the 1960s, the whole country was in full berserko mode. Everyone under 30 was zonked on everything from peyote to paint thinner, and every stretch of asphalt from sea to shining sea was smeared with fat black patches of rubber." It wasn't that Brock Yates denied his or *Car and Driver*'s part in any of it, when asked to look back on what the hell was going on in America in the 1960s. Both he and the magazine always took fair credit for their share of the mayhem—which, in the heart of the decade, seemed to come from all possible directions, often all at once.

1964 Mercedes 600 Grosser.

1963

Pope John XXIII
dies, succeeded by
Pope Paul VI

Martin Luther King Jr.
delivers "I Have A
Dream" speech in
Washington, D.C.

President John F.
Kennedy is killed by
Lee Harvey Oswald
in Dallas, Texas

<

Historians who call the 20th century the American Century may pause when the 1960s come to mind. America was in outright cultural rebellion. Social progress was countered by social upheaval. Soaring achievements, like putting the first man on the moon, were tempered by the tragedies incurred on the way: assassinated presidents and preachers, neighborhoods demolished by riots, a sense of righteousness tested and ultimately damaged in a faraway theater of war.

America still displayed its might regularly, though, and in the automotive arena the 1960s were utterly unlike any other era. In terms of raw power and expressiveness, the cars of the time were without rival. It was a golden age, for sure, and in the short window before smog and Arab boycotts brought down the muscle-car era, it hit dazzling peaks of horsepower and style.

"Muscle-car madness was at its peak, in its last hours of glory, before a goofy Luddite in surplus army shoes teamed up with a gang of blue-nose bureaucrats to throw the red flag," Yates recalled. "The party was nearly over, but we went out with the "tach pegged and the throttle wide open."

Among the roadside debris were some of the most outrageous examples of automotive history. They ranged from the 128-mph, 300-hp, 5,380-pound Mercedes-Benz 600 "Grosser" four-door überwagen, to the feather-light Meyers Manx dune buggy that prompted more knockoffs than creator Bruce Meyers could count. There continued, of course, production of Carroll Shelby's masterpiece Cobra, upgraded now with a 427-cubic-inch V-8 and a claimed (but never proved) record-setting 0-to-100-to-0 time of 14.5 seconds. Along with the Chevy 302s and Hemi-powered Chryslers of the day, those engines were crammed under the hoods of dream machines that captured the essence of rebellion: unbridled power unfettered by regulation or control.

There to capture it all—and to spin it all into unforgettable words and pictures—were the staffers of *Car and Driver*. Chief among them, Yates and David E. Davis, Jr. fueled the magazine with outrageous commentary, bawdy road tests of some of the most powerful cars ever built, and the sharp vision to see the crackup looming down the road for the American car industry.

David E. Davis, Jr., stumbled into motorsports in his youth and never looked back. In magazine print and in a standing ovation commencement address at the University of Michigan in 2004, at which he earned an honorary doctorate, Davis hints that his father's own interest in journalism was doubly recouped when he turned to a career in print. "He never saw me race, but I think he got a kick out of the idea, and I know that he was pleased when I drifted into writing by way of *Road & Track* magazine," Davis recalled. "One of his own dreams was a career in journalism."

Davis teamed his urge to race with words. But a horrific accident in 1955 almost brought an end to his driving career, and his life. At 24 years old Davis flipped a car during a championship race in Sacramento, California. He survived, but endured multiple surgeries that saved what remained of the side of his face. Davis lost his left eyelid, the bridge of his nose, most of his teeth, and

the roof of his mouth. "I was uglier than a mud fence," he later wrote. "I actually frightened children and sometimes caused their parents to call the police on me."

Healed and undeterred, Davis found himself seven years later at the helm of *Car and Driver*. In 1962 the magazine was as old as his injuries, but Davis might argue that he was in better shape. The departure of Ludvigsen had crippled the staff, and the editor who followed had departed from the editorial formula that had doubled circulation. Davis descended into the job on a sort of suicide mission to revive it, and did so without much fear. After his 1955 accident, he said "I suddenly understood with great clarity that nothing in life—except death itself—was ever going to kill me. No meeting could ever go that badly. No client would ever be that angry. No business error would ever bring me as close to the brink as I had already been."

Davis had been hired, he wrote, to save *Car and Driver* from an early demise. "My predecessor had, in eleven short months, alienated everybody, run up bad debts with every steno and file clerk in the company, and energetically undermined the strong editorial foundation built by Ken Purdy, John Christy, and Karl E. Ludvigsen. Halfway through his administration, circulation had gone into a spin, spiraling down from over 210,000 to bottom out at about 175,000 a few months after I took over.

"It had been the magazine's great misfortune to undergo a name change from *Sports Cars Illustrated* to *Car and Driver* and to lose Ludvigsen all at the same time, and it was reeling. Mine was a suicide mission, though the incumbent staff saw my role as more essentially homicidal. Years later, I was told by Gene Butera, the remarkable art director who made by far the greatest one-man contribution to my 'new' *Car and Driver*, that every time my office door was closed the staff would do a quick head count to see 'who was in there getting it this time.'"

What *Car and Driver* needed, Davis determined, was a return to the vision that had been the hallmark of Purdy, Christy, and Ludvigsen. *Car and Driver* had to be what the other magazines were not—not the private domain of effete European sports cars, nor the province of unrecognizable hot rods that you couldn't buy off a Detroit showroom floor. The mainstream was where *Car and Driver* belonged, with an appreciation for good cars from every country, even, and especially, if they were from America.

"We believe that there is a place for an American magazine with an American point of view that talks about cars from all over the world. We do not believe that small cars enjoy some mystical advantage over large cars. Neither do we believe that Detroit has all, or even most, of the answers on automobiles. We judge them purely on their goodness or badness, applauding the former, cursing the latter. We love cars and everything even remotely connected with them. We've bought them, sold them, built them, wrecked them, raced them, and necked in them. We never grow tired of them. We count ourselves among the most fortunate of men: our greatest love is the thing that makes us our living. If we can communicate that pure, unadulterated automotive joy to you, tempered occasionally with a little wholesome outrage, *Car and Driver* will be doing its job," he wrote early in his tenure at the magazine.

In 1964, Davis picked up the lightning rod that would recharge the magazine's image and threw it at shocked readers unprepared to put American cars in the same breath as the finest from Europe. The car was Pontiac's new Tempest GTO, a plain sedan stoked to full power with a massive V-8 engine. "My first ride in a GTO left me with a feeling like losing my virginity, going into combat and tasting my first draft beer all in about seven

52

1965

CAR and DRIVER
DECEMBER 1963 • 50 CENTS

ROAD RESEARCH REPORT
'64 BUICK RIVIERA

NEW GP CAR CUTAWAYS

Studded Tires Revolutionize Winter Driving

CAR and DRIVER
FEBRUARY 1964 • 50 CENTS

Road Research Report:
Lotus Elan 1600

Road Tests:
Citroën DS-19
Hillman Minx

The Case for
Fast Driving

JIM CLARK— GREAT SCOT!

Malcolm X is shot dead in Harlem

Riots in the Watts section of Los Angeles claim 34 lives

"The Sound of Music" premieres

Winston Churchill, Nat "King" Cole die

1966

CAR and DRIVER

MARCH 1964 · 50 CENTS

Tempest GTO: 0-to-100 in 11.8 sec
Who Killed Studebaker? – Page 75
Rover 2000 Road Research Report

54

The Supreme Court establishes Miranda rights in Miranda vs. Arizona

Henri Grandsire has a Formula Three car, but the wheels fall off

Truman Capote's "In Cold Blood" hits bookstores

<

"Star Trek" begins its five-year mission

seconds," Davis wrote. The GTO marked the beginning of the muscle-car era, a generation of cars dominated by breathlessly powerful V-8s and coveted by squadrons of street racers from Detroit's Woodward Avenue to Los Angeles's newly minted freeways. It would be considered heresy, but the GTO grabbed so many *Car and Driver* staffers that Davis, softened up to the approach by Jim Wangers, a clever Pontiac PR man, put the GTO on the cover of the magazine alongside the Ferrari GTO and declared the Pontiac the superior car.

Davis knew the GTO cover was a turning point. The cover read, "Tempest GTO: 0-to-100 in 11.8 sec," which he later noted that the technical department "still hasn't lived down." The GTO had been a ringer—a specially prepped test car that carried a much larger, more powerful engine than any real GTO customer could order. And the technical measurements of the car's acceleration weren't carefully obtained. But it almost didn't matter if the GTO from Detroit wasn't as fast as the one from Maranello—it was the comparison of the two that staked out the ground where *Car and Driver* would thrive. "It accomplished just what we had been trying to do for months: to get the attention of the audience and clearly establish us as a contender in the automotive publishing biz. *Car and Driver* was finally on its way, and the GTO did it," Davis said. *Car and Driver* readers had been primed, unsuspecting, for what the GTO cover represented since Davis had taken office. *Car and Driver* broke cleanly from the car-magazine pack and took an attitude. It taunted its readers in the letters section, it goaded them with road tests of pure American irony, and its writing style changed from casual observation and clinical descriptions to a wilder, freer-flowing tone inspired by Tom Wolfe.

"Damned few important writing talents have shown much interest in automobiles or automobile racing," Davis lamented over the state of car journalism in the 1960s. "But then along came Tom Wolfe, who changed all that. In fact, if we had to give credit for the development of *Car and Driver*'s present personality, we'd say that Ken Purdy established our rules for content almost ten years ago, while Tom Wolfe has had a deceptively strong effect upon our editorial style.

"He can most regularly be found in the pages of *The Trib*'s Sunday magazine, but he also does a lot of stuff for *Esquire*, much of it automotive. Both the title story—'The Kandy Kolored Tangerine-Flake Streamline Baby' and 'The Last American Hero'— originally appeared in *Esquire*, and both must rank as minor classics. 'Tangerine-Flake Baby' is a beautiful exploration of the weird and wonderful world of custom cars, and their creators and enthusiasts, while 'The Last American Hero' is an outrageously accurate portrayal of stock car driver Junior Johnson, the squire of Ronda, North Carolina.

"Tom Wolfe's style is colorful and rebellious. He writes with a tumbling, crazy kind of antidiscipline that is occasionally confusing, but never dull. He may be our only truly contemporary writer, in that both his style and his subject always reflect what's really happening out there—we are a nutty, amusing, ragtag kind of a country and he has an uncanny knack for catching us at our silliest and most pretentious moments."

Wolfe's tone fit in with the tradition of the ballsy, opinionated voice already cemented into the pages of the magazine. And it was beginning to resonate with its readers, too. The GTO story had given established car enthusiasts fits, and so did the success of *Car and Driver*. "When we took this magazine over, there wasn't enough reader mail in the files to make up a letters column," Davis recalled. "Now we can expect hundreds of

The first human heart transplant is performed

The Beatles release "Sgt. Pepper's Lonely Hearts Club Band"

<

1968

The Tet Offensive begins in Vietnam; the My Lai massacre happens

letters—filled alternately with camaraderie, support, or slanderous invective—on any given subject. We used to deplore the fact that no magazine in the automotive field ever surprised anybody with a real honest-to-God statement of opinion. Now the enthusiasts know that there is one that will stand up and holler its editorial head off when it doesn't like something. Now *Car and Driver* maintains a standard of automotive criticism and comment that sets it apart from all the rest."

The GTO story had kicked off a new era in the magazine's history. And, at least by one account, it brought the other chieftain of *Car and Driver* history to the tribe. Yates had been on the periphery of auto journalism when, after the GTO story, *Car and Driver's* editor John Jerome quit the magazine. Davis hired Yates on the staff, and save for a time in the late 1970s and early 1980s when Davis fired him for "terminal writer's block," he showed no signs of leaving. Journalism was already a family tradition before Yates decided *Car and Driver* needed a staff "assassin." Yates's father had been a writer and managing editor of *Popular Science* magazine, as well as an author of more than 80 books.

Writing took a back seat among Yates's loves: racing and the sleek machines of his youth. "I saw my first race when I was a 12-year-old kid. The year was 1946 and it was a midget race at the Niagara County Fairgrounds in Lockport, New York. The track was a flat, rutted half mile and the cars were a sad collection of pre-war Ford V-8 60s, Elto outboards, and Ferguson-Fords. Except for two. There was a pair of white Kurtis Kraft Offenhausers there that night, and I can remember sitting in that rickety, cavernous old grandstand and feeling the nerve ends across the back of my neck prickle with excitement every time they went onto the track. The two drivers were very good, big names, if you will, and they murdered the local boys. I haven't

a clue as to who they were, but I sometimes wonder what I'd be doing today if they hadn't been there," he wrote.

Writing about cars didn't really appeal to him until about the age of 30, Yates says. In part, that was because the field of automotive journalism barely existed in the U.S. British magazines such as *Motor and Autocar* were in existence, but were rarely seen in the U.S. *Hot Rod* had become popular, but as Yates recalled, "'Hot rod' at that time was considered pejorative. It was not a nice word. Hot rodders were not nice people."

Yates nonetheless ended up in automotive journalism, and joined *Car and Driver* only a few months after the GTO story triggered a blizzard of reader letters at the *Car and Driver's* offices at One Park Avenue. "An incredible story," he remembers. "Hopelessly bogus and full of absolutely incredible hyperbole. I remember getting the magazine at my home and I looked at it and said, 'Are these people nuts? A Ferrari GTO being beaten up by this piece of Detroit iron?'"

As the magazine's new managing editor, Yates had to do two things he swears he was and is not capable of—managing and editing. But his other important duty was to be Davis's swashbuckler, putting into print what Yates says was mostly an act of revenge against *Car and Driver's* chief competitor, *Road & Track*. At that point, *Car and Driver* still was the underdog of the two, with a circulation of about 250,000 compared with *Road & Track's* 400,000.

Car and Driver, under Davis's and Yates's command, used its envy of its California competition to hone its verbal edge. "We tried to tell the way it was," Yates says. "We were the first magazine ever to do comparison tests. We did comparison tests and lost all kinds of advertising. No one had ever said, 'This car's better than that car.' It rattled the industry. Nobody had ever done

57

this before because they were terrified that they were going to lose advertising. It changed the dynamics of the industry radically."

At the height of the muscle-car era and at a peak of creativity—and only three years after Davis shook the magazine into shape—a series of title changes left both of these founding fathers out of ultimate control of *Car and Driver*. On January 1, 1966, Davis withdrew the editor from his title of editor and publisher and left Yates with the daily duties of editing. Within a year Davis would also leave behind the publisher's title, and within another few months Yates would drop the editor title. Both would continue to shape the magazine and stay on as senior editors.

The job of editing *Car and Driver* was, and still is, the most coveted title of enthusiasts everywhere. But among those who've written for the car magazines, it's the senior editor post that is blissfully free of paperwork and devoted to the chore of writing. Davis reminded readers of that fact when he handed off the reins to new editor Steve Smith: "I'll actually get to write more stuff for the magazine than I have during the past 18 months. I have a lovely five-year contract to write feature stories and columns, and to act as an editorial advisor to editor Steve Smith and his staff. Steve Smith is the editor-in-chief. He's been through this whole metamorphosis and feels exactly as I do about what the magazine is, and why it's important. Brock Yates will share the title of senior editor with me, and we'll work closely with Steve as writers, editors, and planners."

Smith's tenure would be short; in turn, Leon Mandel would take over the magazine for three years through the end of the 1960s. What Davis had founded took on a life of its own, though. The 1968 road test of an Opel Kadett wagon stands as one of the most controversial road tests the magazine had done yet—

more a hit piece than a review, recalls editor-at-large Patrick Bedard, who joined the magazine in late 1967.

"This was a ritual assassination. The trigger had already been pulled when I interviewed for the job of technical editor in November 1967, but the impact wouldn't occur until a month after my hiring.

"Leon Mandel had just moved into the editor-in-chief's chair. Our address was One Park Avenue, New York, New York. New journalism was dawning. Tom Wolfe was the print media's sensation. Mandel was passionate: '*Car and Driver* is the best f***king magazine in the world,' he told me. 'It just happens to be about cars.'

"To get the world to notice us, he decided to kill a car. The cringing Opel station wagon was handy. The hit man was Cook Neilson.

"We got noticed, all right. General Motors canceled all of its advertising in all Ziff-Davis magazines (*Modern Bride* even lost Frigidaire, a General Motors division then). Honeywell, involved somehow, dropped its ads in *Popular Photography*.

"Collateral damage was everywhere, and we staffers at *Car and Driver* had to suffer snubs from the innocent victims as we walked the halls of One Park. We didn't care. We were hot."

The end of the decade wouldn't close out the era of Davis and Yates. More brickbats were to be tossed and more mutual admiration would be doled out in decades to come. But the end of the 1960s did mark the end of the muscle-car era. Smog choked cities and in return the Feds clamped down on the stuff coming from those glorious muscle-car tailpipes. Muscle cars didn't so much die as they were strangled by regulation and geopolitics. And they nearly took *Car and Driver* along with them to their graves.

March 1963
Road Research Report:
AC Cobra

Very simply stated, the AC Cobra attained higher performance figures than any other production automobile we have tested. And it did it with the "street" engine.

When Carroll Shelby builds a hot rod, he doesn't settle for any old chassis. In this case he has chosen one that has figured largely in hybrid projects for some time, and with great success. Coupling the stout AC chassis and lightweight AC body with a souped-up Ford engine, Shelby has come up with an extremely track-worthy sports car of very high performance indeed.

AC introduced the Tojeiro design as the AC Ace in 1954, powered by the ancient long-stroke, six-cylinder, overhead-valve two-liter. In 1956 AC made a deal with Bristol to use the famous BMW-derived Bristol power plant, and the AC-Bristol became a respected competitor in sports-car racing. The next engine option was the 2.6-liter Ford Zephyr engine, introduced in 1961, and now we have the Cobra.

As a fourth-generation hybrid, the car must be considered in light of its true purpose—SCCA class warfare. For such usage, it is accurately aimed, and viewed in that light the secondary considerations such as street use must necessarily come off second best.

Traffic, for instance, presents some uncomfortable problems. With the Cobra's very powerful engine developing maximum torque at 4,800 rpm, its high gearing, and its fierce clutch, every stop and start presents an interesting challenge in turning noise into motion. Its poor steering lock makes parking and maneuvering highly complicated. And finally, the battery does not get enough input current to cope with low-rpm

running under normal conditions, let alone when using the heater, headlights, wipers, and the inadequate electrical fan mounted in front of the tilted radiator.

Tasca Ford of Providence, Rhode Island, which supplied the test car, suggested a smaller generator pulley to cure the constant discharge problem. A better solution might be the alternator, since it is already optional for the 260-cubic-inch Ford V-8 that is used in both Fairlanes and Galaxies.

If the car presents problems in traffic, one would assume that they would be dissolved by the open road—the opener and the more like a race course the better. In fact, the effortless sort of cruising that the car's performance would seem to promise is considerably handicapped by the encroachment on passenger space that the big V-8 makes. The engine is set back in the chassis enough so that the driver's accelerator foot gets cramped after a while in the only position possible (with the right leg bent inward toward the other at the knee). Some relief is afforded by the long pedal travel of the throttle control, but it only comes with variations in speed.

On the credit side, with regard to the driver's creature comforts, is an interesting refinement in the clutch and brake pedals. These are hinged below floor level and also at the pedal faces. As a result, the pedal faces maintain a constant total contact with the sole of the driver's shoe regardless of the depression angle. The pedals are set closely enough together to allow room for the left foot beside the clutch.

Classic simplicity is the term that first comes to mind for describing the AC chassis (designed by John Tojeiro for his own sports-racing car in 1952 and subsequently taken over by AC). The frame consists of two large-diameter steel tubes with heavy cross-members front, center, and rear. Narrow-diameter tubes are used to support the all-aluminum body. All wheels are independently suspended by means of lower wishbones and upper transverse leaf springs. The result is a chassis that has given away nothing, as far as handling goes, in production-class racing since its introduction. John Tojeiro also designed the body, a sleek shape reminiscent of the Ferrari 166 Mille Miglia.

Design work on Ford's Challenger V-8 engine began in 1958 under the leadership of Robert F. Stirrat. Weight reduction became a main objective during this period, and Ford aimed at producing a cast-iron engine that could compare in weight with an aluminum power unit of similar displacement. The decision to use cast iron was based on such advantages as the graphite content in its matrix, which serves as a lubricant in itself and also attracts and holds minute particles of engine lubricant, thus further reducing engine wear. Cast iron also has excellent sound-damping qualities, and tends to damp vibrations. Thermal expansion characteristics are nearly ideal, assuring proper clearances at all operating temperatures.

Aided by Ford Foundry's latest techniques in thin-wall casting with extensive use of resin-bonded cores, Stirrat came up with an engine that weighed only 450 pounds complete.

Its dimensions are very compact: 8.93 inches high, 16.36 inches wide, and 20.84 inches long. A study of the short and stiff five-bearing crank shaft indicated that about 70 percent of the total unbalanced couple could be balanced by means of normal crankshaft counterweights. Two external counterweights provide the other 30 percent, one mounted in front of the timing sprocket and the other as an element of the flywheel. No vibration damper was needed. Crankshaft stiffness is such that the fourth harmonic occurs beyond the normal engine operating range.

Shelby modifications include higher compression, a hotter camshaft and a four-barrel carburetor (Ford or Holley). As a power option, four Weber carburetors will be available, and in racing tune the engine puts out 355 bhp.

The cars are shipped complete from AC, except for engine and transmission, and engines and transmissions are shipped from Ford to those dealers whom Shelby has authorized to carry out the installation. Our test car had the lesser state of tune (and had not been test-driven by Carroll Shelby).

Even with the mild engine, the torque characteristics were incompatible with most street driving, with a flat spot below 2,000 rpm and a really devastating noise at maximum torque. We suspect that the valve clearances were off on the test car, not only because of the terrific clatter but also because the engine seemed to peak out before the 7,000-7,200 rpm that Shelby claims to get with ease.

During our acceleration tests, upshifts were made below 6,000 rpm, as no improvement could be seen by staying longer in the lower gears. The gearbox was not fully run in on the test car and its movements were inclined to be stiff. The short lever and its precise gate should be just perfect, though, after another 5,000 miles or so.

As has every other American high-performance car of recent times, Ford uses a Warner all-synchromesh transmission. The gear ratios are very well chosen, and close enough for racing, but it is a question whether a five-speed unit

PAGE 60: Three USRRC Shelby
American Cobra roadsters
1963 parked in front of the Shelby
American, Inc. shop.
BELOW: 1963 Cobra Daytona Coupe in
production at Shelby American.

Road Research Report
AC Cobra

Importer:	Shelby American, Inc. 1042 Princeton Drive Venice, California
Number of U.S. dealers:	16
Planned annual production:	1,000
Value of spare parts in U.S.:	Not available due to origin of components.

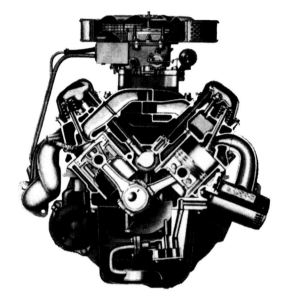

PRICES:

Price as tested...$5,995

OPERATING SCHEDULE:

Fuel recommended ....Premium
Mileage ....12-18 mpg
Range on 19-gallon tank ....230-340 miles
Oil recommended..........................SAE 10W-30 HD
Crankcase capacity.................................5 quarts
Change at intervals of..........................5,000 miles
Number of grease fittings.............................8
Lubrication interval.........................1,000 miles
Most frequent maintenance.......Grease steering-swivel pins every 200 miles for the first 2,000 miles.

ENGINE:

Displacement..........................260 cu in, 4,261 cc
Dimensions..........8 cyl, 3.80-in bore, 2.875-in stroke
Valve gear..................Pushrod-operated overhead valves
Compression ratio.........................10.0 to one
Power (SAE) ....260 bhp @ 5,800 rpm
Torque.........................269 lb-ft @ 4,800 rpm
Usable range of engine speeds ....2,000-7,000 rpm
Carburetion..................Single four-barrel Holley carburetor

CHASSIS:

Wheelbase ....90 in
Tread ....F 51 in, R 52 in
Length ....154 in
Ground clearance ....7.0 in
Suspension: F: Ind., lower wishbones and transverse leaf spring, anti-roll bar. R: Ind., lower wishbones and upper transverse leaf spring.
Steering ....Worm and sector
Turns, lock to lock 1⅔
Turning circle diameter between curbs...............40½ ft
Tire size.............................6.50/6.70 x 15
Pressures recommended ....Normal F 26, R 28 psi
                                        Racing F 42, R 42 psi
Brakes........Girling 12-in discs front, 11-in rear, 512 sq in swept area
Curb Weight (full tank) ....2,120 lbs
Percentage on the driving wheels..........................51.5

DRIVE TRAIN:

Clutch ....Single dry plate

Gear	Synchro	Ratio	Step	Over-all	Mph per 1,000 rpm
Rev	No	2.42	—	8.54	—9.65
1st	Yes	2.36	33%	8.36	9.9
2nd	Yes	1.78	26%	6.30	13.1
3rd	Yes	1.41	41%	4.99	16.6
4th	Yes	1.00	—	3.54	23.4

Final drive ratio.............................3.54 to one

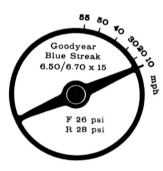

Goodyear
Blue Streak
6.50/6.70 x 15

F 26 psi
R 28 psi

Steering Behavior

Wheel position to maintain 400-foot circle at speeds indicated.

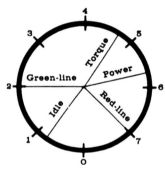

Torque
Power
Green-line
Red-line
Idle

Engine Flexibility
RPM in thousands

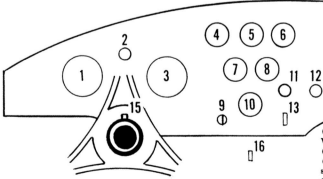

(1) Tachometer; (2) Turn-signal warning light; (3) Speedometer; (4) Water temperature gauge; (5) Oil temperature gauge; (6) Ammeter; (7) Oil-pressure gauge; (8) Fuel gauge; (9) Ignition key and starter; (10) Clock; (11) Light switch; (12) Wiper switch; (13) Heater switch; (14) Glove compartment; (15) Turn-signal switch; (16) Radiator fan switch

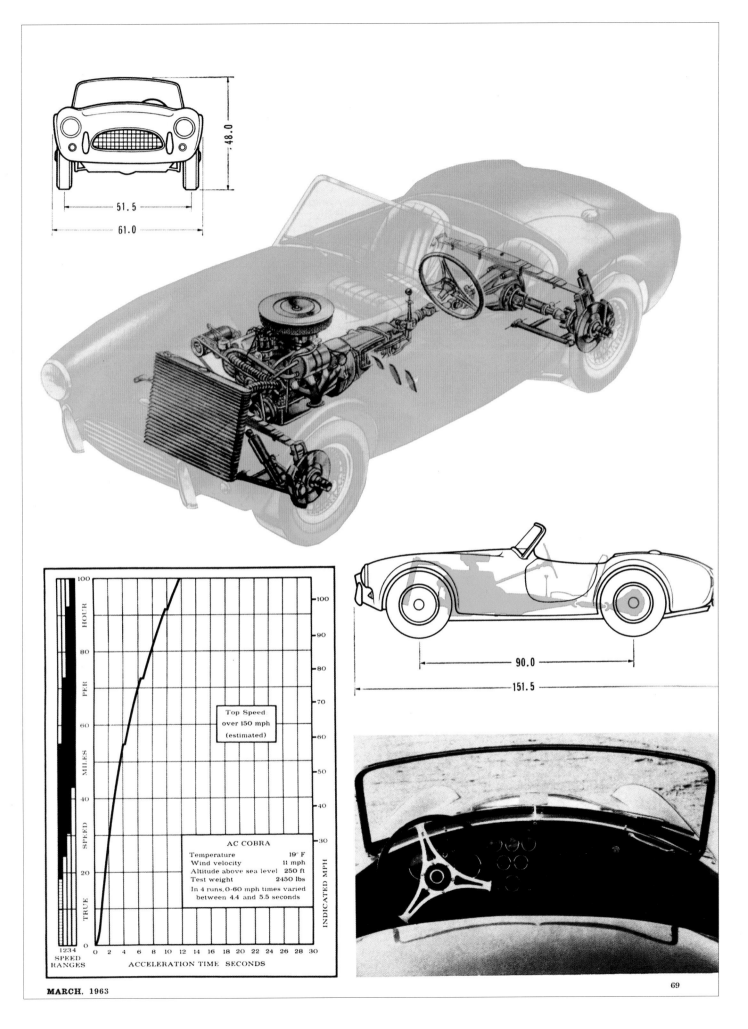

48.0

51.5

61.0

90.0

151.5

65

Top Speed
over 150 mph
(estimated)

AC COBRA

Temperature   19° F
Wind velocity   11 mph
Altitude above sea level 250 ft
Test weight   2450 lbs
In 4 runs, 0-60 mph times varied
between 4.4 and 5.5 seconds

HOUR   PER   MILES   SPEED   TRUE

INDICATED MPH

1234
SPEED
RANGES

ACCELERATION TIME SECONDS

0 2 4 6 8 10 12 14 16 18 20 22 24 26 28 30

would not give better results. With the 3.5-to-one final drive, a starting gear is needed, and with a higher ratio, the car would be undergeared for many circuits. Perhaps next year will see further experiments in this direction.

Placed in a chassis with less of a racing tradition, the power of the V-8 Ford would have been an embarrassment rather than an advantage. The center of gravity is located slightly toward the rear, and the rear wheels have a negative camber of about 3° in their neutral position, with just a trace of toe-in. This setup is obviously made to reduce or annihilate oversteer—but it is still the tail that begins to swing wide when the limit is approached. Correction of such slippage is easy enough with judicious use of power.

The existence of an actual limit of adhesion on a dry smooth surface seems to be a purely hypothetical question with the wide-section flat-profile Goodyear Blue Streak tires. Michelin X tires have always been an inherent part of the AC Ace design and if the Blue Streaks fitted to the Cobra are superior on a dry track, they certainly are not in the wet, on ice and snow, or on a rough or irregular surface. Among the many advantages of independent rear suspension, the one that stands out on the Cobra is the unloading of the rear drive shafts and the resultant lack of wheelspin, in spite of the lack of a limited-slip differential.

As for comfort, the independent rear suspension makes absolutely no contribution, since the springing is so stiff and wheel travel so restricted. The whole car feels like so much unsprung weight at low speeds, and it does not begin to soften up until about 50 mph. At racing speeds it is highly satisfactory, each wheel staying on the ground and no more than one deflection per bump being permitted by the

hard springs and the efficient shock absorbers. This ride gives the driver great confidence and helps improve his feel of the forces acting on the car, with the result that after a few hours at the wheel at high speeds he begins to feel like an integral part of the machine. Few modern sports cars can really give this impression—but then the AC Cobra is not so much a modern sports car as a traditional sports car brought up to the minute.

And this feeling is obtained more in spite of than because of the driving position. We were a little disappointed in the seats, which do not have enough backrest rake (and only fore-and-aft adjustment of the whole seat). The upright seating position is allright on a twisty circuit with plenty of arm and footwork, but far from ideal on a fast course with sweeping top-gear bends. Since the steering is quite heavy at low speeds, turning the wheel is easier when it is located at less than arm's length. At speed, however, the steering becomes lighter, and as wheel movements are ultra-small, with 1 percent turns lock to lock, most drivers would certainly prefer a more reclining position with almost straight arms.

Road shocks are felt in the wheel, but with such direct and ultra-sensitive steering, wheel movements are kept small and bumps could never alter the course of the car to any extent. Road feel is excellent, and corrections can be made almost before they become necessary.

Directional stability at speed is unusually good, regardless of crosswinds and road surfaces. The car can be controlled with a fingertip on a good road, and gentle curves call for no extra force. Under racing conditions, a reduction of steering-wheel work can be achieved by throttle steering, but even on a normal road it pays to look ahead, and with intelligent driving, it is possible to reduce the physical effort considerably.

Caution when using the brakes on a slippery surface is imperative. The 12-inch discs have no power booster, yet so little pedal effort is required that under extreme conditions most drivers are likely to apply too much force on the pedal rather than not enough. The ultimate stopping power on a dry surface is limited by locking of the rear wheels. The handbrake is well placed and comfortable to use, but it is not of the fly-off type as on Ace-Bristols.

Without going the whole hog, HRG-fashion, the AC Cobra has a well-equipped instrument panel, with gauges to tell you the temperature of the oil as well as the water, large dials for MPH and RPM, and an oil pressure gauge—but why the clock? It is obscured by the driver's right fist most of the time, and when a clock *is* needed, it would hardly be considered reliable enough anyhow. There is a roomy (relatively) glove box, but we were surprised to find there's no map-reading light.

English soft tops usually sacrifice a lot on the altar of lightness, and that of the AC Cobra is no exception. It is not flimsy, and the fastening is clever, but there is continual buffeting, rattles from the side windows, drafts and leaks everywhere. In addition to the side clips at the windshield edges, there is a slide at the center of the top of the windshield frame, with nailheads on the top securely fastened. The frame for the top is removable and may be stored separately in the trunk.

Every time we test a genuine 150-mph road car, the question crops up whether there is really adequate justification for their existence. In every case, we have been convinced that there is. For people who enjoy traveling fast, the

tremendous importance as a safety factor of a generous power reserve at all times cannot be overestimated. High-speed highway merges become routine and overtaking distances become amazingly short, so if not abused, the 150-mph sports car can be the safest, yet simultaneously the fastest (it goes without saying), car on the road.

The AC Cobra is not as sophisticated or as well-integrated as the cars it is competing with both in price and in racing classification. It will be interesting to see if the phenomenal performance bias will "bring the car off" as a commercial success. Commercial or not, the hair-curling level of performance the Cobra provides will certainly give the ranks of big-production car racers pensive moments.

Top speed: estimated 150 mph+
0-60 4.4-5.5 seconds
260 bhp, 269 lb-ft of torque
Price: $5,995

April 1963
Road Research Report:
Corvette Sting Ray

Waiting lists of great length and duration for the Corvette Sting Ray at all Chevrolet dealers are the best proof of the public's acceptance of the new model. We hailed the car's technical advances with great enthusiasm (October 1962 *Car and Driver*) after our brief test drives last fall.

Now it's time for an exhaustive report on America's leading grand touring car (which many drivers think of only as a sports car). We chose the 300-bhp version of the coupe, because it seems to enjoy some market preference over models equipped with the 250-, 340-, or fuel-injection 360-bhp engines.

However, the key to the personality of the Corvette Sting Ray lies neither in the power available nor in the revised styling, but in the chassis. Up to now the Corvette has been struggling to rise above a large number of stock components, notably in the suspension, where their presence created all kinds of problems that required extensive modifications for any competition use beyond normal road rallies. The new all independent suspension has completely transformed the Corvette in terms of traction and cornering power, but it still has some faults. The standard setup on the test car seemed a bit more suitable for race tracks than for fast back-road motoring. A rigid front anti-roll bar in combination with a relatively stiff transverse leaf spring in the rear reduces the resilience and independence of the suspension of each wheel with the result that even on mildly rough surfaces the car does not feel perfectly stable. On bumpy turns it's at its worst, veering freely from one course to another, making high-frequency corrections s.o.p., but on a smooth surface it comes incredibly close to perfection. Cornering stability under conditions permitting minimal wheel deflections is remarkable, and an initial feeling of pleasant surprise rises to sheer astonishment when one discovers that the car can be taken off the predetermined line with ease and still complete the turn in perfect balance.

There is some understeer but the car has such a tremendous power surplus, even with the next-to-bottom engine option that the tail can be slung out almost any old time, and after a while throttle steering seems the natural way of aiding the car around a curve. This is so easy to do that a newcomer to the car can master it in half an hour of fast driving.

Given surface roughness, the rear end becomes skittish. We experienced this with a full tank as well as one almost empty, indicating that normal loads don't appreciably affect its behavior in this respect.

One of our test cars had the new Saginaw power steering: three turns lock-to-lock with enough road feel to satisfy the most critical tester and observer while eliminating all difficulties of parking and maneuvering in tight spaces. We also tested a car with manual steering and found it so light in comparison with previous Corvettes that there can be no conceivable need for power assistance. While the power system is every bit as good as those used by Rover and Mercedes-Benz in terms of feed-back and road feel, it seems strange that Chevrolet should get around to introducing it when there is no longer any need for it. The three-spoke wheel is steeply raked (15 degrees 23 feet)

71

with a total span of 1.24 inches. The result is a range of adjustment adequate to let our test drivers (ranging in height from five-seven to six-four) find a nearly ideal seating position. Maximum effective leg room (to the accelerator) is 43.7 inches and the maximum vertical height from the seat to the headlining is 33 inches. In view of the overall height of only 49.8 inches, this is a good example of the care that has gone into designing the living quarters of the new Corvette Sting Ray.

As the engine and drive train are offset one inch to the right to provide wider leg room for the driver, he sits facing exactly in the direction he is going, with the pedals straight in front of him. The accelerator is nicely angled for normally disposed feet, but the clutch pedal has a rather excessive travel. With standard adjustment, you cannot release it without taking your heel off the floor, causing a bit of annoyance in traffic. Instead of a fly-off handbrake, the Corvette has a T-handle under the instrument panel labeled "Parking Brake," one of the few features of the new model that reminds you of its relationship with Chevrolet's mass-produced sedans.

Compared with previous Corvettes, the Sting Ray is improved in almost every imaginable respect: performance, handling, ride comfort, habitability, and trunk space. The trunk is only accessible from inside the car, however, since the tail is full of a fuel tank and a spare wheel, but the storage space behind the seats is even larger than outside dimensions indicate. A third person, sitting sideways, may come along for short rides, but will soon feel cramped from lack of headroom. An occasional extra passenger will actually be better off sitting on the console between the seats and sharing legroom with the shotgun rider.

Having driven the Corvette Sport Coupe in all kinds of weather conditions, we found the heater and defroster units

as on previous Corvettes, and its relatively thin rim offers a good grip. The entire semicircle between nine and three o'clock is free of spoke attachments, providing a clean hold for any but the most eccentric drivers. The steering column has a three-inch adjustment for length, but our test drivers all kept the wheel in its foremost (bottom) position while making the most of seat-adjustment possibilities. There are four inches of fore-and-aft travel but backrest angle is variable only by setting screws at its floor abutments. In addition, there are three seat-height positions eminently satisfactory. The heater fan has three speeds and air entry is variable by a push-pull control. Warm-up is not extremely rapid but seems to be faster than average. The body proved absolutely draft-proof and watertight.

We liked the ball-shaped interior door handles but were not convinced of the advantages of the wheel-type door lock buttons. A minor complaint is the location of the window winders, as you cannot set your knee against the door panel for bracing on a sharp turn without coming in contact with the window handle.

Brakes have long been a sore point with Corvettes and further advance has now been made without taking the full step of going to disc brakes (which the car really deserves). The Delco-Moraine power brakes have one-inch steel drums cast into the wheel rims, with 58.8 percent of the braking force being directed to the front wheels. Sintered iron brake linings are optional and will certainly be found necessary for anyone planning to race, as fade is easily provoked with the standard linings, although the cooling-off period required to restore full efficiency is very short.

Chevrolet is prepared for a fair-sized demand for special performance parts, but has restricted their application to the structurally stronger Sport Coupe. The sintered-iron heavy-duty brake system also includes vented backing plates and air scoops and a dual-circuit master cylinder. There is a heavy-duty anti-roll bar, heavy-duty front and rear shock absorbers, aluminum wheels with knock-off hubs, and a 36-gallon fuel tank. The brake mechanism, in contrast to that fitted as standard, automatically adjusts the brakes when applied during forward motion. To be ordered, this special performance kit (RPO Z06) also requires the 360-bhp engine, the four-speed Warner T-10 gearbox and a Positraction limited-slip differential.

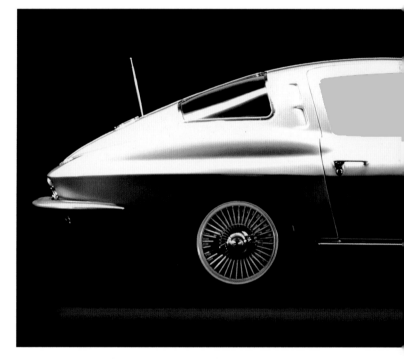

Race preparation of the 327-cubic-inch Corvette engine has been thoroughly treated by Bill Thomas in an article for the *Corvette News* (Volume 5 No.3), a General Motors publication invaluable to both the active Corvette competitor and his "civilian" counterpart. For information, readers are advised to write to *Corvette News*, 205 GM Building, Detroit 2, Michigan.

For all kinds of non-competitive driving, the 300-bhp version gives more than ample performance for anyone, with our average standing quarter-mile time at 14.4 seconds.

Road Research Report
Chevrolet Corvette Sting Ray Sport Coupe

Manufacturer:

Chevrolet Motor Division
General Motors Corporation
Detroit 2, Michigan

Number of U.S. dealers:　7,000 (approximately)
Planned annual production:　16,000

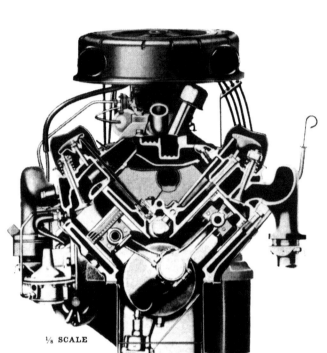

⅛ SCALE

PRICES

Basic price $4,252

OPERATING SCHEDULE

Fuel recommended .... Premium (99-101 Octane)
Mileage .... 10-18 mpg
Range on 20-gallon tank .... 200-360 miles
Oil recommended

	Single grade	Multi-grade
32° F and over	SAE 20 or 20W	SAE 10W-30
0° F	SAE 10W	SAE 10W-30
below 0° F	SAE 5W	SAE 5W-20

Crankcase capacity .... 5 quarts
Change at intervals of .... 6,000 miles
Number of grease fittings .... 10 (9 with manual steering)
Most frequent maintenance .... Lubrication at every 6,000 miles

ENGINE:

Displacement .... 327 cu in, 5,370 cc
Dimensions .... 8 cyl, 4.00-in bore, 3.25-in stroke
Valve gear: ...... Pushrod-operated overhead valves (hydraulic lifters)
Compression ratio .... 10.5 to one
Power (SAE) .... 300 bhp @ 5,000 rpm
Torque .... 360 lb-ft @ 3,200 rpm
Usable range of engine speeds .... 600-5,500 rpm
Carburetion .... Single four-throat Carter WCFB carburetor

CHASSIS:

Wheelbase .... 98 in
Track .... F 56.3 in, R 57.0 in
Length .... 175.3 in
Ground clearance .... 7.5 in
Suspension: F: Ind., coil springs and wishbones, anti-roll bar
　　　　　R: Ind., lower wishbones and unsplined half-shafts acting as
　　　　　　locating members, radius arms and transverse leaf spring
Steering .... Saginaw recirculating ball with power assistance
Turns, lock to lock 3
Turning circle diameter between curbs .... 36 ft
Tire size .... 6.70 x 15
Pressures recommended .... F 24, R 24 psi
Brakes ... Delco-Moraine 11-in drums front and rear, 328 sq in swept area
Curb weight (full tank) .... 3,180 lbs
Percentage on the driving wheels 53

DRIVE TRAIN:

Clutch .... Borg & Beck 10-in single dry plate

Gear	Synchro	Ratio	Step	Over-all	1,000 rpm
Rev	No	2.61	—	8.78	−9.0
1st	Yes	2.54	34%	8.52	9.3
2nd	Yes	1.89	25%	6.36	12.4
3rd	Yes	1.51	51%	5.08	15.6
4th	Yes	1.00	—	3.36	23.5

Final drive ratio .... 3.36 to one

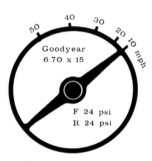

Goodyear
6.70 x 15

F 24 psi
R 24 psi

Steering Behavior
Wheel position to
maintain 400-foot circle
at speeds indicated.

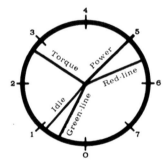

Torque　Power
Idle　Red-line
Green-line

Engine Flexibility
RPM in thousands

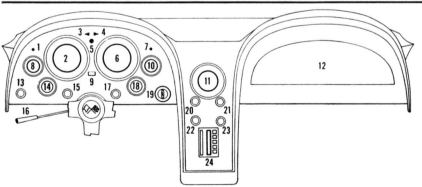

(1) Turn signal warning light (left); (2) Speedometer and odometer; (3) Warning light for headlights on in closed position; (4) Parking brake warning light; (5) High beam warning light; (6) Tachometer; (7) Turn signal warning light (right); (8) Water temperature gauge; (9) Trip odometer; (10) Oil pressure gauge; (11) Clock; (12) Glove box; (13) Light switch; (14) Ammeter; (15) Windshield wiper and washer; (16) Turn signal lever; (17) Cigarette lighter; (18) Fuel gauge; (19) Ignition key and starter; (20) Heater fan and fresh air control; (21) Defroster control; (22) Radio volume and tone control; (23) Radio tuning selector; (24) Radio dial.

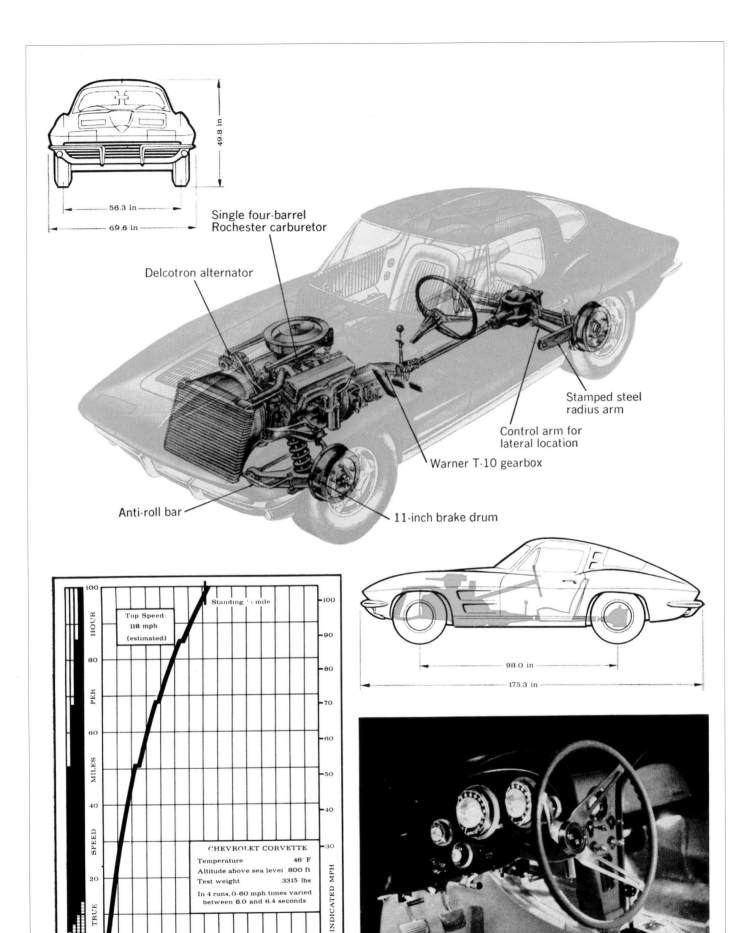

49.8 in

56.3 in

69.6 in

Single four-barrel
Rochester carburetor

Delcotron alternator

Stamped steel
radius arm

Control arm for
lateral location

Warner T-10 gearbox

Anti-roll bar

11-inch brake drum

75

98.0 in

175.3 in

Top Speed:
118 mph
(estimated)

Standing ½ mile

CHEVROLET CORVETTE

Temperature   46° F
Altitude above sea level   800 ft
Test weight   3315 lbs

In 4 runs, 0-60 mph times varied
between 6.0 and 6.4 seconds

HOUR   PER   MILES   SPEED   TRUE

INDICATED MPH

1234
SPEED
RANGES

ACCELERATION TIME SECONDS

APRIL, 1963

This was achieved with the "street" gearbox and an axle ratio that limits top speed to about 118 mph, a combination that results in extreme top-gear flexibility as well. Top-gear starts from stand-still to limit wheelspin present no problem with regard to stalling, but detonations were inevitable.

Fiberglass bodies usually have peculiar noises all their own, but the Corvette was remarkably quiet, no doubt due to the steel reinforcement surrounding the entire passenger compartment. The car is also notable for low wind noise and high directional stability. Engine noise is largely dependent on the throttle opening—it will respond with a roar to a wiggle of the toe if you're wearing light shoes, and this holds true within an extremely broad speed range. Top-gear acceleration from 50 to 80 is impressive indeed, both in sound and abdominal effects. In this connection the gear lever has a set of speeds at which it vibrates and generates a high-pitched rattle (this is in the lever itself and not in the reverse catch), and there are intermittent peculiar noises from the clock, probably when it rewinds itself.

The now-familiar Warner T-10 gearbox has faultless synchromesh and when fully broken in can be as light as cutting butter. One interesting aspect of its operation is the fact that the owner's handbook specifies double-clutching for down-shifts.

We are in complete agreement with this recommendation, over which there has been some controversy. Some people feel that double-clutching will wear out the synchromesh. This can be true only if on down-shifts the engine is accelerated so much that the synchromesh has to work harder than it would with a single-clutch change, a situation that does not seem to occur very often.

While we agree that the Buick Riviera, for example, is the kind of car where automatic transmission has a function, we cannot see its place in the Corvette, and our testing was done exclusively on a pair of manual-shift cars, one with power steering and one without, neither with Positraction limited-slip differential, which perhaps should be standard equipment on this car.

As the majority of new Corvettes are built with four-speed transmissions, it is hard to understand why the three-speed remains listed as standard equipment. We can see no reason for even continuing to offer it, and recommend that both the Power glide and the three-speed manual gearbox be dropped. This would let Chevrolet standardize the wide-ratio four-speed transmission throughout and make the close-ratio version optional for the 340- and 360-bhp models.

Our testers preferred the car with the fewest automatic "aids," and probably most of our readers will, too. That keen drivers prefer manual controls is not baffling at all—except possibly to advanced research personnel who forget that nowhere else can they get an effective 180-pound corrective computer that can be produced at low cost by unskilled labor.

Vastly more practical than any previous Corvette, the Sting Ray Sport Coupe appeals to a new segment of buyers who would not be interested in a convertible, and production schedules at the Saint Louis assembly plant have been doubled from the 1962 models. As an American car it is unique, and it stands out from its European counterparts as having in no way copied them but arrived at the same goal along a different route. Zora Arkus-Duntov summed it up this way: "For the first time I now have a Corvette I can be proud to drive in Europe." We understand his feelings and are happy to agree that the Sting Ray is a fine showpiece for the American auto industry, especially since it is produced at a substantially lower price than any foreign sports or GT car of comparable performance.

76

1963 Corvettes at the track.

March 1964
Road Research Report:
Pontiac Tempest GTO

Most knowledgeable enthusiasts reacted negatively when Pontiac announced that their new Tempest sports model was to be called the GTO. They felt, as we did, that Pontiac was swiping a name to which it had no right. Like Le Mans, Grand Prix, Monza, Spyder, and 2+2, this was another of those hard-to-digest bits of puffery from the Detroit-Madison Avenue axis.

O ur first look at the car made us feel a little better, because it is handsome, and then we got a call from correspondent Roger Proulx, raving about the car's acceleration and handling, so we arranged to test a Pontiac Tempest GTO. This was the most exhaustive and thorough road test we have ever done. We used two nearly identical cars, the differences being that one car had the shorter-ratio manual steering while the other had power; the manual steering car was also equipped with metallic brake linings. We drove our two cars unmercifully. One was driven from Detroit to New York City, used for ten days by every member of the staff, and then driven from New York to Daytona Beach, Florida, carrying the managing editor, his wife, and three active children. This car—the manual steering, metallic brake version—was driven over 3,000 miles. The other car was driven about 500. We ran dozens of acceleration tests on the two cars, plus many, many laps of the Daytona International Raceway's tri-oval and road circuit.

It was our original intention to borrow a Ferrari GTO and to run the two against each other at Bridgehampton's road racing circuit and on the drag strip at Westhampton. We had engaged Walt Hansgen to drive the Pontiac and Bob Grossman to run his own Ferrari. Unfortunately Grossman's

Ferrari was tired from a season of racing and was not considered fast enough to really be a match for our Tempest. We then canvassed all the GTO owners in this country and simply could not get one of those lucky gentlemen and the weather to cooperate simultaneously. As a result, we drove two Ferrari GTO's, but we were never able actually to run the Tempest against either one of them.

Although it would have been great fun and quite interesting to run the Ferrari racing car against Pontiac's similarly-named touring car, our tests showed that there really was no effective basis for comparison—the Pontiac will beat

the Ferrari in a drag race, and the Ferrari will go around any American road circuit faster than the stock Tempest GTO. We are positive, however, that a Tempest like ours, with the addition of NASCAR road racing suspension, will take the measure of any Ferrari other than prototype racing cars or the recently announced 250-LM. We should also point out that our test car, with stock suspension, metallic brakes and as tested 348-bhp engine will lap any U.S. road course faster than any. Ferrari street machine, including the 400 Superamerica. Not bad for an actual delivered price of $3,400 dollars, wot?...

Were we to buy a GTO (and there's a good chance at least one of us will), our selection might go something like this. A GTO is basically a $2,480 Tempest Le Mans with a $296 extra-equipment package that includes a floor shift, 389 engine, dual exhaust, stiffer shocks, "exterior identification" and a choice of super-premium tires or whitewalls. The four-speed, all-synchro transmission is $188 extra, and we'd gladly pay $115 to get the hottest (348-bhp) engine. The shorter axle ratios are only available with metallic brakes, HD radiator, and limited-slip differential ($75 for the lot). Quick steering (20:1) is part of the handling option, though HD shocks and springs alone are only $3.82. The "wood"-rim steering wheel is $39, and from there on in, it's trimming the window with fuzz (like $36 for custom-wheel covers). With every conceivable option on a GTO it would be difficult to spend more than $3,800. That's a bargain....

When you drive a Tempest GTO with the right options on it, you're driving a real automobile. Can Pontiac help it if they're too dumb to know that a car can't go that fast without a prancing horse decal on the side?

May 1964
Road Research Report:
Ford Mustang

It's easily the best thing to come out of Dearborn since the 1932 V-8 Model B roadster. But for all Ford's talk of Total Performance, it's still clear that the Mustang has been designed and built to a price. The necessity of meeting cost goals meant that it had to share a maximum number of components with other models in the Ford line.

Out of this situation sprang the advantage of an extremely wide availability of options for the Mustang, selected from the Falcon, Fairlane and Galaxie series. Briefly, it gives the customer a choice of four engines, three clutches, seven transmissions, two driveshafts, four brake systems, four wheel types and three wheel sizes, three suspension systems, and three steering systems. This seems slightly overwhelming until one remembers that only certain combinations are authorized, for either technical or commercial reasons. But it's still very impressive and approaches the Tempest's profusion of power team options. In two departments Ford even has the lead on Pontiac. Disc brakes are optional on the Mustang, and an independent rear end will be homologated and made available in small series for racing purposes. Lee Anthony Iacocca, vice president and general manager of Ford Division, sees the Mustang first of all as a family car, which meant that it had to have four seats, with better rear seat accommodation than is offered in the "two-plus-two" category. It's also aimed at a not clearly defined market consisting of customers looking for a not clearly defined combination of luxury and status. In addition to all this, the Mustang is intended as a sports car (or sporty car).

The Mustang constitutes an entirely new and separate line of Ford cars (bringing the total up to five, not counting the products of the Lincoln-Mercury Division). It will be produced exclusively in a factory within the River Rouge plant. Its production capacity is not stated, but Ford aims to sell about a quarter of a million Mustangs in its first 12-month period on the market. With the versatility of this design and the plentiful options, the demand might even exceed that figure.

Top speed: 110 mph (estimated)
0-60 8.0-8.6 seconds
210 bhp, 300 lb-ft of torque
Price: to be announced

PAGE 82: Mustang grille design seems a poor disguise for an air intake, and frontal appearance is marred by gaps between body panels.

PAGE 83; OPPOSITE, BOTTOM AND RIGHT: The door vent panes and rear light units are gracefully integrated with the body design as a whole.

OPPOSITE, TOP: A rakish windshield indicates the sporty character of the Mustang, and the sleek, squared-off body does not betray the presence of a genuine rear seat. Both soft and hardtops leave sufficient headroom for the rear seat passengers, and interior width will allow two Tessie O'Sheas to be comfortably seated in front. Well-styled bumpers do not add to the overall length but may offer inadequate protection.

OPPOSITE BOTTOM, LEFT: The lively emblem is well chosen and well executed, with framing to match the grille outline.

BELOW: All Mustangs have bucket-style front seats, and the convertible also displays the "rally pac" clock and tachometer. The lack of elbow room in the rear seat can be seen, as the padded ashtray shelves are located too far forward to permit their use as armrests.

Road Research Report: Ford Mustang

Manufacturer: Ford Motor Company, Rotunda Drive, Dearborn, Michigan
Planned annual production: 250,000
Price as tested: To be announced.

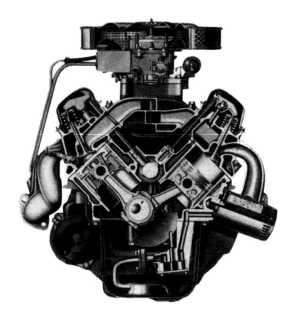

⅛ SCALE

ENGINE:

Water-cooled V-8, cast iron block, 5 main bearings
Bore x Stroke................4.00 x 2.87 in, 101.6 x 72.9 mm
Displacement................................289 cu in, 4727 cc
Compression ratio...................................9.0 to one
Carburetion............................Single 4-barrel Ford
Valve gear............Pushrod-operated overhead valves, hydraulic lifters
Valve diameter..........Intake 1.662-1.677 in, exhaust 1.457-1.442 in
Valve lift.................Intake 0.368 in, exhaust 0.380 in
Valve timing:
    Intake opens............................20° BTC
    Intake closes...........................66° ABC
    Exhaust opens..........................56° BBC
    Exhaust closes.........................20° ATC
Electrical system.............12-Volt, 55 Amp-hr battery
Power (SAE)....................210 bhp @ 4400 rpm
Torque.........................300 lbs-ft @ 2400 rpm
Specific power output......0.73 bhp per cu in, 44.5 bhp per liter
Usable range of engine speeds...........1000-5000 rpm
Fuel recommended...............................Regular
Mileage.....................................12-20 mpg
Range on 16-gallon tank.................192-320 miles

DRIVE TRAIN:

Clutch......................10-inch single dry plate
Transmission ....4-speed all-synchro

Gear	Ratio	Over-all	mph/1000 rpm	Max mph
Rev	2.78	8.34	-8.7	-43.5
1st	2.78	8.34	8.7	43.5
2nd	1.93	5.79	12.6	63.0
3rd	1.36	4.09	17.8	88.0
4th	1.00	3.00	24.2	110

Final drive ratio.............................3.00 to one

CHASSIS:

Platform frame, all-steel semi-integral body.
Wheelbase ....108 in
Track...................................F 56, R 56 in
Length......................................181.6 in
Width..68.2 in
Height.......................................51.0 in
Ground clearance..............................5.2 in
Curb weight.................................2861 lbs
Test weight.................................3150 lbs
Weight distribution front/rear...............53/47%
Pounds per bhp (test weight)...................15.0
Suspension F: Ind., unequal-length wishbones and coil springs, anti-roll bar.
    R: Rigid axle and semi-elliptic leaf springs.
Brakes........10-in drums front and rear, 251.3 sq in swept area
Steering...............Recirculating ball (16.0 to one ratio)
Turns lock to lock.............................3½
Turning circle.................................38 ft
Tires......................................6.50 x 13
Revs per mile..................................865

MAINTENANCE:

Crankcase capacity.............5 qts (incl filter)
Oil change interval...................6000 miles
Number of grease fittings.....3 (every 36,000 miles)

ACCELERATION:

Zero to	Seconds
30 mph	2.2
40 mph	3.6
50 mph	6.1
60 mph	8.2
70 mph	11.9
80 mph	16.1
90 mph	21.0
100 mph	28.1
Standing quarter-mile	81.5 mph in 16.4

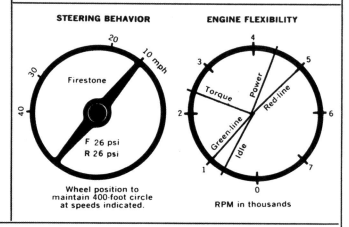

STEERING BEHAVIOR

Firestone
F 26 psi
R 26 psi

Wheel position to maintain 400-foot circle at speeds indicated.

ENGINE FLEXIBILITY

Torque
Power
Red-line
Green-line
Idle

RPM in thousands

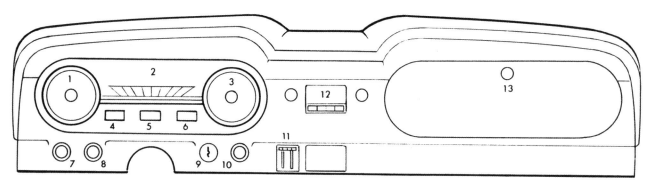

(1) Fuel gauge, (2) Speedometer, (3) Temperature gauge, (4) Oil pressure warning light, (5) Odometer, (6) Generator warning light, (7) Windshield wiper, (8) Light switch, (9) Ignition key and starter, (10) Cigarette lighter, (11) Heater and defroster controls, (12) Radio controls (13) Glove box.

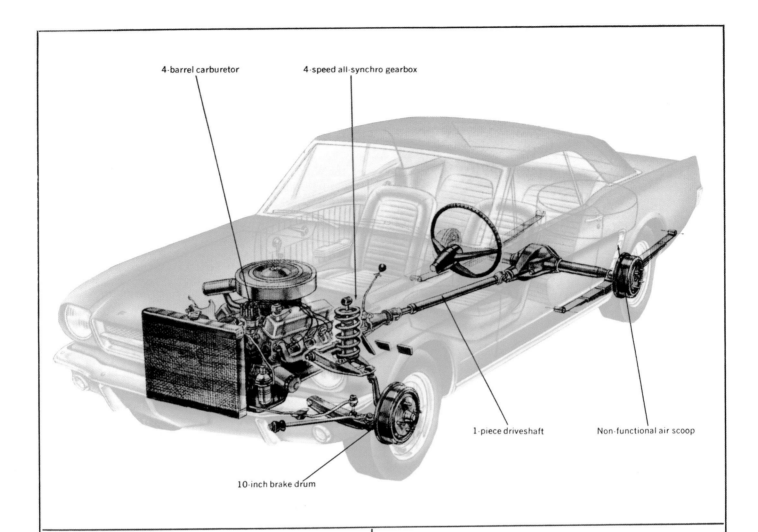

4-barrel carburetor

4-speed all-synchro gearbox

1-piece driveshaft

Non-functional air scoop

10-inch brake drum

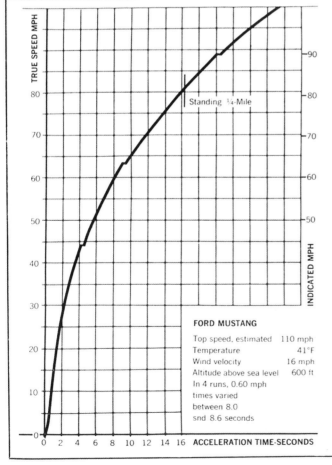

TRUE SPEED MPH

INDICATED MPH

Standing ¼-Mile

FORD MUSTANG

Top speed, estimated	110 mph
Temperature	41°F
Wind velocity	16 mph
Altitude above sea level	600 ft

In 4 runs, 0.60 mph times varied between 8.0 snd 8.6 seconds

ACCELERATION TIME-SECONDS

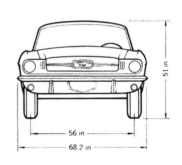

51 in

56 in

68.2 in

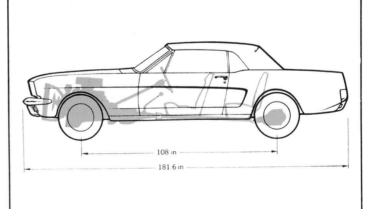

108 in

181.6 in

July 1964
From The Driver's Seat

By David E. Davis, Jr

DAN GURNEY FOR PRESIDENT!
Car and Driver's Candidate for This Great and Honored Post!

As we sit in our office watching the parade of poltroons, charlatans, earnest amateurs, and fuzzy idealists that constitute the current assortment of presidential aspirants, we rebel. We will not let the major political parties lead us down the garden path again this year. We'll run our own candidate, a man who can represent each of us who counts himself a car nut.

Enthusiasts Unite! Join with us in supporting the candidacy of Dan Gurney, running on a platform of unbridled automotive enthusiasm. Neither the Republicans nor the Democrats have taken any interest in the keen drivers' needs, hopes, desires, or innermost dreams, so we say the hell with them! We'll create a third stream—a vital new force in American politics that will sweep old ladies and small town speed traps from the highways and restrict winding two-lane roads to drivers of proven enthusiasm and skill. All drivers will have to pass through something like Carroll Shelby's school at Riverside, or one of the good English or European driving schools—the failures to be banished to public transportation. This will serve the dual function of improving local and state revenues, making railroads, airlines and local surface transportation companies solvent again, and clearing the jerks off the roads so that we paragons of impeccable, high-speed driving can have our way.

Who could possibly be better suited to champion our cause than Daniel Sexton Gurney. He goes like the wind. He can drive anything better than most anybody. He has the enduring love of 300,000 fans at Indianapolis. His name inspires countless stock car partisans in the Southeast. He is the patron saint of American sports car racing. European GP aficionados speak his name in the most reverent tones imaginable. He has become a legend in his own time.

Look at him from a purely political, non-automotive standpoint. Say his name aloud: Daniel Sexton Gurney. President Daniel Sexton Gurney. What a sound—as though he was preordained to take the job. Dictionaries variously define his given name as "An Exemplary Judge," or "God has judged." Even if those definitions were not so reassuring, we have to but point to Daniel in the Lion's Den or Daniel Boone for further inspiration. His middle name, Sexton, brings to mind selfless men laboring in little country churches, working night and day for the benefit of their friends and neighbors—significance that will not be lost upon the fundamentalist rural electorate. Then Gurney—a solid Anglo-Saxon name borne with pride by countless generations of soldiers and men of the soil, merchants and artisans, the very stuff of which America was formed. Daniel Sexton Gurney! The name that shall be a rallying cry for thousands of disenfranchised enthusiasts!

What about his competition? Goldwater likes horses and Thunderbirds and doesn't stand a chance. Rockefeller has been pictured with a variety of farm tractors and Model A Fords, but he seems to lean toward various American-made limousines, so we can disregard him. On form, Nixon's name is too easily linked with Edsel and Studebaker and shares their "loser's psychology." Lodge's car enthusiasm is pretty well limited to jeeps and half-tracks and things, so he should be a pushover for enlightened enthusiasts. Scranton refuses to commit himself.

April 1965
Road Research Report:
Porsche 911

No contest. This is the Porsche to end all Porsches—or, rather, to start a whole new generation of Porsches. Porsche's new 911 model is unquestionably the finest Porsche ever built. More than that, it's one of the best Gran Turismo cars in the world, certainly among the top three or four.

Porsche enthusiasts used to insist that the 356 model was as nearly perfect an automobile as had ever been designed, an immutable classic that couldn't be improved upon. Oh, no? Put a familiar 356 up alongside a 911. Only yesterday, the 356 seemed ahead of its time. Today you realized its time has passed; the 356 leaves you utterly unimpressed and you can't keep your eyes off the 911. The 911 is a superior car in every respect...the stuff legends are made of.

Top speed: 130 mph
0-60 6.8-7.9 seconds
148 bhp, 140 lb-ft of torque
Price: $6,490

—Jim Hall

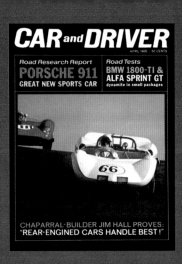

Road Research Report: Porsche 911

Importer/manufacturer: Porsche of America Corp.
107 Wren Ave.
Teaneck, N. J.

PRICES

Price as tested: $6490 POE East Coast

ENGINE

Air-cooled, horizontally-opposed 6-cyl. light alloy block. 8 main bearings

Bore x stroke	3.15 x 2.60 in, 80 x 66 mm
Displacement	121.5 cu in, 1991 cc
Compression ratio	9 to one
Carburetion	6 Solex 40 PI
Valve gear	1 overhead camshaft per bank of cylinders
Valve diameter	Intake 1.54 in, exhaust 1.38 in
Valve lift	Intake 0.451 in, exhaust 0.412 in

Valve timing (at 1 mm checking clearance; operating clearance is .1 mm)

Intake opens	29 BTC
Intake closes	39 ABC
Exhaust opens	39 BBC
Exhaust closes	19 ATC
Power (SAE)	148 bhp @ 6100 rpm
Torque	140 lbs-ft @ 4200 rpm
Specific power output	1.22 hp per cu in, 74 hp per liter
Usable range of engine speeds	1000–6800 rpm
Electrical system	12-Volt, 45 amp-hr battery, A.C. generator
Fuel recommended	Premium
Mileage	16–24 mpg
Range on 15.5-gallon tank	248–372 miles

DRIVE TRAIN

Clutch	8.5-inch single dry plate
Transmission	5-speed

Gear	Ratio	Over-all	mph/1000 rpm	Max mph
Rev	2.69	11.911	6.0	41
1st	2.833	12.535	6.5	44
2nd	1.778	7.873	9.5	65
3rd	1.218	5.393	13.7	93
4th	0.962	4.259	17.3	118
5th	0.821	3.635	20.3	138 (theoretical)

Final drive ratio .... 4.428 to one

CHASSIS

Wheelbase	87.1 in
Track	F 52.7, R 51.9 in
Length	164 in
Width	63.4 in
Height	51.9 in
Ground clearance	5.9 in
Dry weight	2177 lbs
Curb weight	2376 lbs
Test weight	2566 lbs
Weight distribution front/rear	40/60%
Pounds per bhp (test weight)	17.36

Suspension F: Ind., MacPherson strut and lower wishbone. telescopic dampers, longitudinal torsion bars, anti-roll bar
R: Ind., semi-trailing arms, transverse torsion bars, telescopic dampers

Brakes .... Ate-Dunlop discs, 10.8-in discs front, 11.3-in discs rear, 376 sq in swept area

Steering	ZF rack and pinion
Turns, lock to lock	2.8
Turning circle	33 ft 9 in
Tires	165 x 15 Dunlop SP
Revs per mile	808

MAINTENANCE

Crankcase capacity	8 qts (dry sump)
Oil change interval	3000 miles
Grease fittings	0

ACCELERATION

Zero to	Seconds
30 mph	2.3
40 mph	3.3
50 mph	5.2
60 mph	7.0
70 mph	9.8
80 mph	12.4
90 mph	15.6
100 mph	20.0
Standing ¼-mile	90 mph in 15.6

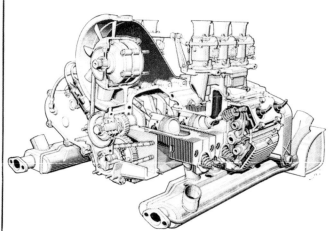

Above, the 901 engine of the prototype; below, the 911 production engine. The primary difference is in the carburetion; the 901 used two triple-throat Solex carburetors, the 911 uses six single-throat Solexes. The factory has quoted 130 DIN horsepower for both engines, but we suspect that this may be on the low side; it's probably more like the 148 SAE hp figure. The single overhead cam and rocker arms are easily seen in the above drawing, though only part of the chain drive is shown. The ram tubes (or "velocity stacks") are fitted to the production engines, hidden under the air-cleaner.

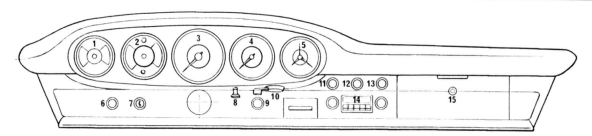

(1) Fuel level and oil level, (2) oil temperature and pressure, (3) tachometer, (4) speedometer, odometer and tripmeter, (5) clock, (6) lights, (7) ignition, (8) tripmeter return, (9) cigarette lighter, (10) fresh air control, (11) fog lights switch, (12) parking lights, (13) auxiliary heater and fan control, (14) optional radio, (15) glove compartment. Warning lights in (2), (3) and (4) indicate: turn signals on, oil pressure low, hand brake on, and malfunction in the electrical system.

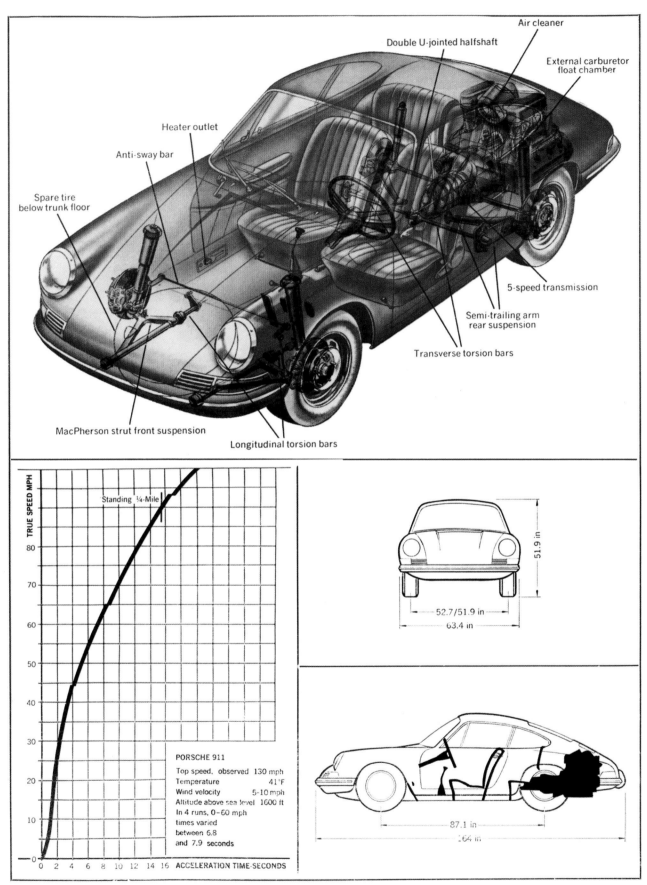

Air cleaner

Double U-jointed halfshaft

External carburetor float chamber

Heater outlet

Anti-sway bar

Spare tire below trunk floor

5-speed transmission

Semi-trailing arm rear suspension

Transverse torsion bars

MacPherson strut front suspension

Longitudinal torsion bars

TRUE SPEED MPH

Standing ¼-Mile

80

70

60

50

40

30

20

10

0

0 2 4 6 8 10 12 14 16   ACCELERATION TIME-SECONDS

PORSCHE 911

Top speed, observed 130 mph
Temperature 41°F
Wind velocity 5-10 mph
Altitude above sea level 1600 ft
In 4 runs, 0–60 mph
times varied
between 6.8
and 7.9 seconds

51.9 in

52.7/51.9 in

63.4 in

87.1 in

164 in

Enzo off guard

BELOW: Enzo Ferrari and John Surtees at the Cavallino. Enzo has just set up drinks: "Formula One, Two or Three Cocktails"—with the Formula One reserved for "hard men only." Surtees is being ribbed by the Commendatore because he wisely chose the "Formula Three," a concoction heavily diluted with water. A Ferrari aide shares in the fun.
RIGHT, TOP AND BOTTOM: Ferrari makes no secret of his grief for his son, Dino, whose brilliant career in engineering ended with his death from leukemia. Here, in Ferrari's Maranello office, the boy's photograph dominates an otherwise stark décor. The bare desktop is a Ferrari trademark—the result of his well-known aversion to paperwork.

—Julius Weitman

President Johnson has the enormous advantage that accrues to any strong incumbent, but the fact that he travels in helicopters, DC-8s and various ill-handling bubble-top limousines ought to hurt him. Besides, we've seen pictures of him on horseback too, so he really suffers the same potential mayhem at the hands of the muckrakers as the junior senator from Arizona. Let's face it, none of these men is worthy of Gurney's steel. Dedicated, yes; honest, yes; capable, probably; but worthy of our support as *Car and Driver* candidates? Never.

We don't know why we didn't think of this before. Gurney is a natural. He is the mold from which all of history's strong, silent, American heroes were cast. He is handsome enough to be a film star, with features rough-hewn from native American oak. He's as brave as Dick Tracy. He never says anything dumb (in fact he hardly ever says anything at all, which is one more powerful point in his favor). He comes from the great American middle class, with neither wealth nor poverty to embarrass him in his quest for greatness. He is a superlative husband and father, which won't hurt him a bit. Finally, he's a good driver. It has been said that no adult male American will admit to being less than an expert at golf, lovemaking, or driving. We hold that truth to be self-evident, and we predict that large numbers of Americans will identify with Mr. Gurney and lend him their wholehearted support.

We have included a coupon on page 82 to make it possible for you to join our crusade. We are offering campaign buttons and bumper stickers for one dollar, to cover the cost of production, handling, and mailing. Send your dollar today—join us to form a tidal wave of public opinion that will sweep the non-enthusiasts out, and our man Gurney in. Make 1964 the Year of the Car Enthusiast! Send Dan Gurney to Washington!

February 1966
The Editorial Side

By Brock Yates

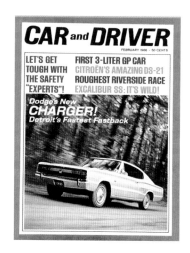

Now that I'm up here on this soapbox, feeling kind of exposed and wind-buffeted, it might be appropriate to introduce you to my particular brand of automotive likes and dislikes. After all, any magazine—and this one in particular—reflects the personality of its editor in a multitude of subtle ways, and it therefore seems fair to forewarn you about the editorial stance you can expect *Car and Driver* to take in the coming months.

96

Don't expect any radical changes. If you purists are looking for me to part the seas and lead us all back into the promised land of pur sang two-seaters, be prepared to get your feet wet. Conversely, there will be no danger of the journal turning into a series of vicarious rides down a quarter-mile drag strip. We will continue to view the automotive scene with as much liberalism as possible, treating each automobile, each race, each personality on the basis of its own merits, and not on its relationship to any particular subspecies of automotive enthusiasm.

I enjoy automobiles. Oh, there are times when I despise them, when I find them assuming an exaggerated role in our daily lives; when they clog highways and reduce their drivers to the level of cattle in a loading chute; when they call forth the most primitive urges for status-seeking and idol worship; and when they indiscriminately kill innocent citizens. Yet, I suppose these drawbacks are important because they add real dimension to the automobile. There is no social force which is all good or all bad, and therein lies our basic fascination with this machine—a device that is unequalled in terms of its widespread impact on the human race.

To give you an idea of my mixed bag of automotive tastes, I find myself vehemently defending the hot rodders when I'm around sports car people and vehemently defending the sports car people when I'm among hot rodders.

There's simply too much going on out there in the world of the automobile to operate, ostrich-like, in one limited realm, and I frankly admit to fiendish pleasure in assaulting the little duchies of smugness that have been built up throughout the sport.

CYCLONE GT

LINCOLN-MERCURY DIVISION OF Ford

Top spine tingler in the Comet line: Cyclone GT convertible.

This one will start a glow in any red-blooded American driver. For getaway, there's a new 390 4-barrel V-8 with a high-lift cam. Quite a start. And console-mounted transmission. (The optional 4-speed manual is specially geared for blazing getaway.) Buckets, of course. And heavy-duty, wide-rim wheels. And high-rate front and rear springs, big-diameter stabilizer bar, and HD shocks front and rear. And twin scoop GT hood. Engine dress-up kit, too. Add the optional tach and you're ready to rally. You get the idea: This Comet omits nothing that could add to the sport of driving. It has a special, spirited luxury, too. In the upholstery, trim, carpeting, everywhere. This new Comet Cyclone GT is also available as a hardtop—one of the thirteen bigger new-generation Comets: sedans, hardtops, convertibles, station wagons . . . all roomier, livelier and more beautiful than ever. The complete lineup includes sporty Calientes, stylish Capris and rakish Comet 202's, as well as racy Cyclones. Choose your 1966 Comet at your Mercury dealer's now.

the big, beautiful performance champion

Mercury COMET GT

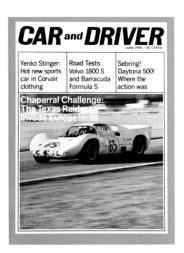

June 1966
From The Driver's Seat

By David E. Davis, Jr

This fella named Ralph Nader may be about to kill an old friend of mine: I went to work for Chevrolet's advertising agency in the spring of 1960 and found myself plunged right into the middle of what was then called "the Corvair problem."

The Corvair was introduced in the fall of 1959, along with the Falcon and the Valiant. The Falcon represented the high water mark of the Robert S. McNamara "dumb-cars-for-dumb-people" concept that seemed to guide the Ford Motor Company at that time, and the Valiant was a generally more palatable, "European looking" version of the same thing. Not the Corvair, though.

Ed Cole, now Executive Vice President at General Motors Corporation, was the General Manager of Chevrolet Division in those days, and he had sparkplugged the Corvair project from its beginning in 1956. He and his supporters on the engineering side had decided that since the Volkswagen was the hot setup in the raging imported car boom, a Volkswagen was what Chevrolet should build—an American Volkswagen, but a Volkswagen nonetheless.

The Volkswagen was very much the darling of the foreign car enthusiasts back then—it hadn't yet become a member of the automotive establishment. As such, it was held up as the cure for all of America's automotive ills, the perfect protest against Detroit's late-1950s excesses by everyone from college professors to gas station attendants. You could hardly pick up a copy of any car magazine, or the science and mechanics magazines, without getting slugged by statements to the effect that the VW was the Good Car. *Consumer Reports* used it as the standard of comparison for about half the cars it tested—luxury sedans, station wagons, *ad nauseam*.

So who can blame the powers that were at Chevrolet for selecting the VW as the way to go? Anybody who'd ever driven one knew that they oversteered like mad and that a gusty crosswind could blow one clean off the road, and so did the people at Chevrolet. But, at the same time, here were the experts—the automotive literati and culturati singing the Beetle's praises to the skies. And there was the public buying Beetles in ever-increasing numbers, so maybe that was what they wanted.

The Corvair was duly introduced and the car magazines went quite ape over it.

For example Karl Ludvigsen, writing in *Sports Cars Illustrated*, said: "...Most of all it [the Corvair] personifies what we feel is important in the field of automotive safety: its fine steering and stable braking restore to the driver of an American car the kind of honest precise control that he has had to do without for some three fast-moving decades. It has live nerves and quick reflexes that are worth more than all the seat belts and crash pads in the world."

Ludvigsen also mentioned the fact that the car oversteered, but he didn't see it as a serious drawback. *Road & Track*, on the other hand, said, "...The Corvair positively understeers under any and all conditions, up to the point of total loss of adhesion." They even went farther later in the piece calling attention to "gossip about the car's dangerous

IF YOU WANT
THE WORD
ON CORVAIR, ASK
1,500,000
OWNERS

IF YOU WANT A GOOD DEAL, ASK YOUR CHEVROLET DEALER

We think we know what you'll hear when you ask around about Corvair. Praise
for Corvair's independent four-wheel suspension. Comments on how Corvair turns,
parks and maneuvers. Compliments for Corvair's one-of-a-kind styling.
Awe for its great rear-engine traction. Buy one now and you'll like it so well
you might want to buy another one in '67!

handling characteristics," saying, "It definitely understeers at all times." They loved it.

So, while Chevrolet's management might well have pondered over *Road & Track*'s definition of understeer, they certainly had no reason to think they'd done the wrong thing. But then came the fan-belt-throwing problem, which had everybody nattering about the Corvair in America's bars and barbershops, followed by the word that Falcons got much better gas mileage than Corvairs, followed by the information that Falcons also sold much better than Corvairs, and the panic was on.

The basic hang-up was that a lot of people at Chevrolet had really wanted a Falcon all along, and they were terrified of the Corvair's nonconformity of design. (In some quarters in the Motor City, nonconformity ranks with dope peddling and sexual perversion as a capital crime.) Those Chevy engineers loved the Corvair, and a tiny handful of enthusiasts scattered through the organization loved the Corvair, but the sales department hated it.

At the agency, I inherited the mantle of "official company enthusiast" from a great copywriter and one-time automotive journalist named Barney Clark. The Corvair and the Corvette were Barney's raison d'etre, and it infuriated him to grind out ads that tried to make the Corvair—Ed Cole's baby—into a Falcon. When I moved in, I got all worked up about the enthusiast oriented qualities of the car, and became a Corvair missionary.

I used to ache for a chance to forget about "economy transportation." I wanted to turn the enthusiasts on about this neat, quick, little car, the way I was turned on. That was part of it, but I figured I owed it to Barney Clark too, and to that ragged little band of enthusiasts who were getting shot down in flames every time they tried to promote the Corvair's strengths, instead of pretending that it had no weaknesses.

Then Ed Cole saved us again. In 1961 he sent us off into the wilds of Canada to run Corvairs in the Winter Rally and the Shell 4000, and the cars turned out to be just as good as we'd always said they were. He got together with Bill Mitchell, the boss at GM Styling, and they created the Monza, which appeared at the Chicago Auto Show that year, and knocked the enthusiasts dead. We got to do ads that sold the Monza for what it was, not what somebody wished it was. And they sold. The Monza became the biggest seller in the Corvair line—the "family sports car"—and "economy transportation" was forgotten.

When it became clear that the Corvair was at last going to be an enthusiast's car, Ed Cole approved the release of a heavy-duty suspension package that made it even more desirable. In 1964, the whole Corvair line got a modified and improved version of the old swing-axle rear suspension, and in 1965 the swing-axles were dropped completely, replaced by a new version of the same independent rear suspension that Zora Arkus-Duntov had designed for his experimental CERV-1, and later adapted to the '63 Corvette.

It was beautiful. Half the car manufacturers in Europe were falling over each other to mass-produce Corvair copies. The Corvair was outselling the car that had been rushed into production to replace it—the Falconesque Chevy II. It was even outselling the Falcon. It was so hot that Ford brought out the Mustang, just to capitalize on the booming Monza

phenomenon, and did so well that they took over the market for such cars and expanded it beyond the wildest dreams of anybody at Chevrolet.

Now Chevrolet is going to bring out a new car to counteract the car that Ford brought out to counteract the car that Chevrolet had in the first place. Beautiful.

In all the confusion, Corvair sales have started to fall off. Why? Because the weirdest collection of legislator-lawyers, zealot-lawyers, ambulance-chasing lawyers, hack automotive writers, and has-been race drivers ever assembled under the banner of a single cause, has decided to make it the scapegoat for our country's traffic death toll.

A short time back, I met Ralph Nader, the author of *Unsafe At Any Speed*, on a TV show. Nader figures that Chevrolet is probably going to be forced to drop the Corvair, because of the bad publicity caused by his book and by the Senate safety hearings—not to mention all the lawsuits brought by people who've suddenly and mysteriously come to the realization that the accident they had four years ago was really their car's fault. Nader smiled like a kid with an all-A report card when he told me that Ed Cole himself had said that the growing pressure could someday finish the Corvair off altogether. Beautiful.

The man who first conceived the Corvair is an enthusiast. Enthusiasts built it. Enthusiasts sold it, enthusiasts bought it, and enthusiasts love it. The 1965 and 1966 Corvairs are rare examples of fresh, unorthodox thinking in Detroit car design, and the 1967 will be even better. But in spite of that, Ed Cole has to fear for the Corvair's continued existence, because almost ten years ago he built one that handled like a 1966 Volkswagen.

November 1967
Amphicar

The Amphicar's modest commercial success should be more than enough to enshrine it forever in the hearts of all the nutball inventors in the world. Dinners and wives will grow cold and stale while mechanics, mad scientists, and tweedy chemistry professors work late in workshops all over the world, figuring that if the Amphicar people can do it, so can they. The Amphicar is the rolling, floating embodiment of a fantasy fueled by years and years of *Popular Science* and *Popular Mechanics*, not to mention Tom Swift and Buck Rogers. Somebody is always trying to perfect the airplane you can drive to work, or the sports car you can fly, and the Amphicar is a logical extension of that dream. As a car, unfortunately, it behaves a bit too much like a boat, and its water-borne performance is hampered by a lot of purely automotive shortcomings. And although there are many beautiful cars and an endless variety of beautiful boats, combining the two concepts in one machine has brought out all of the ugliest characteristics of each. The Amphicar is not beautiful. In fact, we are hard-pressed to come up with any hard-and-fast definition of what the Amphicar really is—unless it was never meant to perform any genuinely important function in the first place. If that's true, if it was meant to be nothing more than a moderately expensive automotive novelty, then it succeeds. But if they meant it to be a fully functional proposition—interchangeably useful as either boat or car—then they dropped the ball somewhere.

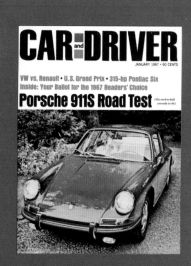

February 1967
Road Research Report: Shelby GT 500

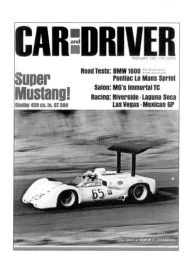

Seven liters! Four hundred and twenty-eight cubic inches in a Mustang! We were expecting a cataclysm-on-wheels, the automotive equivalent of the end of the earth. We were pleasantly surprised to discover that the GT 500 isn't anything like that.

The old corollary to that old adage, "There's no substitute for cubic inches," is "except rectangular money" and who would know better than Carroll Shelby? When the Cobra 289 peaked out on the race track, there were several ways of making it go faster—most are expensive, one is cheap. One of the more expensive ways was the Daytona coupe body. The late Ken Miles found a better way. At Sebring in 1964, he shoehorned a Ford 427 NASCARized engine into a Cobra roadster. The experiment came to rest, sorely bent, against a palm tree, but Miles persisted. By the end of the season, at Nassau, he had another one bolted together. It blew up, but the die was cast. Early in 1965, Shelby announced the Cobra II with a 427-cubic inch V-8 replacing the 289. That June, at Le Mans, two of Ford's rear-engined GT prototypes appeared with the big 427 instead of the 289. The Europeans hooted and jeered at the bulky, heavy, unsophisticated V-8 with its pushrods and single four-barrel carburetor. A year later, Ford 427s swept the first three places at the French classic, with Shelby's two entries dead-heating the final lap. What the 427s had beaten was a team of 270-cubic inch Ferrari V-128 with multiple carburetion and four overhead camshafts. The Italian engine developed almost as much horsepower as the Ford —425 hp vs. 485—but it was much more tautly stressed and, therefore, fragile. Which is the whole point of 7-liter Fords, Cobras, and now, Shelby Mustangs.

For 1967, Ford offered the Mustang with its tried-and-true 390 V-8, which has a bore and stroke of 4.05 x 3.78 inches. Ford also builds a 428 V-8 on the same block with a bore and stroke of 4.13 x 3.98 inches. "Why not use this engine in the 1967 Shelby Mustang?" reasoned Shelby. Why not indeed. The car is called the GT 500 and its engine is called the Cobra Le Mans.

Somebody is telling a little white half-truth. Please note that the Cobra Le Mans engine displaces 428 cubic inches. That sounds a hair better than the 427. In fact, they are two entirely different engines. Both have the same external dimensions, but the 427 is more oversquare, with a bore and stroke of 4.23 x 3.78. The 427 is a racing engine, full of the kind of intestinal fortitude that makes it capable of enduring 500 miles at Daytona and 24 hours at Le Mans. The 428 is a passenger-car engine, and nearly $1,000 cheaper than the 427. Few people would be happy with the 427 unless they were racing it. It's noisy, balky, and an oil burner at normal highway speeds. The GT 500 is not a racing car, although, but for a few subtle differences, its engine is the same as the one that propelled Shelby's Fords to victory at Le Mans. Seven liters in a Mustang! The early GT 500 engineering prototype was the fastest car ever to lap Ford's twisty handling loop, except for the GT 40s, of course. And the same car cut a quarter mile in 13.6 seconds at 106 mph. Super car!

So we braced ourselves when we stuck our editorial foot

PAGE 102: Hairy air scoops are a
Shelby trademark, as on the GT 40.
BELOW AND OPPOSITE: The Shelby
Mustang conversion includes a new
nose and a big fat Kamm-type rear
deck treatment. The GT 500 isn't quite
as fast as we expected, but it does
with ease what the old 350 took brute
force to accomplish.

into the first-production GT 500. And when it only turned 15.0 at 95, we were a bit disappointed. That's only two-tenths of a second quicker than the Mustang 390 automatic (*Car and Driver*, November 1965) and last year's GT 350H automatic (*Car and Driver*, May 1966), and not quite as fast as the original GT 350 four-speed (*Car and Driver*, May 1965). But then we thought back on the earlier GT 350s and realized that what the old Shelby Mustang does with difficulty, the GT 500 does easily.

The GT 500 is an adult sports car. Shelby's Mustangs have come a long way in three years—from adolescence to maturity. The 1965 GT 350 was a hot rodder's idea of a sports car: a rough-riding bronco that was as exciting to drive as a Maserati 300S, and about as marketable a proposition. The traction bars clanked, the side exhausts were deafening, the clutch was better than an advanced Charles Atlas program, and when the ratcheting-type limited-slip differential unlocked, it sounded like the rear axle had cracked in half. It rode like a Conestoga wagon and steered like a 1936, Reo chain-drive, solid-tire coal truck... and we loved it. It was a man's car in a world of increasingly effeminate ladies' carriages. You drove it brutally and it reacted brutally. Every minute at speed was like the chariot-racing scene in *Ben Hur*.

Unfortunately for Shelby, the market for a car as hairy as this was limited. One state's motor vehicle bureau complained that the brakes, although virtually fade-proof, required too much pedal pressure. Apparently, the inspectors' leg muscles had atrophied from years of dainty stabs at over-boosted power brakes.

For 1966, Shelby toned the GT 350 down from a wild mustang to a merely high-strung thoroughbred. It was barely tame enough for the Hertz Corporation, which bought 1,000 of them and put them into service as the hottest rent-a-cars the business has ever seen.

The GT 350 still wasn't acceptable to a large enough body of potential buyers; so, in 1967, an abrupt change in policy has transformed the Shelby Mustang. The $1,000-or-so above the price of a comparable Mustang that used to go into expensive, unseen mechanical improvements is now lavished instead on exterior styling changes. The back lot at Shelby American's remanufacturing plant is littered with stock Mustang front and rear sheet metal and engine and trunk lids. In their place go fiberglass panels stylized by Ford's Chuck McHose, working in close cooperation with Shelby American.

The new nose piece arches tautly forward, forming a deep cowling for the headlights (changed from duals to quads, with the high-beams centered in the grille, driving-lamp style). The hood features an air-scoop even larger than last year's, now divided by an air-splitter, and it's still functional. At the rear, the new trunk lid and tailpiece combine to form a racy-looking aerodynamic spoiler lip. No one would say for sure if high-speed tests had proved the efficiency of this styling gimmick or not—but it looks right. Finally, the side louvres have been replaced by scoops—big hairy scoops that poke out into the

airstream beyond the boundary layer. Actually, these are to let the air out; stale interior air exits through the inconspicuous slot behind the scoop. The forward-facing scoop leads to a narrow venturi area that helps draw air out the rear slot. That light behind the scoop flashes when the turn signals are on and glows steadily when the brakes are on. Another pair of funnel scoops are installed at the rear of the sculptured side panel—this time to blow air at the rear brake drums. A pair of giant taillights running almost the full width of the Kamm-inspired tail completes the Shelby look. As a whole, the Shelby Mustangs make the regular Mustangs look sick.

Underneath, the Koni shock absorbers have given way to less expensive adjustable Gabriels; the traction bars are gone; the noisy racing differential has long since disappeared; and the Shelby Mustang has become a lot less like a NASCAR stocker without becoming any less roadable. The engineering is now built into stock parts instead of having to be included in extra hardware. The front suspension geometry was determined by Klaus Arning and the same computer he used in setting up the suspension of the Ford GT 40 and Shelby's Cobra II, and the front anti-sway bar has been reduced from an almost immovable one inch to a more compliant .94 inch. The rear leaf springs are now equipped with little rubber bumpers called "hopper stoppers" that are designed to prevent axle hop under hard acceleration. Most of the competition-bred racing equipment is still available, if necessary, as options. Oddly, the rear springs are stiffer this year (135 lbs./in. vs. 115 lbs./in. in 1966), but the actual ride is smoother. The front springs of the GT 500, at 365 lbs./in., are naturally stronger than those of the GT 350, at 330 lbs./in.

We drove, briefly, a 1967 GT 350, and noted how busy and mechanical the engine sounds. Jumping from that into the GT 500, the most marked difference was in engine noise, which is practically nonexistent in the 428-engined car except for a motorboating exhaust throb. Our test car also had an automatic transmission (it will be difficult to get a GT 500 with a four-speed manual), power brakes, fast-ratio power steering, air conditioner, shoulder harnesses, and roll bar. (More about these last two items later.) All the viciousness had gone out of the car, without any lessening of its animal vitality. It still reacts positively, but to a much lighter touch. The power brakes, we felt, were a little oversensitive, but the automatic transmission was near perfect. The GT 500 accelerates powerfully at any legal speed, gets off the mark with little wheelspin, despite the absence of a limited-slip, and shifts very crisply. The automatic is a beefed-up Ford C-6, and each gear change feels like "a shift and a half," in the words of one staffer. The power steering is among the best we've driven, partially because it's quick, but mostly because we could actually feel the road through the wood-rim wheel (standard equipment).

In softening the car to make it more acceptable to a wider market, some of the sheer handling virtuosity of the old GT 350s has been lost, but not much. As you might expect, the car understeers until you get the throttle open. It tracks well in a corner and is exceptionally agile in evasive maneuverability tests for a 3500-lb. car. Our handling tests were made with 40 psi in the Goodyear Speedway E70-15 tires (similar to Firestone's Wide Ovals), so the harshness control was not all it would be with normal pressures (28 psi front and 2.4 psi rear). The acceleration was not all it might have been either. With less than 100 miles on the odometer, the engine was tight and breathless at anything much over 5,000 rpm. The redline is 6,000, but we got the best acceleration times letting the

want
more

F.P.M.?*

try a Shelby GT

That's Fun-Per-Mile—yours aplenty in these *two* great new GT cars from Shelby American.

There's more F.P.M. when you have reserve performance. The GT 350 carries a 306 horsepower 289 cubic inch V-8. The GT 500 is powered by the 428 cubic inch V-8, descended from the 1966 LeMans winning Ford GT.

The F.P.M. is higher when steering is competition-quick, suspension is firm. Driving's *fun* with the safety of an integral roll bar, shoulder harnesses, disc front and drum rear brakes, wide-path 4-ply nylon tires.

Driving's *fun* with the Shelby brand of comfort and style. For more F.P.M., see your Shelby dealer P.D.Q.

 **SHELBY G.T.** 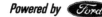 350 and 500 **The Road Cars** Powered by Ford

Shelby American, Inc., 6501 W. Imperial Highway, Los Angeles 90009

TURN SIX AT RIVERSIDE

SHELBY MUSTANG GT 350

American. SCCA Class B production sports car champion in 1965 and 1966. Body style: two-door fastback. Engine: Ford overhead valve V8. Bore and stroke: 4″ x 2.87″. Displacement: 289 cu. in. Compression ratio: 10.5 to 1. Brake horsepower: 306 @ 6000 rpm. Torque: 329 lbs.-ft. @ 4200 rpm. Induction and exhaust: special free-breathing Shelby design. Transmission: 4-speed synchromesh. Suspension: independent coil spring, front; semielliptic leaf spring, rear. Shelby-modified for 30% less cornering roll. Brakes: disc, front; air-cooled drum, rear. Steering ratio: 16 to 1. Wheelbase: 108″. Overall length: 186.6″. Weight: 2723 lbs.

Autolite speaks a performance language all its own

And that language is Ford *total* performance. Total performance knowledge requires participation in every phase of racing. So everywhere racing goes—Ford, and only Ford goes. To Indy, Le Mans, Darlington, Riverside, Daytona, drag strips. And where Ford goes . . . Autolite goes. Designing, building, and testing new performance techniques. For Indy cars. For dragsters. For stockers. For your car, too. Racing is the only road to high-performance know-how. And only Autolite has traveled every inch of it.

AUTOLITE
...the spark behind the total performance company...

MARCH, 1967

automatic shift by itself at 5,100 rpm. The .74 G braking ability might have been better if the power brakes were more controllable. Wheel lock-up was hard to avoid and harder to correct—pedal pressure has to drop to near-zero before the locked wheel begins rolling again. This is a trait common to Ford powerbrake systems, and a better compromise between the touchy Dearborn system and the old GT 350 leg-buster could be worked out.

We're sure someone will utter a cry of protest, but to our knowledge, the 1967 Shelby Mustang is the first production car to offer a true rollover bar as standard equipment. Not a thicker roof section, but a real-live roll bar. The shoulder harness is not standard equipment, but, like the GT 500's automatic transmission, it will be difficult to get a Shelby Mustang out of the showroom without one.

The roll bar itself is a tubular structure, covered with padding and welded to the chassis. Where it curves up into the roof, tabs poke out and bolts secure the bar to the car's top in the threaded holes intended for the upper attachment point for Ford's over-the-shoulder shoulder harness. Shelby's shoulder harness is the double type. Another pair of tabs are welded to the roll bar, and to these are bolted a pair of inertia reels made by Advanced Safety Devices. The reels exert a half-pound pull—thus requiring no adjustment by the user—and lock at .5 G, something like a window-shade mechanism in reverse. The shoulder harness strap divides just behind the user's neck, the halves passing over his shoulders to fasten at points on either side of the seat. A standard lap belt is used in conjunction with the shoulder harness, but because the halves don't come together at the lap buckle, like racing harnesses, it's the only

shoulder harness we've seen that women can wear. These devices have to be seen and felt in action to be believed. At the risk of encouraging showroom traffic by curiosity seekers, we'd recommend that our readers stop by Shelby American dealers and try the shoulder harnesses. Then no matter what other car you may buy, drop a line to the manufacturer and suggest that he offer shoulder harnesses like this on his cars.

The rest of the GT 500 interior is stock Mustang, except for a few points. An oil cooler is standard equipment, but had been removed for some obscure evaluation on our test car and an oil temperature gauge had been mounted under the dash. It never got over 2,300°F, incidentally. Our car also had the optional folding rear seat and an instrument cluster (ammeter and oil pressure gauge—the pressure was a steady 60 psi). The presence of the shoulder harnesses greatly complicated entry to the rear seat, what with climbing through a mass of nylon straps and ducking the inertia reels.

The air conditioner controls were confusing in an otherwise well laid out interior, but this small annoyance was more than made up for by Shelby's special wood-rim steering wheel. It has much less dish than Ford's, thus placing it in a perfect position for effortless control.

That, then, is the GT 500. A grown-up sports car for smooth touring. No more wham-bam, thank you ma'am, just a purring, well-controlled tiger. Like Shelby says, "This is the first car I'm really proud of." Right. We've come a long way since bib overalls too, Shel.

Top speed: 128 mph (estimated)
0-60 6.5 seconds
355 bhp, 420 lb-ft of torque
Price: $5,034.60

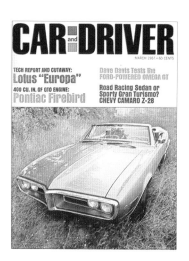

CAR and DRIVER
MARCH 1967 · 60 CENTS

TECH REPORT AND CUTAWAY:
Lotus "Europa"
400 CU. IN. OF GTO ENGINE:
Pontiac Firebird

Dave Davis Tests the
FORD-POWERED OMEGA GT
Road Racing Sedan or
Sporty Gran Turismo?
CHEVY CAMARO Z-28

March 1967
Road Research Report: Chevrolet Camaro Z-28

Almost! Inch by cubic inch, Chevrolet warily circles the enthusiast, closing in for the kill. With the Camaro Z-28, they're getting warm—very close to what we'd like to see the Camaro become.

The Z-28 designation refers to an engine option, a 302.4-cu. in., 290-hp V-8, the heart of a sedan racing package. The option adds $437.10 to the Camaro's $2,572 base price...the Z-28 option includes heavy-duty springs and shocks front and rear, shot-peened front ball studs, a rear radius rod, 15 x 6-inch wheels with 7.35-15 nylon red-stripe tires, and a pair of broad fore-and-aft racing stripes that all but say, "Awright kid, let's see your license and registration."

Basically, the Z-28 is Chevrolet's version of the Shelby Mustang—a Gran Turismo disguised as a Detroit sporty car. The Z-28's performance is remarkably similar to the Shelby GT 350, at a price almost $1,000 less.

The engine is obviously the Z-28's strongest point...the 290-hp figure quoted for the Z-28 engine seems ridiculously conservative; it feels at least as strong as the 327 cu. in., 350-hp hydraulic-lifter engine offered in the Corvette.

The 302 engine is without a doubt the most responsive American V-8 we've ever tested.

With the Z-28, Chevy is on the way toward making the gutsy stormer the Camaro should have been in the first place. It's an appealing car; as tough and purposeful as an F-5 jet fighter, but a car you could be happy living with.

 Top speed: 124 mph (estimated)
 0-60 6.7 seconds
 290 bhp, 290 lb-ft of torque
 Price: $4,051

As a racing car, we expect the Z-28 to do quite well. Modified to the legal limit, the 302 engine should be capable of 390 horsepower.

September 1967
Street Racing

By Brock Yates

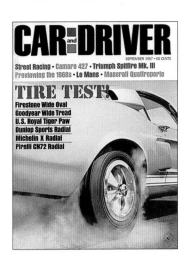

Organized drag racing was supposed to have turned hot rodding into something as respectable as apple pie and as legal as little-league baseball, but the truth is that drag racing on the public highways—street racing—is bigger than ever, and Detroit's Woodward Avenue is the street racing capital of the world.

So here comes the Cheater, tooling his GTO down Woodward Avenue, looking for a little action. He eases away from the lights with the big engine rumbling ominously and the rear slicks making noisy whispers against the pavement. Very cool, the Cheater. Across the mall, in the opposite lane, a Chevelle SS 396 and a Plymouth with the rear suspension jacked up maybe two feet in the air run side-by-side for a few seconds before their drivers nail the wood and they spurt ahead like scalded dogs. They roar away into the night with the Cheater casually watching their progress in his rear-view mirror. Then a Mustang pulls alongside and a pair of high school kids—just strokes—gawk at the Cheater. He looks straight ahead, not bothering to acknowledge their presence.

In the pecking order of the Woodward Avenue racing scene, a guy driving a very strong street racer like Cheater's doesn't pay any attention to the strokes. Guys in other GTOs and 442s and Chevelles, yes, and guys in 427 'Vettes and Mopars, very definitely yes, but you want to watch it before you take a shot with them. A good 'Vette or a sharp Mopar will suck the doors off a GTO, so the Cheater has to be very cautious about what cars he chooses to race down Woodward.

The Cheater is operating in a very wild scene. By day, Woodward Avenue is a wide street that all the fat daddies from Royal Oak, Birmingham, and Bloomfield Hills use to drive into stolid old downtown Detroit—Motor City, by golly. But come sunset, Woodward Avenue becomes the street racing capitol of the world. Oh yes, there's some action around L.A.—out in the Valley and in Downey and along the beach, and a lot of guys talk about Palm Beach and Miami and there's even a little street racing going on up in the Bronx and on the south shore of Long Island. But they don't cut it with the scene on Woodward, where maybe two thousand—really—cars are milling up and down the five-mile-long "strip" on any given night. Woodward is the Indianapolis of the street racers, and if you can make it there, baby, you will be very tough behind the wheel no matter where you go.

The Cheater is very tough. Mostly he sits in Ted's Drive In, one of three or four spots along the strip where real racers hang out. A lot of the high school strokes come in there too, revving their stock engines and showing off their mags and their uplift shocks, and guys like Cheater can tell them a mile off. But when some cat chugs through in a big Mopar with some wild grind that makes it idle rumpa-rumpa-rumpa, you know there is going to be some serious action.

The Cheater wheels into Ted's and scans the scene. Like every night, it looks like the garage area at a big race. Lined up in the stalls are rows and rows of Super Cars with giant tires and hunched-up suspensions and hood scoops and fuel injection and blowers and mag wheels and smooth, cool looking paint jobs. In each car are a pair of guys—because you usually street race in pairs—and the scene, with all these stalls, reminds you of those Amsterdam prostitutes who sit in the windows, patiently awaiting the call to action.

Out in front, parked along the street, are some Corvettes and GTOs with nobody near them. They belong to very cool guys who hang out at nearby gas stations, bars, and coffee shop counters, and if you want to take a shot with them, you have to know enough to be able to find them and ask something like, "Will that thing run?" and they answer, "You want to take a shot?" and then you'll go out to Interstate 75 and settle it. For cash.

As a matter of fact, it's not much of a secret that there are factory teams operating on Woodward. Not kids getting a mother's price on parts, mind you, but employees of the Detroit corporations that make and sell automobiles right out there racing on Woodward Avenue like it was Daytona International Speedway. Call it "market research."

The factory guys don't have the blessing of the chairmen of the boards, mind you; nobody ever bothered to ask. And they race for kicks, to keep up with what's happening, not cash. One guy's favorite trick used to be to show up with a very stock automobile, arrange a rendezvous somewhere else for the race, then stop off along the way and switch cars. The second car was definitely not very stock. But hardly anyone falls for that gag anymore, and certainly not the Cheater. The Cheater recognizes some of the regulars sitting in front of Ted's Drive In. The Shaker is out tonight, and so is Moses. He spots an open slot and backs in beside a rough looking GTO that belongs to a little guy wearing shades who they call Peanuts. Now, Peanuts has a 430-inch engine in that wreck with the license plates wired on, and it is known to be a very tough machine to deal with.

Peanuts doesn't shift too well, so he has another guy at the wheel tonight, but neither of them pays much attention to Cheater as he backs in, cuts the engine, and orders a cup of coffee over the squawk box. Pretty soon this haggard looking broad comes out of the drive-in with the coffee and the Cheater sits there scanning the action. Out on Woodward, the strokes are roaring up and down, screeching their tires, and every once in a while the fuzz will snap on their gum-ball revolving lights and pull some guy over and lay maybe a $200 fine on him. This is really a very good deal for the fuzz in Royal Oak and those other suburban towns, because the city fathers can make a lot of bucks off the racers in a given evening. Oh, they talk very big about the menace for the street racers, but they never make any really big push to shut down the action. After all, if you can make a few grand in fines every night, why spoil a good thing? But even then, pros like the Cheater watch it very closely when they run Woodward, but mostly they save their racing for the open spaces of I-75.

Pretty soon the cheater looks over at Peanuts and says, "How's that thing running tonight?"

And the guy who is driving for Peanuts says, in a very cool tone, "Peanuts has the fastest '65 on the street."

So the Cheater says, "Is it worth twenty bucks?"

And then Peanuts turns his head and scans the Cheater from behind his shades so you can't tell whether he's bluffing or not and says, "Man, it ain't worth spinnin' the key for twenty bucks."

The Cheater lets that ride for a few seconds and then he looks Peanuts right square in the shades and says, "Like they say, man—money talks, but bulls--t walks."

Now that is a very tough thing to say to a guy like Peanuts,

but sometimes you have to be that way to deal with some cats, and sure enough, it is all that is needed for Peanuts to accept the challenge.

Because there was so much action around the drive-ins on Woodward, a law was recently passed that forbids car-hopping by the customers. Big signs proclaim that leaving a car on foot is illegal and most of the places have a rent-a-cop to enforce the regulation. This is kind of a drag, but it doesn't prevent the word from passing around the place that Cheater and Peanuts are about to take a shot.

There's a guy sitting in a red Mopar with American mags who calls over to the Cheater, "You better watch it man, you're dealin' with big heads and a Holley."

"Maybe," replies the Cheater, kind of under his breath, "but I've put the lunch to better equipment than that on the way to work. Peanuts never dealt with nothin' like this, so I wouldn't spend my money on him if I were you." The Cheater hunches forward in his seat and reaches for the ignition key. It is time to go. Cheater is a guy in his early twenties, with a clean-cut Caucasian profile and short, athlete's blond hair. He is wearing a lightweight windbreaker and a pair of narrow-cut pants with the creases still in them, and moms and pops all over the country would take him into their arms and gladly call him one of their own. This is the way it is on Woodward; there are very few punks running equipment out there. The suburbs are rich, and the street racers are the products of fat-cat midwestern households that don't really care if their sons are out running $6,000 race cars up and down the public roads.

Sanctioned drag racing meets are supposed to have stopped all the illegal action on the streets and turned hot rodding into something as apple-pie sweet and legal as little-

115

league baseball, but nobody really believes that. The drag strips have become so crowded that a guy is lucky if he can make three runs during an entire afternoon or evening, but on Woodward you might get 50 shots in a few hours. And they're all free, baby. Of course, pros like the Cheater can make a lot more coins on the street than on the track, where you get these 19-cent trophies with a phony gold car stuck on top of a cheap wood pedestal.

The word has passed around the drive-in and a couple of cars full of guys who want to watch ease out and head up Woodward toward 1-75. Then Peanuts takes off, followed discreetly by the Cheater.

The Cheater takes it very slow up Woodward so the cops won't notice, then swings onto a deserted side street that heads toward the expressway. The engine seems to be running all right, but he lays it on the wood anyway, just to be sure. The exhaust noise swells inside the car as it leaps ahead in second gear, then reaches a frantic, instantaneous peak as he makes a lightning, full-throttle shift to third. The slicks yelp against the pavement and the GTO yaws sideways under power for a few feet before straightening out. The Cheater is ready.

He rolls onto the dark expanse of the expressway and heads west toward the rendezvous. Headlights pop into the rearview mirror, one of the spectator cars. Then Peanuts shows up and eases into a steady 60-mph formation in the center lane. A few more cars enter the convoy from the rear and they all roll down the expressway, waiting for the traffic ahead to clear. Good street racers don't use the traditional wheel-spinning drag-type start from a standstill. First of all, you have to stop to do that sort of thing, and that means brake lights flashing—a sure tip-off to the fuzz. Secondly, screeching tires get the

neighbors uptight, and finally, starts from a full stop are hard on clutches and rear ends. So a flying start is used, usually from about 30 mph, and the race goes up as high as necessary to determine the winner, which is sometimes 140 mph.

Peanuts pulls alongside the Cheater and rolls down his window. Cheater already has his down, so they rumble along, fender-to-fender for a while, until they're in position. Then Peanuts yells, "Go!" and the race is on.

The sound of Peanuts' voice transforms the Cheater into a dervish on wheels. He throws his entire body against the gear lever as he rams the transmission from first to second. Wham! The Pontiac begins to moan in second and Wham! into third while Peanuts' ol' '65 hangs on maybe half a car length behind. Suddenly the GTO is running 100 mph and the Cheater flings it into fourth gear. Now he's beginning to get the advantage and Peanuts is falling farther back. He touches 120 mph and then eases off, letting Peanuts roll alongside once again.

"One more time," Peanuts shouts into the wind, and the two cars line up and scream into the night with their support vehicles trying to keep up. Once more the Cheater puts ol' Peanuts in paradise and it is all over.

They pull off at the next exit and stop at a deserted shopping center. They all talk quietly for awhile, and Peanuts tells the Cheater why he wasn't getting the kind' of rpm he should have, and how it was leaking oil and how maybe he had 15 bent pushrods and how next time....

Old Peanuts hadn't really lost, because nobody ever really loses a street race. And by the same token, the Cheater hadn't really won, either, not really, except that he feels good enough to stuff his winnings into his wallet and head back toward Woodward for a couple more shots.

April 1968
Turn Your Hymnals to 2002:
David E. Davis, Jr. Blows His Mind
on the Latest From BMW

As I sit here, fresh from the elegant embrace of BMW's new
2002, it occurs to me that something between nine and ten
million Americans are going to make a terrible mistake this
year. Like dutiful little robots they will march out of their
identical split-level boxes and buy the wrong kind of car. Fools,
fools! Terrible, terrible, I say.... To my way of thinking, the 2002
is one of modern civilization's all-time best ways to get
somewhere sitting down. It grabs you. You sit in magnificently
adjustable seats with great, tall windows all around you.
You are comfortable and you can see in every direction.
You start it. Willing and un-lumpy is how it feels. No rough
idle, no zappy noises to indicate that the task you propose
might be anything more than child's play for all those 114
Bavarian superhorses.... The BMW 2002 may be the first car
in history to successfully bridge the gap between the
diametrically opposed automotive requirements of the
wildly romantic car nut, on one hand, and the hyperpragmatic
people at *Consumer Reports*, on the other.   —*David E. Davis, Jr*

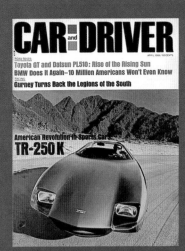

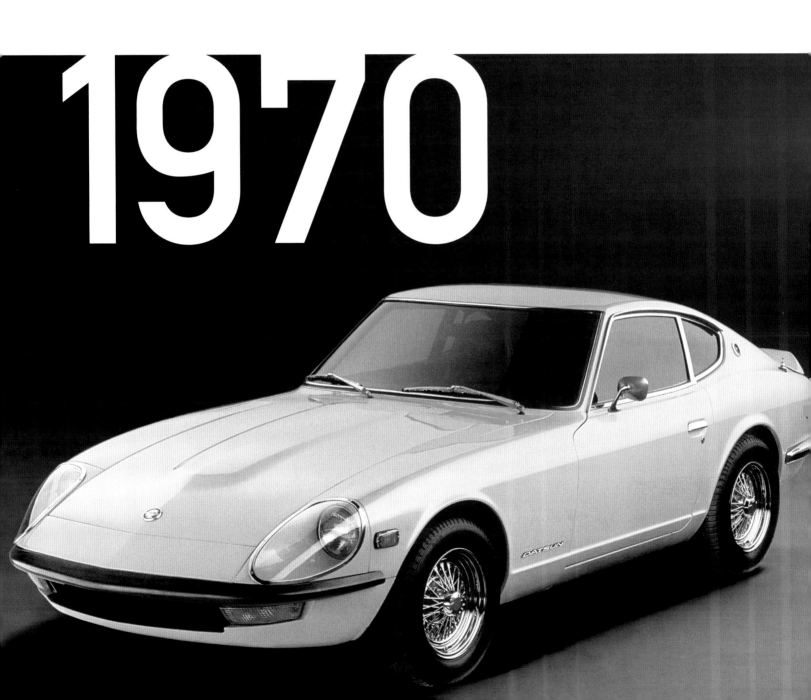

1970

1977

Gas Pains

In the 1950s, *Car and Driver* had been
the field guide for an emerging generation
of car nuts, who gladly spent weekends
tooling in the garage, subscribing to the
new American car magazines, and
discussing the merits of race drivers as
readily as Eisenhower versus Stevenson.
In the 1960s, the country's enormous
power grew, and one of the most obvious
symbols of national strength was the
auto industry. American cars were brassy,
ballsy, ungodly powerful, and, in deep
contrast to the vehicles from Germany and
Japan, they were big. Muscle cars ruled
the car magazines, and a great 0-to-60
time could make a sales success as readily
as it could doom a would-be sports car.

1970

The U.S. military
invades Cambodia

Four students die at a
Kent State U. protest
against the Vietnam War
when the National Guard
opens fire

Jimi Hendrix and
Janis Joplin die of
drug overdoses

>

The 1970s, as the staff of *Car and Driver* would predict, were about the dark side of cars—how many people were dying in them and how much pollution they were releasing into the atmosphere.

Editor-at-large Patrick Bedard, who joined the magazine as a technical editor in 1967, saw the end of the glory days appear in *Car and Driver*'s pages. "My heart was still pounding from the mid-1970 Chevrolet Camaro Z28 and Pontiac Firebird Trans Am—they of the Italianesque proportions—when the whole car thing got sideways and spun off into deep gloom," he recalled. "Horsepower went away in 1971 as compression ratios plummeted in anticipation of no-lead gas. The first energy crisis hit in 1973, which some wise guys in Washington tried to fix with a 55-mph speed limit. By 1974, we couldn't drive cars and we couldn't stand to look at them either, because the big-bumper mandate had made them so ugly."

What could a magazine whose universe centered around speed do? "We chewed our editorial paws in despair as the calendar flipped out of 1974, and the wise guys voted four days later to make the double-nickel permanent. I applied for transfer to the Uranus desk."

Depending on your point of view, 1970 either was the end of the world or the beginning of a new one. The Vietnam war had faltered, and protests against it around America had turned fatal. The Woodstock generation lost Hendrix and Joplin to drugs and Morrison was in Paris, drinking away his last months on earth.

The muscle car was dying, too. Pollution controls, unleaded fuel requirements and fuel-economy bogeys steamrolled out of Washington and Detroit could hardly counterpunch. Within a few years, Mustangs were based on Pintos, the Corvette V-8 had been choked nearly to death, and the Japanese had one of the most compelling sports cars on the planet.

In 1970, it was easy to see the hairpin curve coming ahead and to see that Detroit hadn't corrected for it. In 1955, Congress tried to set the first national air-quality standards, with little effect. But the issue would not and could not go away. Smog snuffed out the sky in cities from Los Angeles to New York and legislators were determined to do something about it. California enacted its own air-quality laws in the late 1960s, and Congress tried again with the 1967 Air Quality Act, which set regional standards and adopted some California standards nationally. But a lack of enforcement brought about even tougher action: in 1970 Washington set up the Environmental Protection Agency (EPA) and enacted the Clean Air Act, setting limits for all kinds of pollutants, but in particular those coming from the tailpipes of cars.

The punches to Detroit's big, V-8-powered vehicles came in quick succession. In 1973 the phaseout of leaded gas began, and in 1974 unleaded became the new standard. In 1975 the Corporate Average Fuel Economy (CAFE) rules meant that Detroit's big fleets would have to downsize and de-power.

Coupled with the creation of the Department of Transportation in 1966 and the new rules that mandated bumper strength, seat belt interlocks and, eventually, airbags, the early 1970s were pretty much a disaster for Detroit. For the first time, safety and emissions controls were required on all cars. "For the

123

| Anwar Sadat takes power in Egypt | **1971** | "All in the Family" premieres on CBS | The voting age is lowered to 18 | Phyllis George wins the title of Miss America |

most eloquent portrayal of just how much our Motor City didn't get it in those days, look to the American Motors Gremlin, which we covered in April 1970," Bedard says. "It was a compact sedan turned into an import fighter by hacking off one foot of wheelbase and almost everything of substance behind the rear wheels. Detroit thought import buyers wanted less. Japan knew better, and the Datsun 240Z arrived as a 1970 model with dream-car specs overhead-cam power, all-independent suspension, and front disc brakes—all standard for as little as $3,526. While it lacked tail-flicking torque, it gave us something we needed far more— it gave us hope."

And in the middle of the downsizing, politics gave Detroit's cars another untimely kick. The Middle East simmered from the mid-1960s until a series of wars erupted between Israel and nearly every other neighboring Arab state. In 1948, the wars came about after the creation of Israel; in 1956, the Israelis raced to the Suez Canal and grabbed the port of Aqaba. In the 1967 Six-Day War the Israelis took the Sinai, Jerusalem and the Golan Heights. And in 1973, the sides lined up as before, with the United States siding with Israel and the Arab states increasingly hostile to the U.S. position.

On October 6, 1973, the Syrians and Egyptians invaded Israel on Yom Kippur and forever changed the car culture of the U.S. as well. In the short war Israeli soldiers repelled the invasion and forced a cease-fire at the end of the month. And in response to the U.S. support of Israel during the war, the Arab nations belonging to the Organization of Petroleum Exporting Countries (OPEC), a cartel of Middle Eastern and other oil-producing nations, shut off the flow to the U.S. and other nations, like the Netherlands, and raised prices to Western European nations as much as 70 percent.

It was a disaster for the American economy, and the auto industry in particular. America had produced all the energy it needed as recently as 1950, yet now depended on foreign oil for 35 percent of its energy needs. The price of a barrel of oil quadrupled in a year. Arab nations had grasped the extent of their power over the U.S., and sent the Nixon administration hunting for answers. Year-round Daylight Savings time was tried; the Alaska pipeline was begun. Even or odd license plate numbers dictated whether you could buy gas or not on a particular day. The worst consequence to some drivers, the 55-mph speed limit, was enacted in 1974 and not raised until 1987. Gas prices in the U.S. nearly doubled to about 50 cents a gallon by the time the embargo was lifted in March of 1974.

The after effects forced structural changes in the American economy and in international policy. It also forced the reconfiguration of the U.S. car fleet to smaller, more frugal vehicles that were the specialty of Japanese automakers. While the VW Beetle had already elbowed its way into the U.S. because of its charm and simplicity, the Japanese economy cars had to wait until the oil embargoes and clean-air acts caught Detroit off-guard. When the time came, Japan was ready and American car companies were not. After this era, America's highways would never look the same.

Car and Driver didn't quite look the same during this time, either. Davis's departure for an at-large position in 1966 turned into a total departure for most of the 1970s. Yates had decamped from New York City for upstate New York. Leon Mandel had given way as editor to Gordon Jennings, a West Coast *Car and Driver* writer who had spent years with *Road & Track* and *Cycle* magazines. And Jennings gave way for Bob Brown, who in turn hired future editor William Jeanes to be a feature editor.

124

PUMPS CLOSED

OPEN – 1PM – 2PM DAILY ONLY

SORRY 3⁰⁰ LIMIT

90⁵

$ 9.5

your car
to the

CAR and DRIVER

DECEMBER 1974 · ONE DOLLAR

ROTARY RECORD AT BONNEVILLE
Car and Driver's 160-mph Mazda

★

HERE COMES THE DRESSERATOR
The Miracle Carburetor That Works

★

A BOLD NEW CHALLENGE TO THE SUPER-COUPE CROWD
Volkswagen's Scirocco

126

While the staff tussled with how to write about cars in an age where there were few great cars, Don Sherman arrived at the magazine in 1971. A fellow Iowan with Bedard, a Michigan grad and a Chrysler engineer, Sherman signed on at the nadir of the American car and held out long enough to become editor himself. Being a real car guy, as opposed to a real advertising guy, another chief career path into the magazine's halls, won him the job. During the course of his interview with *Car and Driver*, "As he was flipping through the pages, talking to us about thermodynamics and fluid dynamics, out from the back pocket of his leather covered book floated a Kodacolor snapshot. Bob Brown picked it up, took one look at it and, in astonishment asked Don, 'Is this a Valkyrie? Did you actually build one of those things?' Sure enough there was Sherman, in fatigues, sans moustache, standing beside a nearly completed Fiberfab Valkyrie. From that point on, the interview ceased to be about what was required of him before the University of Michigan would grant him his Masters, or even much about Don's responsibilities at Chrysler. Instead, there were questions like, 'How much did it really cost?' 'How long did it take?' 'What sort of condition was the thing in when you got it?' 'What the hell did the Army think of you building this thing on its time?' 'How does it perform?' 'What kind of modifications did you make to Fiberfab's way of doing it?' 'Can you license and insure it?' And, of course, 'Would you ever do it again?'"

The staff still was populated by car lovers, at least. And great cars were still the focus of the magazine, but the lack of them made it difficult to justify a big staff and to hold on to roving talent. Some writers deserted. Editors landed for months-long stints. For more than a few years the comings and goings were as uncertain and disruptive as all the new laws that were knocking the wind out of Detroit. As publisher Martin Toohey catalogued it once, it was like a chaotic eddy of personalities floating into the offices at One Park Avenue almost by chance.

"Bob Brown came off a surfboard nine years ago when David E. Davis Jr. was editor. Brown was hired to write promotion copy for *Car and Driver* and Davis had no plan of leaving at the time, let alone ever making Brown editor. But that's the way it eventually worked out. After Davis departed for Detroit gold, Brock Yates jumped into the lurch and found out that an editor not only had to put up with the flaky writers but also rewrite the gems, which always arrived late. 'I'd rather write than edit,' stated Brock as he ran for sanity.

"After Yates, Steve Smith occupied the editor's desk for about a fortnight. To the best of my memory, I believe Steve wanted to turn *Car and Driver* into *Rolling Stone*. Leon Mandel then took over as editor and set out to produce the Great American Social Commentary. Three years later, Leon left to become publisher of *Autoweek* and write books on motor racing. He was followed by Gordon Jennings, who was later found out: he didn't like cars.

"This loony bin has been led by editors who photographed the 1968 Opel in a junkyard. Through 'the magic of retouching,' they removed the eyebrows from a photo of John DeLorean, the man who was scheduled, we thought, to eventually head General Motors. The fabled Denbeigh make-believe car of all time was dropped into the Readers Choice Ballot one year and damned near beat all of the competition.

"Are these the accomplishments of Pulitzer Prize winners? Is this what schools of journalism espouse to be qualifications for scaling the heights of publishing? Where is the guidebook on how to rent the right editor for *Car and Driver*? Is there no manual to help us avoid making the same mistake over again?"

WHY THE COSWORTH VEGA ALMOST DIDN'T MAKE IT

CAR and DRIVER ®

OCTOBER 1975 · ONE DOLLAR

1976 New Cars From GM, Ford and AMC

★

Chevette
The Most Important Car Detroit Has Ever Built

oohey didn't have the time to wait for an answer. Editor Brown left quickly, as seemed to be the custom, to be replaced in 1974 by Stephan Wilkinson, who parachuted in from *Flying* magazine. "I am of the opinion, quite frankly, that my arrival at *Car and Driver* as editor is a stone bore as far as the readers are concerned. I wouldn't mention it. These are the helpful and encouraging words of Stephan Wilkinson in answer to my request that we publish something in recognition of Bob Brown's departure to *Sports Illustrated* and Wilkinson's arrival at *Car and Driver* as editor. We were aware of Wilkinson as executive editor of *Flying*, a Ziff-Davis magazine with editorial offices on the other side of our 6th-floor wall, but aside from a chance meeting in the men's room or the annual get together at company flu-shot time, not too many of us really knew Steve. Rumor had it he once rebuilt a 1936 Ford Phaeton. There were also fragments of Aston Martin and Porsche Club references but nothing concrete. Wilkinson refuses to cooperate. And with nothing further forthcoming, one might ask, how does a guy with 'credentials' such as these get to be editor of *Car and Driver*? Consider the past. It reads like a lunatic personnel man's dream. I'm afraid not. Not with Wilkinson standing diffidently astride his Ducati motorcycle (Gad, not another Jennings) in the lobby of One Park Avenue awaiting an empty elevator to avoid speaking with colleagues. As an associate editor of *Holiday*, he not only refused to wear cruise clothing to work in Philadelphia but instead wore rags. Spiteful rags. Wilkinson was arrested for vagrancy late one evening as he wended his way through the ghetto streets of Philly toward his low-rent garage, which housed two Porsche Speedsters. The fuzz had guns drawn as Wilkinson opened the doors to prove solvency. And you ask about personnel hiring procedures? Manuals? Guidebooks? I say we'll follow history. One

look at the unqualifieds who have preceded Wilkinson and there is no doubt that we have found the right editor."

Wilkinson, now the car guy at *Conde Nast Traveler*, would serve as editor during two of the darkest years in the magazine's short life. "We wanted so badly to put our shoulders to the wheel of environmental correctness that *Car and Driver*'s cover line for the 1976 Chevrolet Chevette read, 'The Most Important Car Detroit Has Ever Built.' Still, Brock Yates managed to get the word "shitbox" onto the opening page of the road test. The Chevette was a nice try. (Really? No, not really.) If nothing else, it demonstrated Detroit's sudden, abject willingness to get with the less-is-more program."

Though the Japanese had yet to hit their stride, it wouldn't be long before Hondas, Toyotas, and Datsuns became the car of choice for millions, replacing the stock and trade of Chrysler, General Motors and Ford. "The Datsun F-10 I tested in July 1976 was significant if only because it was the last totally clueless Japanese car, a grotesque coda to the years during which Nissan and Toyota were still occasionally creating automobiles of exceptional ugliness and mechanical incongruity. It also helped get me fired, because I wrote the road test that said so."

And yet, all the 1970s wasn't a wash. Hyperexotics still would dribble out from corners of Italy and Germany. "There was the Lamborghini Countach, the car that invented a category: exotic. Never mind that it was ugly and barely drivable, that it was rumored to have often been purchased with ill-gotten gains, and that it afforded Italian craftsmanship almost exclusively for guys who wore excessive jewelry. The Countach was to fast cars what silicone was to breasts.

"Porsche's 911 Turbo, an elemental machine tool of a car, was the first firm affirmation that awesome performance could

still crawl ashore and survive the ooze of primitive EPA and DOT regulations. In an era when decals were thought to contain horsepower, sports cars were agricultural TR7s and MGBs with all the looks and power of body bucks on sawhorses—until the Huns sent this monster our way, like the Bismarck shouldering its way into a marina full of bass boats."

After sticking out most of the 1970s with regulations crumbling its foundations, Detroit began to stabilize with vehicles like, of all things, the Cadillac Seville. And *Car and Driver* followed suit late in 1976 when David E. Davis returned to the editor's chair. First there'd have to be a big yard sale, though.

"I've just parted with my 1976 Nova Q-car. It was a silver four-door with the California Highway Patrol suspension, Koni shock absorbers and trick wheels, and I'll miss it. Neat car. Steve Smith bought my old Baja-racer Blazer, and I'll miss that too. (It was as tall as a two-story tool-and-die shop, Wehrmacht flat green, with a roll cage and big old white Jackman wheels, whip antenna for the CB, a winch, a little refrigerator, and all the suspension bits painted bright blue or yellow.) A splendid device, but not for New York City. Oh, my boat's for sale too, if you know of anybody that wants to own a gorgeous 26-foot Lyman, built in 1973, one of the last of the great lapstrake woodies. Ninety-five hundred bucks takes it away. Why am I doing all this? Well, I've decided to leave Detroit and the advertising business and come back to my first and greatest love, *Car and Driver*. It was exactly ten years ago that I became restive here at *Car and Driver* and decided to try my hand at something else. Within six months I knew I'd made a mistake, that this magazine was practically my whole life, but I gritted my teeth and took my best shot at the advertising business, did well enough and made more money than I ever thought I'd see, let alone put in the bank, but it wasn't the same."

The landscape Davis had returned to looked more like a moonscape, but he saw a coming reconstruction. "Nobody knows what it's going to be like out there in the misty void between here and the year 2000, but it doesn't require the futurist bravado of a Herman Kahn to know that it's going to be exciting as hell. Cars, and the games we play with them, are in for some changes."

Davis told readers the magazine hadn't wavered. And in a summon-the-troops column, he reconnected with *Car and Driver's* readers to promise them good times ahead. "*Car and Driver* has grown and prospered since I left in 1966, and we're all terribly proud of it. Now it's going to be my job to take the magazine all the way. Ziff-Davis, the company that owns *Car and Driver*, wants it to be the most prestigious, most respected, and most successful car magazine in the world. I read most of the car magazines from around the world, and I have some idea just what an enormous challenge that is. But the writers and editors that you've come to know and enjoy here at *Car and Driver* have the knowledge and the skills, and we all share the desire, so we're accepting the dare. You're involved too. You buy this magazine, so you pay the bills, and you're the final judges of whether or not the magazine is going where it has to go, doing what must be done. We'll be depending on you for guidance and criticism as we launch ourselves on the great automotive crusade. We'll strive to be the best writers/artists/editors in our field, but we can't out-guess you. Tell us how you feel about cars, your cars, our cars, all cars. If we do our job properly, and you participate fully as readers and payers of our salaries, *Car and Driver* can be the greatest car magazine in the world, and I'll never need to regret leaving my boat and my Super-Omigod Blazer and coming to the least automotive city in the western world."

1976 Porsche 911 Turbo 3.0 Coupe.

1977

"Star Wars" and
"Saturday Night Fever"
dominate the box office
at theaters

Elvis Presley dies at his
Graceland mansion

Upset winners
Marquette down North
Carolina for the NCAA
men's basketball title

Seattle Slew wins horse
racing's Triple Crown

June 1970
Road Research Report:
Datsun 240Z

The difference between the Datsun 240Z and your everyday three-and-a-half-thousand dollar sports car is that about twice as much thinking went into the Datsun. It shows. For the money, the 240Z is an almost brilliant car.

The people at Datsun balk at calling the 240Z a sports car. To them it's a "personal" GT car. Even so, they know perfectly well who the customers will be: sports car buyers, adventuresome young Americans who were collecting their dollars for an Opel GT or MGB-GT or Porsche 914 until something better came along and changed their minds. Still, the "personal" GT car description somehow fits. It separates the Datsun from whimsical, superficial sports cars like the Opel GT and moves it off into a mature class of automobiles that has more to offer than just amusement. The Z-car, as it has come to be called, is a very real transportation automobile, meant as much for coast-to-coast journeys as it is for playing around on idyllic summer days. Datsun is probably right. The Z-car really isn't a sports car.

It is exactly the kind of car we have come to expect from Datsun, however. You can't really consider Datsun to be an innovator—it didn't invent the overhead cam engine or disc brakes or independent suspension—but it is one of the most ambitious car manufacturers alive these days and it has a habit of incorporating these sophisticated systems into easily affordable cars. The budget-priced PL510 sedan is the envy of all its competitors, and the vitality in the engine and gearbox of the 2000 sports car makes a Triumph feel like a first-round loser in the soapbox derby. With that kind of siblings, the Z-car would naturally be a gifted performer.

And it is. Curiously, a double standard has grown up through the years concerning sports cars and equivalently priced family sedans—the sedans are always more powerful. Not so with the Z-car. It will keep right up with your neighbor's Bonneville and leave all of the sports cars in its class scuttling along in the slow lane. At Orange County Raceway the test car ran through the quarter in 16.1 seconds at 86.5 mph—more than one second and 9 mph quicker than a Triumph TR6. It is also several mph faster than a 2-liter Porsche 911T, although the elapsed time is not quite as good because the Z-car continues Datsun's practice of using axle ratios suitable for the Bonneville salt flats.

Of course, it should also be obvious that the Z-car continues Datsun's practice of using exceptionally powerful engines, in this case a 2.4-liter single-overhead-cam six. It's a new engine for Datsun, yet not really new because it is actually one and a half of the Fours used in the PL510 sedan. With the help of two SUs and a 9.0-to-one compression ratio it generates 151 horsepower at 5,600 rpm, and if you are so inclined you can turn it all the way to 7,000 rpm before you hit the red-i line, We aren't inclined, however. Like all Datsuns, the torque curve is as flat as Nebraska and the engine noise is so unpleasant above 6,500 that there is just no reason to ever go up there.

Datsun tackles the exhaust emission problem with three separate external devices: an air pump to inject air into the exhaust manifold, a valve that admits air into the intake manifold immediately after the throttle is closed to aid combustion of fuel that is already in the manifold, and a diaphragm that prevents the throttle from closing for several seconds after you lift your foot off the accelerator. Only one of these is noticeable to the driver—the last item. It keeps engine speed too high, making smooth upshifts impossible, and seriously detracts from the pleasure of driving. Throttle response, particularly at low speeds, also suffers due to subtleties of the system.

In most other ways the Z-car is kind to its driver. The steering effort is moderate, the shifting motions are light and acceptably precise, and the driving position is excellent. The brakes—discs in front and leading-trailing shoes in finned aluminum drums at the rear—stop the car well enough, 259 feet (0.83G) from 80 mph, but very high pedal effort is required for a panic stop. In addition, the system is spongy and offers very little feel to help the driver control lock-up. In the rain things get even worse, at least in the test car. Water somehow splashes up onto the braking surfaces and sharply reduces stopping ability. In this respect the Z-car is not satisfactory.

The Datsun's suspension system—a fully independent MacPherson strut arrangement both front and rear—also has a few quirks. The test car would understeer more in right than in left turns. You would never notice it on the road, but on the test track the car was very well balanced when cornering to the left yet would plow heavily when turning right. There is no reason that this should be typical of all of the Z-cars. The test car had expanders between several coils in the left front spring to overcome a sag, and the asymmetric handling can probably be blamed on that spring. We don't know what to blame for the

poor directional stability, however. When you'd like to be going straight down the road the Z-car would rather weave back and forth. The wiggles are small and they seem to correct themselves, but they are annoying, nonetheless.

Neither we nor Datsun are entirely satisfied with the choice of tires. Bridgestone 175 SR 14 radials were selected as standard equipment because of their good handling characteristics, but they are also responsible for an abnormally high level of road noise, particularly over tar strips and small bumps. The ride quality of the Z-car is actually quite comfortable for a sporting car of its class but the noise tends to make you think otherwise. Knowing this, Datsun engineers were deeply involved in tire testing at the time of our road test and hoped to have a more compatible tire before very many Z-cars were imported.

While there are problems in the chassis that still must be worked out, it's an altogether different story in the cockpit. At times during the test we found ourselves being very critical of the Z-car—judging harshly where it fell short of perfection and completely forgetting that it sells for $3,601. It seems far more expensive than any competitive similarly priced sports car. We are back to the double standard for family cars and sports cars again. The Z-car has certain qualities that up to now were available only in sedans or very expensive GT cars. Silence is the best example. The engine noise level in the Datsun under normal operating conditions is roughly equal to that of an American intermediate sedan, which is to say that you hardly know it's there. That doesn't seem like a monumental achievement except that no one else in this price class has ever done it before.

And the 240Z is very comfortable, which also makes it

134

seem more expensive. The bucket seats are elaborately contoured and wrap around you slightly to keep you from sliding around. The backrest angle is adjustable in notches through a small range so you can find a position that suits. Head room, leg room, and shoulder room are ample and the final little detail that makes it just right is the dead pedal.

The feeling of getting your money's worth is reinforced by the complete instrumentation and rather complex looking controls. The speedometer (which for some reason starts at 20 mph) and the 8,000-rpm tach are directly in front of the driver, and all of the normal small gauges and a clock are angled toward him from three pods centrally located on top of the instrument panel. A curious rod projects out of the right side of the steering column, which has turntype switches for lights and windshield wipers and a button for the washers on its outer end. It works quite well when you get used to it but its biggest advantage is that it can be easily reached, even when you are strapped in with the shoulder belt. On the console are two levers that look like they should be for lowering the landing gear or adjusting the flaps—it turns out that one is a hand throttle and the other is the choke (the 240Z always has to be choked to start).

The 240Z is obviously well conceived by standards universal to good automobiles, but there has been an East-West struggle in the interior trim. When you consider the tremendous cultural differences between the Japanese and the Americans it's surprising that any automotive styling could bridge the two. In some areas, like the 1953 Tijuana quilted vinyl on the console and on the sides of the luggage area and yellow wood rim on the steering wheel, the difference in taste is conspicuous. The instrument panel, too, has a characteristic flavor that is found in all Datsuns. It's a one-piece affair, molded of soft energy absorbing plastic foam and deeply contoured in a way that suggests nothing but a Datsun instrument panel: not a GT car in the fashion originated by the Italians, not two-ton nickelodeon in the style championed by Detroit, but just plain Datsun. Elsewhere, the Z-car seems international in its appearance. The exterior styling is smooth and appropriately GT-like, drawing remarks like, "That's not a Datsun, is it?" and "Man, how much did that thing cost ya?" It's obviously attractive enough to generate a little envy in everyone who sees it and that is at least half the value of any automobile other than a four-door sedan.

But while they are envying you for having a sports car, the Z-car doesn't shackle you with the normal sports car limitations. Not only is it comfortable and quiet but it also has a generous luggage area. From just behind the seats all the way back to the rear of the car is a flat area that will easily carry enough luggage for two people. Tie-down straps have been provided to secure small objects that like to roll around. And loading is easy because of the huge tailgate. It would be handier if the seat backs would fold forward so that small things could be unloaded from the front. As it is, the headrests are so high that there is little room left for passing bulky objects around them. Even so, the 240Z sets the new standard for utility in two-passenger cars of this price.

And it's inevitable that we should come back to price because that ultimately decides the desirability of any car. At the time of the test, the Z-car followed Datsun's typical pricing policy for its sporting cars—everything is standard equipment. Every car as it comes from the factory has radial ply tires and an excellent push-button AM radio with a power antenna. It's as simple as that. There will be options in the future, however. Tinted glass and a heated rear window will soon be available. Price is the least of the Z-car's problems—and it does have a few problems. Although it is splendidly conceived, we have the feeling that it's not quite done yet. There is an annoying vibration somewhere in the drivetrain that you feel under full power, and as near as we can tell it is present in varying degrees in all cars. And as we mentioned before, the brakes are sensitive to splashed-up water which is a serious deficiency. Still, we are optimistic. After the test we sat down in a truth-telling session with the key men of Datsun USA, the importer, and they were intent on hearing any criticisms that we might put forth. It turned out that they were aware of every weakness we had found and were working closely with the main engineering department in Japan to find solutions. We are confident that they will succeed. Since they were obviously bright enough technically to bring the Z-car this far along, the final rung on the ladder is within easy reach.

Even as it is, the 240Z is worth its price. Just between you and us, when Datsun gets it all straightened around, it might be worth a little more.

Top speed: 109 mph
0-60 7.8 seconds
151 hp, 146 lb-ft of torque
Price: $3,601

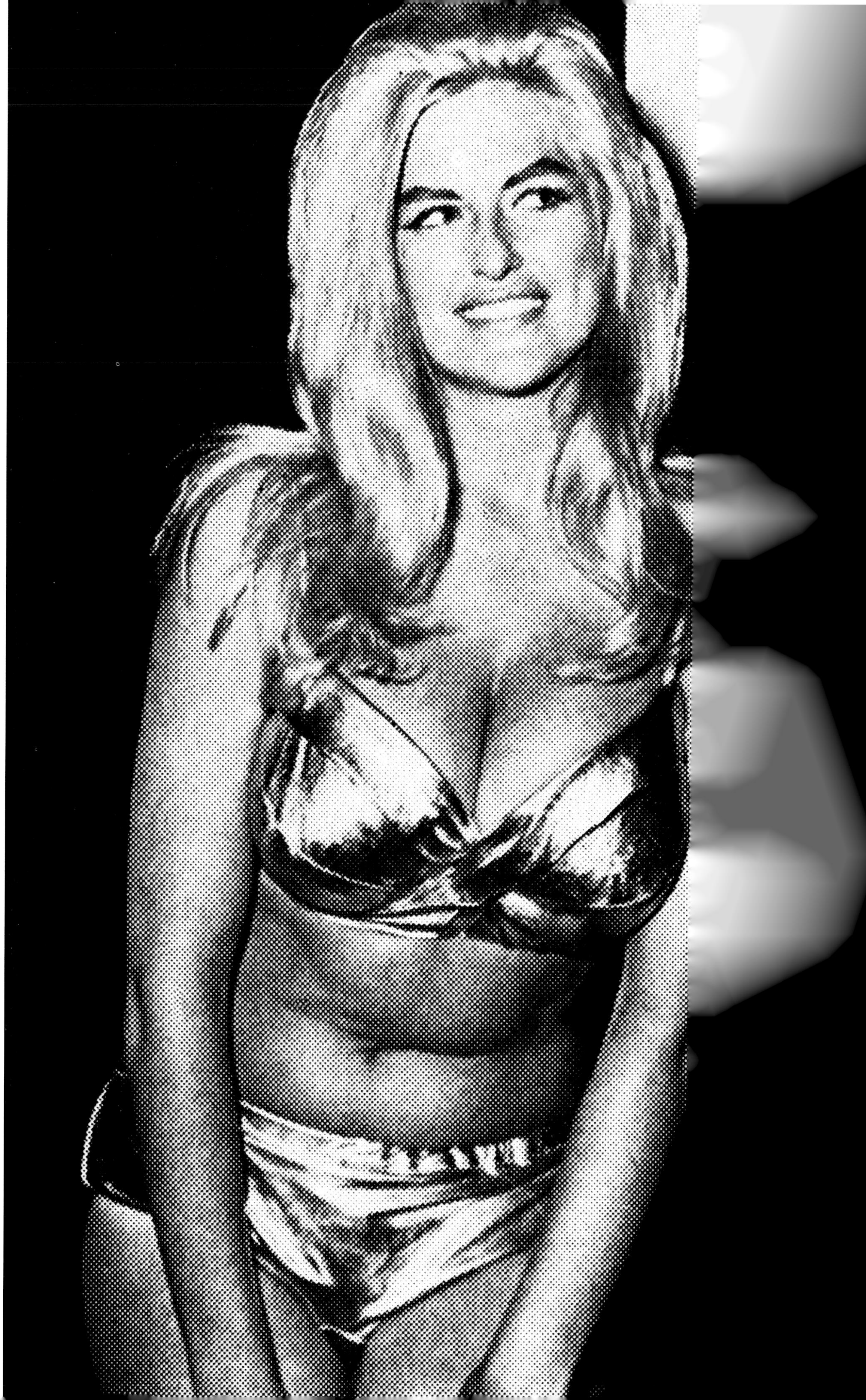

June 1970
Linda

By Brock Yates

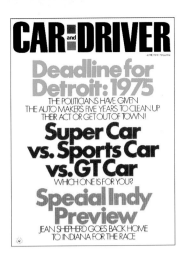

"Ah love 'em all, just like my little brothers and sisters."
The Bakersfield drag races are run on an abandoned military airfield planted in the middle of a treeless, haze-shrouded basin. It is flat and featureless from horizon to horizon save for low rows of bleachers that border the track and a rickety orange control tower painted with a sign that says, "Kern County Racing Association."

The numbing thunder of the machines is silenced. Practice and qualifying are over and the elimination rounds are about to commence. The national anthem is partially digested by the aged public address system. Then it appears at the far end of the track, shimmering and unworldly against a gray backdrop of smog. It is a white convertible with a great pole probing out of its trunk lid—a phallus ten feet tall—a giant shift lever draped with this fantastic, silver-haired, pneumatic woman. My God, it's Linda! "And here she is, ladies and gentlemen, the queen of racing, the lovely Linda Vaughn, Miss Hurst Golden Shifter!"

"Linda, baby, up here!" "Look it that hair." "Unreal!" "Man, oh, man, what boobs!" "Linda, baby, you got a good thing going!" "Bow, Linda, Bow!"

Linda Vaughn faces the crowd and sweeps into an exaggerated bow. Suddenly there is a cleavage that looks like somebody split that glowing skin with an axe. Wolf whistles. Shouts. Arms waving. Hands clapping. Binoculars are focused. Brownie cameras cock and fire. The few women present watch in wooden silence. The lean, golden-sheathed body snaps upright and the long, sharp-chinned face breaks into a wide, innocent grin. An arm flutters, the great bosoms turn in gallant profile, the massive, sensuous streams of hair sway in the breeze and

the voice shouts, in shrill, Southern little-girl tones, "Hi, y'all!"

Then Miss Linda Vaughn, Miss Hurst Golden Shifter, former Miss Pure Firebird, former Miss Atlanta Raceway, former Miss Georgia runner-up, the queen of auto racing, the earth mother of all racers, big sister to brave boy-men, the sweet, indomitable Little Annie Fannie of the Speedways, life and fertility symbol of motorsport, has passed by.

The racing is over. The sun is falling and clusters of men and their women with beehive hair are standing around inert cars. Bored kids are stomping plastic cups under the bleachers, mini-bikes buzz. People squint against the punishment of blowing grit. Accessory company representatives in miracle-fiber warm-up jackets paste decals on the winning cars and a platoon of photographers record the presentation of enormous, polished wood trophies to the victors. In the middle is Linda, resplendent, bright-eyed, loquacious, unmarked by the hours of rubbing and hugging that she has carried on with a thousand, hungry, fantasy-crazed fans. Autographs, kisses, poses for Instamatics and Polaroid Swingers, enough "Hi, y'all's" to rupture a Georgia peach, and miles and miles of smiles.

In a small trailer behind the timing tower another woman is watching the performance. She is Caroline Williams, the wife of Jack Williams, a veteran drag racer who promotes the Bakersfield event. Caroline Williams is no bush leaguer.

139

An ex-Playboy Bunny in mini-skirt and frosted hair, she has assisted Linda with her costume changes throughout the day, thereby becoming a true witness to the legend of the Vaughn physical presence. She leans easily against the trailer door, smiles laconically and says, "One thing about Linda, she sure can make you feel like a boy."

The Lions Drag Strip in Long Beach, California, is dark and sea air makes the pit area damp and chill. It is clogged with racing cars, painted like lace curtains, pickup trucks with camper bodies, delivery vans, raked street jobs with mag wheels, and that awful, seismic, mantle-ripping drum-ruffle sound of fuel-burning, supercharged V-8 engines. Linda is there, too, swirling through the pits, sliding easily into open arms, snuggling against tingling torsos, joking, waving, chattering in a hundred brief encounters. Hovering nearby is a young man in a wheelchair— a bashful youth whose awkwardly canted legs indicate that his occupancy in the chair has been long and difficult. He watches her with the awe and simple affection reserved for untouchables, for idols, for goddesses. Whenever she appears at Lions, he is there, to watch and to roll along behind at a respectable distance. Linda goes to him as she goes to the rest, grasping his hand and carrying on a brief, automatic conversation laden with innocent pleasantries. The boy is pleased, and suddenly the mentality of "fandom" and the relationship of glamour to loneliness gains meaning.

Linda gets hundreds of letters a week. Dozens include earnest proposals of marriage and tokens of affection. Valentine's Day brings boxes of candy and syrupy expressions of love. To most of them she is little more than a plastic doll life symbol mounted on the back of a convertible. To others she exists as a living, breathing, talking human being, and when all of the heated loins and pulsating glands have cooled, she remains for them not the embodiment of sexual fantasy, but a lusty, big sister. "Linda has a way of letting guys down easy," says a friend. "They get all pumped up when they see her, and you'd think she'd have trouble with a lot of them, but she's so sweet and genuinely friendly that nobody can get sore at the way she says no." Others recall an incident at Indianapolis several years ago when a drunken, grease-stained mechanic broke into a cocktail party Linda was attending. He elbowed his way through the crowd and asked her to dance. Dressed in a flowing formal, she accepted instantly. The dance completed and her partner's ardor. dampened, if not satisfied, he staggered away and the party resumed. "Linda handles things like that better than any woman I've ever met," says a friend who witnessed the incident. "If she'd turned up her nose at the boy, there would have been a nasty scene, but she has an instinctive sense about how to handle men and their egos."

Aside from the few serious involvements in her 26 years and the scattered adventures of her early career in Southern stock car racing, her relationship with the racing community is surprisingly asexual. "Everybody thinks I'm in the sack with everybody else," she says, "but the fact is, I really consider the guys in racing my friends. In a sort of general sense I'm married to all of them, but only in the way that they relate to the sport. When I started out in Atlanta, the glamour of racing was a pretty big thing to a little ol' country girl from Dalton, Georgia, and I sort of went off the deep end. But I'm older and smarter now and my personal life is my very own. Forget all the fantasies and you'd be surprised how really cool I am."

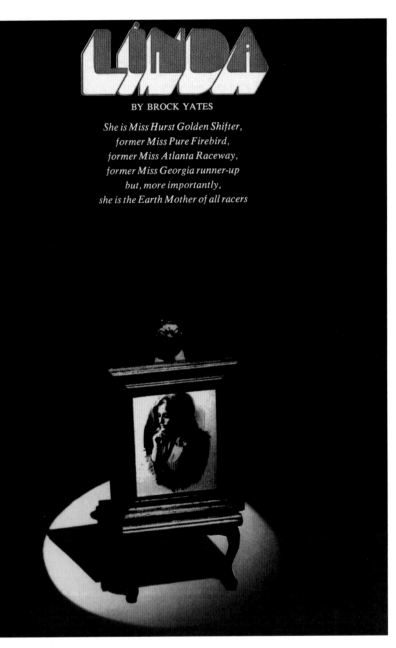

LINDA

BY BROCK YATES

*She is Miss Hurst Golden Shifter,
former Miss Pure Firebird,
former Miss Atlanta Raceway,
former Miss Georgia runner-up
but, more importantly,
she is the Earth Mother of all racers*

They remember her with Fireball. It was a legendary combination. Fireball Roberts, the fastest, smartest stock car driver of the early 1960s and the nubile Linda, first the "Queen" of the Atlanta Raceway, then Miss Pure Firebird, wherein she logged the first of several thousand miles of touring race tracks perched on a performance totem (in this particular case a scarlet, winged bird, symbol of Pure Firebird gasoline). "He used to call me 'Bird,' and he taught me a whole lot about life," she says as she regally raises her chin in an unconscious gesture of sadness and nostalgia. Although Roberts was married throughout his friendship with Linda and at the time of his tragic death in 1964, her devotion to him is obvious. She says she loved him, but for her love is an oft-used euphemism for many subtle gradations of affection, more often relating to family figures than to paramours.

She says she loved Jimmy too, meaning the late Jim Clark, who saw Linda a great deal more than the racing fraternity realized before his fatal crash in 1968. "He had so much class—he was such a gentleman," she says in that sharp voice of hers, full of cornpone country Georgia thickness, but strangely punctuated by precise articulation. If shorn of her accent, she would have extraordinary elocution.

"We used to sit around in the motel room and talk and I'd rub his back. It was a beautiful thing, and one of the proudest things I would ever have done in my life would have been to have borne one of Jimmy Clark's children. He was a great man. Most race drivers are lousy lovers. They are too wrapped up in themselves, too impatient. But he was different. I can remember the day he died. I was working the New York Automobile Show and a call came while I was on the stand. It was Booper calling from Atlanta ("Booper" is Linda's close friend, Betty Drye, a shapely North Carolinian who is something of a legend in her own right). I said, 'Who?' and she answered, 'Jimmy.' I left the show right away and went to my hotel room and called her back. We bawled on the phone for an hour. Most race drivers would make terrible husbands because of their ego problems. But I would have married Jimmy. He has so much class. Sometimes I get so lonely I could bawl my damn eyes out."

Linda Vaughn was engaged to be married once. Her suitor was a balding, fiftyish, ex-General of the Air Force with powerful connections within the military-industrial establishment. He had millions, and he seemed prepared to spend them on his wife-to-be. Linda appeared at the races wearing a diamond ring that would make even Liz and Dick blink. Its center stone was 10 carats, surrounded by a grouping of one carat subordinates. It cost the earth. He owned executive jets and suddenly

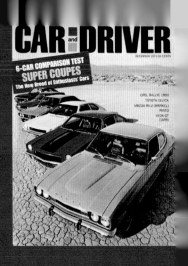

December 1971
Wallaby Balloonfire X-4000
A Commie-Pinko plot to rot your moral fibre?

So there you are dumping along 1-94 at 54 mph in your clapped-out three-year-old Chevy Caprice Concours with "Jerry Vale's Greatest Hits" oozing out of the Muntz Stereo; you're wearing your StaPrest red and gray sport shirt and J.C. Penney KantKrease slacks with the two-inch cuffs and you're still feeling gas pains from that Stuckey's cheeseburger and little Walter in the back seat is going gak-gak-gak with his styrofoam M-16 automatic rifle and you're hoping to get home in time to catch the Colts and Vikings on the tube when, whoooooooooosh, Omigod!—something very solid, very fast and very purple fills up the whole left window for a millionth-of-a-second that feels as long as an extra-innings twinight doubleheader and damn near wrenches that genuine imitation Carpathian burled walnut plastic optional deluxe wheel out of your hands before you can recover your wits; by which time this Thing out there has flashed on past and your bug-stained windshield with the 1968 Idaho Highway Inspection Sticker

is actually trembling in its frame, yes, trembling, with the shock-waves from whatever-it-was, which is now arrowing almost out of sight and the air between its disappearing stern and your Chevy, bumping along at 54 mph on wheezed-out old Monroe Load Levellers is blurry and full of these waves like you were half a mile behind a 747 in the stack-up pattern over JFK or something. No, it's not some trick new paramilitary hunk of hardware on secret test; not even a commie-pinko plot to degenerate the central nervous system of American highway travelers and take over the country while everybody's still in a catatonic state of shock. What that purple thing was, bub, was *Car and Driver*'s current road test car, the new Wallaby Balloonfire X-4000 Coupe de Grace with Jetplume 425 cu. in. V-8, and no matter what all the faceless bureaucrats in their little Insurance company plywood cells may mumble or how the fuzz of 50 states will fulminate in their Friday Night Safety Lectures at the Legion Hall, or what all those mincing goody-two-shoes who pose as "safety experts" behind their $1.95 clip-on Hawaiian ties may sputter about it during the next Committee Hearing on cement bumpers, this dude already has the self-satisfied moguls out in Detroit plenty shook up, faked out, strung-out and blubbering in the shower room of the Bloomfield Hills Country Club. There's old Wallaby, building nice dumb cars nobody but the chorus of Up With People could lust after, the kind of automobile that wouldn't have an image if it looked in the mirror—and bammo!—here comes the Balloonfire from deepest left field to catch the industry with its Italian-silk Size-56 pants down. Beautiful! We can almost hear the myopic dim bulbs on other car magazines clucking over the Balloonfire's undersize drum brakes and reeling off four miles of statistics and facts and figures proving, just proving, how it can't outcorner the average Conestoga wagon and what horrible, terrible things it means to get only two miles per gallon of premium fuel. Of course these poor benighted slaves to the Puritan Ethic miss the whole point of a car like the Wallaby Balloonfire X-4000. What is the point of the Balloonfire? Well it isn't the kind of car that would feel at home trundling down to the corner Finast to pick up a big giant size bag of Krisp-E-Chipz, if that makes things any clearer. The consensus around *Car and Driver* ran something like, if certain other Detroit makers (not Ford, GM or Chrysler, we hasten to add, and not American Motors either) would knock off their Rip Van Winkle number and twig to what the Balloonfire is really, really all about, America could start digging on the real problems of this country and forget those hippie atheist dope-fiend goose-stepping commie red pinko plots, no matter what all those comical knee-jerk liberals and far-out cryptofascists keep bawling every time Ralph Nader buttons up his $29.95 Robert Hall WetherPruf gabardine water-resistant gray overcoat and goes out to call a press conference on the imminent danger to the American public in the crooked business practices of the sinister horseshoe cartel. When you think of it that way, the Wallaby Balloonfire makes as much sense as any car has in *Car and Driver*'s history.

her primary mode of transport was Saberliners and Lears.

"For a while I thought it was the real thing. Then he started to call up at odd times, just trying to catch me cheatin' on him. Then more and more it seemed like I was a big-busted blonde that he could show off. I finally talked him into a trip to Europe—just the two of us, no business, no friends—to really see if we worked together. It was going to be a dream trip; we were going to travel by Lear, you know, first class all the way. Then the first minute we get to our hotel in Paris, surrounded by all this romance, the rat gets on the telephone to make a Transatlantic call!"

"It all ended in this Swiss chateau one night when he had gone off on another of his business things. I was alone and it was raining and I felt terrible. I began reading Rod McKuen—he's my very favorite—and Kahlil Gibran's *The Prophet* and I read a passage that said:

Love gives naught but itself
And takes naught but from itself.
Love possesses not
Nor would it be possessed,
For love is sufficient unto love.

That really got to me. Here I was with all this money, and I was still as lonely as before. The next morning I got on the airplane for home. Then I gave him back that great, big beautiful rock. It damn near broke my heart."

It is 3:40 in the morning and the Delta Airlines passenger lounge at the Los Angeles International Airport is desolate and still. Rumpled forms are sprawled on the green vinyl couches and a few uniformed agents slump at their desks. In the corner a pair of swarthy janitors with 1954 greaseball hair stop their mopping to watch the tall blonde sweep into the room. She is wearing a blue denim slacks suit that covers a great deal of the spectacular figure, but the foliage of platinum hair gives her 5' 6" body a larger-than-life aspect that sometimes makes her look eleven feet tall.

She spots the hunch-shouldered form of a tired man and strides to him. A hug. Chatter. Then silence. The moment is serious. The man is Tommy Lemmons, frontline mechanic for the great Don Garlits. Hours earlier his boss's car had exploded in half at the Lions Drag Strip and now Garlits lies in the intensive care unit of the Pacific Hospital with part of his right foot shorn off and his left leg broken.

Lemmons is a man with soul and he is heartened by the company. Before Linda's arrival it was his job to alone greet Garlits's wife, Pat, who is rushing through the night from Tampa to be at the side of her wounded husband. These are hard moments in racing, when legend says that the insiders—those who understand the hurt—bunch together in a protective cover for the stricken. Linda had heard about the crash at Bakersfield, 150 miles to the north, and had hurried to help. Of the thousands of people in Southern California who tell you they are bosom buddies of "Big Daddy," only Linda Vaughn has stayed up all night in order to do what she could.

It's never far away, the little leather bag with all the cosmetics stuff: the brushes and paint and the powder puffs and mascara, and the mirror that she uses to eye herself a hundred times a day. Riding in the back seat of a friend's Eldorado ("Love those Eldos"), passing a mirror in a hotel lobby, catching a reflection in a store window, it's the same: a detached examination of appearance—to tug a wrinkle from the dress, to finger curl a strand of hair, to blend the makeup shading on a cheekbone—constant tampering with the external self. Then the bag. Out comes a comb or an eyebrow pencil or another application of Jasmine cologne. Inside that bag is a great deal of psychic protection against the world. Don't count the .25 caliber Beretta Jetfire automatic that sometimes lurks in there, because a woman with a visibility quotient like hers can attract degenerates of both sexes. But the cosmetics are meaningful, as is the bulging, grayed wallet full of family pictures—nieces, nephews, brothers, sisters, step-brothers, cousins. There is mother, a fulsome, youthful woman, in a ragged Walgreen color photo leaning against the door of a pink and black Ford hardtop. "My mamma is the greatest," she says. "We've always been very close. I go home to Dalton to see her as much as I can, and keep her up to date on all the things that are happening to me. She was a little mad at me when I wouldn't marry the General, but you've got to understand that life has been pretty hard for my mamma, raising all of us kids like she did. She could just see all that money slippin' away. My daddy, he's a pretty wild '01 boy and they've been divorced a long time now. Last time I saw him he was drivin' around in a big '01 Eldo with a chick younger than me sitting beside him." There is a picture of herself, taken during a brief vacation in Hawaii with "my boy"—a reticent, introspective, hard-running race driver for whom she harbors great affection. She is standing loosely in front of a low, vanilla-colored hotel on the Island of Maui. Her hair is unteased and lays flat against her head. She is wearing slacks and a sweater and a pair of sneakers. Her face is without makeup. She looks childlike, innocent, maybe 16 years old.

Then she snaps the wallet shut and buries it inside the bag. Before she locks the clasp, the mirror comes out for a quick perusal. Everything is in order.

"I've been doing this for eight years. Two more and it's all over."

Nobody has ever stopped to figure out why automobile racing, of all the major sports, has a queen symbol like Linda Vaughn, but the fact remains that she is the best-known female ever to snuggle up to an automobile or the man who drives it. She is a good broad. Somehow through all the madness and sadness, the hustlers and the phony lovers, she has managed to keep smiling, to keep looking forward to tomorrow and another ride around another race track on the trunk of that convertible. She is unsinkable. In the course of her work with Hurst she visits numerous military hospitals and plays big sister to thousands of smashed young men from Vietnam. She plows cheerily through the wards and solariums, a smile glued to her face. Then she flees to a car and cries uncontrollably.

She has been romanced by some of the biggest names in sports and entertainment, married and unmarried. One of America's most famous racing personalities asked her to marry him. Joe Namath squired her briefly until she walked out on him in a nightclub. The father of one of the world's international racing stars offered her big money and a life of leisure if she would become his mistress. She declined.

"Two more years and that's it," she says. "My associations with Hurst, especially with George and his wife Lila, who are among my closest friends, and Jack Duffy (the balding, aggressive, extremely capable Hurst PR boss) whom I respect more than anyone in this business, will stay close, I hope, but I want to develop a career based on advertising and public relations. My idol is Mary Wells, and I figure if she can do it, I can do it."

And why the hell not.

LEFT: Anonymity was hardly the Ferrari's strong suit.
CENTER LEFT: Fred Opert (center) counseled caution; he was ignored.
CENTER RIGHT: Waters, Marbut, and their Little Rock Super Van.
BOTTOM LEFT: Travco team carried on a coast-to-coast card game.
BOTTOM RIGHT: A diary of events experienced by contestants in the Cannonball Baker: the routes they followed, the time they took, the stops they made, the troubles they encountered, the cops they met....

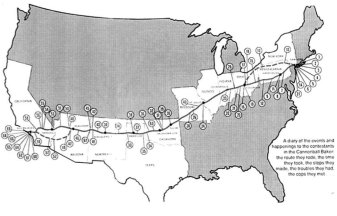

A diary of the events and happenings to the contestants in the Cannonball Baker: the route they rode, the time they took, the stops they made, the troubles they had, the cops they met.

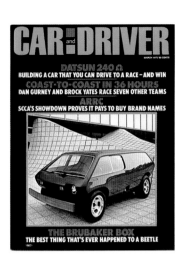

March 1972
The Cannonball Baker Sea-to-Shining-Sea Memorial Trophy Dash

Those damn fools, they went and did it. Shortly after midnight on the 15th of November, 1971, six outlandish vehicles, manned by 16 even more outlandish drivers, codrivers, navigators, mechanics—and a TWA stewardess, for God's sake—scattered out of the Red Ball Garage on East 31st Street in New York and headed west. A few hours passed and two more entrants joined the chase, a coast-to-coast epic that will be remembered as the Cannonball Baker Sea-to-Shining-Sea Memorial Trophy Dash.

Eight vehicles in all, 23 lunatics. Less than a day and a half later (six minutes less to be precise), the first car, a mud-streaked Ferrari Daytona, yowled into the parking lot of the Portofino Inn in the marina of Redondo Beach, California, 2,863 miles from New York. In the next three hours, four more machines had checked in, and the exhausted, red-eyed competitors were lounging around, breathing the gentle Pacific air, stretching their cramped, grubby bodies in the warm sun and exchanging tales of their adventures. Twenty-four more hours passed before the last competitor, a pachydermatous Travco Motor Home with a shrieking police motorcycle escort, rolled sedately over the finish line.

It was over. The Cannonball Baker Sea-to-Shining-Sea Memorial Trophy Dash had entered the annals of sporting minutiae, leaving it to future generations to decide what it meant, if anything. To those involved, it had been an adventure, encompassing difficult endurance driving, nasty weather, brushes with the law—some of the latter bordering on the absurd navigational challenges and a variety of mechanical troubles. The concept had been refreshing in its simplicity. Whereas every automotive competition in the world is encumbered by a thicket of confusing rules, the Cannonball Baker had but one—"All competitors will drive any vehicle of their choosing, over any route, at any speed they judge practical, between the starting point and destination. The competitor finishing with the lowest elapsed time is the winner." There were no other rules. Once this word filtered through the underground of the sport, a substantial discussion arose as to what type car would be best suited, what route would be the fastest, etc., in keeping with the essentially anarchistic underpinnings of the event, there was no organizing body (save for a shadowy group known as "The True Friends of Hernando DeSoto"), and more important, no prize money. The only material award to be gained by the winner was possession of the S-K "Nutmaster" trophy—a free-form sculpture of wrenches, hammers, and pliers fabricated and donated by the S-K tool company. In its simple challenge—getting from New York to Los Angeles in the quickest possible time—lay the fascination for the competitors. Others wanted to go, but were held back by obligations to job and family, or in some cases, fear of censure. Others talked big but disappeared before the start. In the end it was eight cars, 21 guys and two women who ran the Cannonball Baker.

The race began at the Red Ball Garage shortly after midnight on November 15. While the competitors could leave at any time they chose during the 24 hours of the 15th, most chose to depart New York in the dead of night, primarily to avoid the Manhattan and New Jersey normal cheek-to-jowl traffic and to permit them to run the Los Angeles freeways at roughly midday, 36-38 hours later if all went well. While an Indy-type flying start through the Lincoln Tunnel would have been ideal, practical considerations dictated a staggered start with the entrants leaving the Red Ball at informal intervals. The competitors are listed in the order in which they departed: Chevrolet Sportvan, Polish Racing Drivers of America—drivers, Oscar Koveleski, Tony Adamowicz, and Brad Niemcek. This team requested to leave first, based on its obvious claim to the "pole position." This request was not contested by the other teams, so the PRDA rolled away from the Red Ball at 12:11 a.m. with a small cluster of photographers, *Car and Driver* staffers and baffled pedestrians witnessing their departure. The plan was to run non-stop, thanks to a special setup using five 55-gallon fuel drum, and a myriad of hoses, lines and pumps, which gave them a total on-board capacity of 298 gallons. (Note: Others knew they would have to stop: the original Cannonball Baker, run last May by Moon Trash II, an infamous Dodge Van, in 40 hours 51 minutes, had consumed 315 gallons of gas. With nearly an extra ton of gas on board; giving their PRDA van a gross weight approaching 7,000 lbs, mileage had to slump to a point where a stop would be necessary.) Briggs Chevrolet, the New Jersey dealer that entered the van for the PRDA, had also modified the dipstick and filler setup so oil could be added without stopping. A special 3.07-to-one final drive, Corvette dual ignition, heavy-duty Goodyear tires, tachometer, bunk, and modified air cleaner completed the improvements.

Professional racer Adamowicz, one of the two FIA-graded American drivers, was teamed with Oscar Koveleski, a perennial Can-Am competitor, SCCA champion, and racing public relations expert, and club racer Brad Niemcek. They left a substantial tide of publicity (which some of their more paranoid rivals thought the police might have read), claiming that with the aid of multitudes of PRDA members across the country and their non-stop capacity, they would win by maintaining legal speed limits. Decked out in fancy fireproof racing uniforms, they accelerated their wildly decorated van into the night as Steve Smith, Cannonball pioneer and sage of cross-country racing, commented, "They'll need more than Nomex to protect them if they so much as cough. If that thing lets go, it'll make Amchitka look like a wet match."

1971 Cadillac Sedan deVille Driveaway Special—drivers, Larry Opert, Nate Pritzker, Ron Herisko, all of Cambridge, Massachusetts. As this trio rolled away at 12:14 a.m., they had to be strong candidates for the Style Award (if there could be such a thing in an event of this nature). Lawyer Opert, brother of racing car dealer Fred Opert and himself a club racer, plus his law partner Herisko and engineer friend Pritzker had no car that suited the demands of the Cannonball so they found one in the stygian pages of *The New York Times*. They answered an ad from a stuffy New York businessman who wanted his new Caddy transported to California. Our three heroes got the job, provided they did not drive the nearly new (2,500 miles) sedan before eight o'clock in the morning, did not stay on the road after nine in the evening, and under no circumstances exceeded 75 mph. Putting the owner's mind at rest, the Cambridge team snatched up the car, stuffed some extra fuel cans in the trunk, a radar detector on the sun 34 visor, a set of binoculars in the glove

June 1973

The Boys of Memorial Day: Whatever became of the 33 men who ran the 1952 Indy 500?

The answer was simple: many of them died behind the wheel. The list of those who lost their lives racing in the 20 years since included Jimmy Bryan, killed in a dirt track race; Jimmy Reece, who died in an Indy car race in New Jersey; Jim Rigsby, dead in a sprint car crash in Dayton; Joe James, another sprinter who lost his life in a race in San Jose; George Fonder, killed in a dirt track race in Pennsylvania; Bill Schindler, also dead in a big car race in Pennsylvania; Bill Vukovich, the "mad Russian," dead in a crash at the Indy 500 in 1955; Manuel Ayulo, killed at the same Indy race in practice sessions; Johnny McDowell, who died during qualifying in a race the week following Indy in Wisconsin; Bob Sweikert, who also died shortly after the 1952 Indy 500 in a race in Salem, Indiana; Bob Scott, dead in an Indy car race in South Carolina; Alberto Ascari, dead testing a new Ferrari at Monza; and Chet Miller, killed in Indy practice sessions before the 1953 race. Bobby Ball, another 1952 driver, crashed in California in January of the next year and remained in a coma for 13 months until finally passing in February 1954. —*Brock Yates*

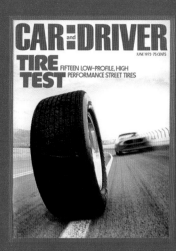

compartment and screeched off toward the Red Ball.

1970 MGB/GT—drivers, Bob Perlow, Baldwin, Long Island, and Wes Dawn, Venice, California. Perlow and Dawn left at 12:15 a.m. in a car they hadn't expected to be driving. Perlow's original entry, a Volvo P1800, had been stolen at the United States Grand Prix (and recovered, although the local authorities never bothered to notify him), so he bought the MGB used with 10,000 miles on the clock. A student at Hofstra University, Perlow met up with Dawn, a West Coast television worker and club racer, a few days before the race. Aside from adding driving lights and cans of fuel and water, their car was dead stock.

1971 Dodge Van, Modified—drivers, Tom Marbut, Randy Waters, and Becky Poston, all of Little Rock, Arkansas. Everyone called them the "Little Rock Tankers," because they'd mounted 190-gallon aluminum gas tanks in the back of their dazzling new Dodge van. Operators of the Sound 'n'Sirloin restaurant in Little Rock, Marbut and Waters, plus Tom's girlfriend, Becky Poston, had put together their van after reading about the exploits of Moon Trash II in Car and Driver. Aside from its special paint and fuel system, the van was equipped with a 2.94 final drive, an outside exhaust system, a radar detector (which sounded an alarm at every airport, but never made a peep in the vicinity of the police) and a thickly rugged interior. Its 360 cu. in. engine had been fitted with a Holley 750 CFM carburetor. "Snoopy II" as they called the van, had made a reconnaissance run from Little Rock to New York and back the week before the race. The "Little Rock Tankers" departed the Red Ball Garage at 12:22 a.m.

1971 Ferrari 275 GTB/4 Daytona coupe—drivers, Dan Gurney, Santa Ana, California, and Brock Yates. This team left at 12:32 a.m. Their Ferrari was entered by exotic car impresario Kirk F. White, of Philadelphia. It was utterly stock (what could be modified?) and

aside from a couple of sacks full of bread and cheese, peanuts, chocolate, Vitamin C tablets, Gatorade, a thermos of coffee and some extra spark plugs, etc., no extra equipment was carried. A dazzling blue paint job, complete with exquisite pin-striping, plus a patchwork of sponsors' decals, made the car about as inconspicuous as Hugh Heffner's DC-9. Everybody was convinced the car would be a wide favorite with law enforcement officers.

Moon Trash II: 1971 Dodge Van—drivers, Steve Behr, Wellesley Hills, Massachusetts, Kim Chapin, New York City, and stewardess, Miss Holly Morin, Boston, Massachusetts. Surely the sentimental favorite, Moon Trash II barely made the starting line. A crash on Manhattan's West Side Drive several weeks earlier had wiped out its front end and work had been carried on until a matter of hours before the start. It was painted a lethal looking flat-black, its headlights were unaimed and the heater was not operable as it left for Los Angeles. Otherwise it was the same machine that carried Yates, Steve Smith, Jim Williams, and Yates's son, Brock Jr., to the first Cannonball Baker record of 40 hours and 51 minutes in May 1971. Job demands kept Smith and Williams from going this time, while young Yates was back in school, but the two former drivers were on hand at the Red Ball when Moon Trash II departed. At the wheel was Steve Behr, a highly-competent SCCA racer who shared, with John Buffum, the honor of being the American to finish highest in the history of the Monte Carlo Rally (12th overall in 1969). In that competition Steve had noted ironically that the police had escorted the racers the entire distance. With him was Sports Illustrated and Car and Driver writer Kim Chapin and Holly Morin, a friend and TWA stewardess who'd just arrived in New York on a flight from Los Angeles. The hope of avoiding morning rush-hour traffic in Columbus kept Moon Trash II from leaving before 1:53 a.m., making it the sixth entry to depart.

1966 Union 76 Travco Motor Home—drivers, Bill Broderick, Phil Pash, both of Chicago, Bob Carey, Arlington, Virginia, Joe Frasson, Golden Valley, Minnesota, and Pal Parker, Waynesville, North Carolina. After driving their aging (five years old, 38,000 miles) but eager motor home nonstop from Lou Klug's motor home rentals in Cincinnati, Ohio, Broderick and Co. caught a few hours sleep and left the Red Ball at 5:56 a.m. While the 65-mph top speed of the old machine made it a long-shot to win, Broderick, who is Union 76's racing public relations man, hoped to set a cross-country record for motor homes and bring some publicity to his company's network of lavish truck stops along the way. Phil Pash, motorsports columnist for *Chicago Today* planned to send daily dispatches on the journey. Pal Parker, a specialist in racing photography, and Bob Carey, editor of *Circle Track and Highway*, intended coverage as well. Joe Frasson, an upcoming Grand National stock car driver, was along to run fast, especially while drafting tractor-trailer rigs.

1969 AMX—drivers, Ed and Tom Broerton, Oakland, California. This team of enthusiastic brothers, with their 90,000-mile-old AMX (veteran of a trip the full length of Baja California among other things), would have left with the rest, but they needed sleep. They had arrived in New York only hours before midnight, after a 44-hour, nonstop reconnaissance run from the Portofino Inn, and sought refuge in a hotel for some critically needed rest before starting out again. Ed, who is a supermarket manager, and Tom, a pharmacy student at Cal-Tech, had made numerous long-distance runs, including a number of Memorial Day weekend jaunts from Oakland to Indy for the 500, leaving a day before the race and running home the day following. When they left the Red Ball at 2:51 p.m. Monday afternoon, they carried a pair of binoculars, some snacks, a stopwatch, a fresh idea of the route, and a certain apprehension about the old AMX holding up for 3,000 flat-out miles.

While the justification (or lack of it) for the Cannonball Baker will be debated for some time, a number of tangible conclusions were forthcoming regarding routes, type of vehicles, tactics, etc.

While the Ferrari won, it was not driven the fastest. The Cadillac's over-the-road average (excluding stops) was faster and Moon Trash's was equal to the winner (see following chart). There is little question that the Ferrari won for other reasons, such as excellent mileage—the highest of the eight competitors at 12.2 mpg-combined with a 29-gallon gas tank that provided a range of 300-350 miles. This, coupled with its extraordinary high-performance capabilities in acceleration, braking, comfort, cornering, and cruising speed (plus Gurney) made the difference.

The Ferrari made nine stops for gas, consuming approximately 50 minutes. The PRDA van made one seven-minute stop. The Ferrari consumed 240 gallons 6t-fuel averaging 80 mph, the PRDA van used 356 gallons while traveling a slightly shorter route and averaging about 3 mph less. On the other end of the scale, the Cadillac and Moon Trash, both with stock tanks, made 15 and 14 gas stops, respectively, but were in the thick of competition, if other factors like police and mechanical troubles are discounted. In sum, the extra-weight, lower mileage, poorer handling, and general hazard of massive fuel loads produce strong limitations. Big car or little car, van or Ferrari, sedan or sports car, economy car or monster machine there is no clear-cut solution. When it is remembered that the first five finishers were separated by less than two hours, the difficulty of deciding on the perfect long-distance vehicle comes into focus.

The problem of tactics provides a clearer answer: to run flat-

151

out or to cool-it; that is the question, and the "cool-it" school seems to be the way in any long-distance journey. Speeds in excess of 100 mph, regardless of how safe they might be on modern Interstates, simply attract too many lawmen. The Cadillac, with five apprehensions that cost them several hours, is a perfect example of the limitations of this mode of travel. By contrast, the two fastest cars, the Ferrari and the PRDA, collected but one ticket between them and both made the trip at carefully paced, ever-watchful speeds in the 90-100 mph range. (The Ferrari was stopped during the period that rule was violated.) Sustained speed is the key to the Cannonball, and any time lost to the police is a disaster. Therefore a happy medium must be found without attracting attention. Sounds simple, what?

Seven of the eight competitors used essentially the same route—the Pennsylvania Turnpike, Interstate 70, Interstate 40 network running through Columbus, St. Louis, Oklahoma City, Flagstaff, etc. Only the Ferrari took a different course. Rather than run Interstate 78 from northern New Jersey to the intersection of the Pennsylvania Turnpike at Harrisburg, its crew cut northward across New Jersey's Route 46, through Netcong and Hackettstown, to Interstate 80 due west across Pennsylvania. From there they cut southwest across Ohio from Akron to Columbus, intersecting with the conventional route. This is a good choice if one leaves in the middle of the night. Otherwise Route 46 is clogged with traffic over much of its two-lane distance. It is unusable during daylight hours.

The Ferrari also used the Ash Fork cutoff west of Flagstaff, Arizona, heading south on Routes 89, 71, and 60 to reach Interstate 10. While a good road, there are several mountainous sections on Route 89 that are extremely dangerous and should only be attempted by expert drivers in excellent cars.

The Ferrari traveled approximately 35 miles farther than its rivals, but the higher speeds attained over that extra distance helped to win. Yet the perfect route, especially with the constant addition of new Interstate highways, is still unknown. (Nearly six hours was lopped off Moon Trash's original record, set last May, primarily because of better route knowledge and the new four-lane sections that were opened this summer. If this trend continues, a 32-hour trip may be possible.)

There has been lengthy discussion of the so-called northern route, taking Interstate 80 westward across Iowa, Nebraska, Wyoming, and Utah, then cutting southwest across Nevada to take advantage of the absence of speed limits in that state. However it is 200 miles longer and winter comes early to Wyoming, making the trip in November extremely risky. The southern route, using Interstate 81 to Knoxville, Tennessee, then cutting west across the deep south to Texas, etc., has been studied, but it is again 200 miles farther. But then, if there were bad weather in the central states....

One conclusion is clear; better roads in the east and central U.S. permit faster average speeds than in the far west. The slowest running comes in New Mexico and Arizona, mainly because many towns have to be safely traversed. And don't forget, five of the ten traffic tickets came near the Arizona-California border. It is ironic that here, in the vastness of the West, there is the heaviest concentration of police. Why? Because, given one-on-one situations in the desert, it's easiest to make arrests. No competitor was even looked at in the heavy traffic of New York, St. Louis, Oklahoma City, or Los Angeles, where the accident probability is highest.

That was the Cannonball Baker Sea-to-Shining-Sea Memorial Trophy Dash. No one who ran, not Gurney, not

June 1974

The Day Ford-Ferrari Became Ford Versus Ferrari

It would have been the most unusual merger in the history of the automobile. But surprisingly few, even in the industry's innermost circles, had an inkling of the potential upheaval until it had already become shrouded history.

Ferrari to merge with Ford. Strangely, in light of the bitter racing duels that would be staged between the two parties just months after the talks fell through, each was anxious for the merger in the spring of 1963: Ferrari, the man, for very personal reasons; Ford, the corporation, as a means of confronting and solving a marketing dilemma.

Those were the reasons that the merger talks progressed as far as they did...and the reason they disintegrated. Leading on one hand to an all-Italian Fiat-Ferrari marriage; on the other, to Ford's almost budgetless involvement in racing during the mid- and late-1960s. So wrote John Clinard for *Car and Driver* of the deal that nearly brought Ford control of Ferrari—a deal that collapsed in rancor as Enzo Ferrari finally refused to give up his son—not Dino, his actual son, but the company with his name—to Ford's labyrinthine structure. "My rights, my integrity, my very being as a manufacturer, as an entrepreneur, as the leader of the Ferrari works, cannot work under the enormous machine, the suffocating bureaucracy of the Ford Motor Company!" Enzo is said to have said. In 1964, the deal quashed, Ford was also approached to buy Lotus, and having seen the workings of such a deal through the Ferrari negotiations, turned it down. And in 1966, Ford's GT finished 1-2-3 at Le Mans, knocking Ferrari on its heels.

—*John Clinard*

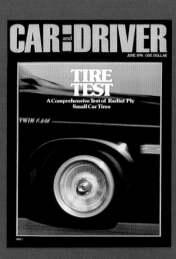

Adamowicz, not anybody, got a dime for the race, making it some kind of milestone in modern automotive annals.

(Editor's Note: Because *Car and Driver*, or any other formal organization for that matter, has no sanction or direct involvement with the Cannonball Baker, this staff, individually or collectively, will recognize, support or publicize any attempts to break any of the records reported in the foregoing story.)

MIDNIGHT/DAWN. MONDAY, NOVEMBER 15

(1) PRDA: Drive briskly west for eight blocks before van's shifter sticks in second gear. Lose five minutes jimmying it loose.
(2) CADILLAC: Passes PRDA, zooms across 34th Street to Lincoln Tunnel in three minutes.
(3) MG: New York-native Perlow misses turnoff to Lincoln Tunnel, wanders around west side docks for 15 minutes.
(4) LITTLE ROCK TANKERS: Zoom out of Manhattan, pass PRDA shortly after reaching New Jersey Turnpike.
(5) FERRARI: Catches seven stoplights in a row on west side of Manhattan.
(6) MOON TRASH: Roads clear, makes quick exit out of City.
(7) PRDA: While bustling along Interstate 78 in eastern Pennsylvania, the engine rattles with an explosion and cab fills with smoke. Adamowicz diagnoses trouble as a faulty crankcase breather system. The team jury rigs a new breather out of a heater hose, hanging it out of right-side window (13 additional tremors occur during trip. without apparent damage).
(8) CADILLAC: Apprehended on the Pennsylvania Turnpike near Harrisburg for 109 mph. Unbelievably, State Trooper lets them go.
(9) MG: Second gear synchro goes; double-clutching tried to no avail.

(10) FERRARI: While everyone else cuts across Interstate 78 to Harrisburg, they head north over two-lane Route 46 to Interstate 80. Road is nearly empty and average speed rapidly rises to 82 mph.
(11) TANKERS: Stopped for speeding near Harrisburg. State Trooper tries hard to hustle Becky Poston, allegedly offering to pay her fine if she will stay behind with him. She refuses, then Trooper threatens an additional charge of smuggling gasoline (due to oversize tanks). They are dragged off to a JP where they pay a $15 fine and lose nearly an hour.
(12) CADILLAC: Narrowly avoids hitting deer on two separate occasions near Washington, Pennsylvania.
(13) FERRARI: Rainstorm in mountains of central Pennsylvania reveals jammed windshield wipers. Situation finally corrected after five-minute stop. Solution; much cursing and jiggling of wiper blades.
(14) TRAVCO: Leaves Red Ball. Parker is sick and remains so for first 14 hours of trip. (Blames illness on Polish kishkes served at lavish PRDA pre-race party held at the Auto Pub restaurant in Manhattan.) Carey has a sprained ankle suffered in loading the vehicle.

MONDAY FORENOON

(15) PRDA: Calculations indicate planned pace is too slow. Up cruising speed to 100 mph.
(16) CADILLAC: Sails into Columbus, Ohio, approximately 6.5 hours after start.
(17) FERRARI: Cuts through Columbus from the north on Interstate 71. Intersects with Interstate 70, placing all eight contestants on essentially the same route.
(18) TANKERS: Pass crippled MG east of Columbus.
(19) MG: Failing transmission seal causes serious clutch

slippage. Stop at a Columbus British-Leyland dealer who indicates cause is hopeless. Perlow drives Dawn to airport, then begins long, slow drive home.

(20) MOON TRASH: Passes Tankers west of Columbus.

(21) TANKERS: Once passed by Moon Trash. they decide their pace is too slow. They trail Moon Trash at discreet distance until it stops for gas (actually running 200 yards shy of the gas station).

(22) CADILLAC: Arrested for speeding (approximately 110 mph) east of Indianapolis. Taken to judge where fine of $33 is levied, 60 minutes lost.

(23) PRDA: Misses turnoff from Indianapolis bypass to Interstate 70, becomes only team to fail to turn left at Indy.

MONDAY AFTERNOON

(24) PRDA: Hard braking permits avoidance of radar trap on western edge of St. Louis.

(25) TRAVCO: Frasson uses stock car experience to draft tractor trailers on Interstate 70. Suction has radio antenna pointing straight forward.

(26) FERRARI: Averaging an effortless 83 mph, team is relaxed, driving one-handed in completely stable machine. Their confidence is building.

(27) AMX: Enters the chase only to find Manhattan streets clogged with traffic. Twenty minutes consumed reaching New Jersey Turnpike.

(28) MOON TRASH: When leaving gas stop near Rolls, Missouri, encounters Tankers once again. The two vans run together for 200 miles, then Moon Trash, being lighter and having more speed, pulls ahead.

(29) CADILLAC: Arrested for speeding on Turner Turnpike near Bristow, Oklahoma. Runs out of gas simultaneously. Explanation

that excessive speed was an effort to coast to nearest gas station is ignored.

(30) MOON TRASH: After falling behind again due to gas stop, repasses tankers in Tulsa freeway traffic.

(31) TANKERS: Stop east of Oklahoma City to add 165 gallons of gas. Twenty minutes lost while trying to clear purchase with a credit card. Three miles down road sediment in gas tank forces a change of fuel pumps, Lose another 20 minutes.

(32) PRDA: Passes Tankers while Little Rock team is adding gas. Great display of honking and waving.

MONDAY EVENING

(33) FERRARI: Perhaps leading, drives into heavy rain, fog, thunderstorms at Texas-New Mexico border.

(34) MOON TRASH: Continues to maintain rapid pace, possibly ahead on elapsed time. Lose five minutes repairing a loose fan belt.

(35) PRDA: Encounters Moon Trash in East Texas Panhandle. After a long struggle in rain, finally gains a 2 to 3-mile lead.

(36) TANKERS: Having run at a conservative pace, they decide they are behind. They up speed, figuring to hell with the police.

(37) CADILLAC: Continues to run on customary flat-out 100-mph schedule.

(38) MOON TRASH: The trouble starts with a mild vibration and a tendency to steer to the right. They stop in Amarillo, Texas, to check trouble, fearing a wheel bearing has failed. Put car on lift; mechanic has no tools to pull wheel. Lose 20 minutes; find out nothing. Two other stops provide no solution. Right front tire tread is critically worn. Limp at 65 mph into Vega, Texas. It is found that wheel weights have been lost. New weights added, but balance not correct. Cragar wheels have special acorn lug nuts. Cannot find conventional lug nuts for spare. Start out

again, although vibration continues at over 70 mph. Are running through heavy rain and fog when a large chunk of tread lets loose on the unbalanced tire. Road is awash, but they manage to struggle to a gas station, where a sleepy attendant cannot find a lug wrench. Try again at Moriarty, New Mexico. No luck. Finally decide to press on at modest speeds. With time ticking away, they manage to chug Into Albuquerque where an extremely cooperative Union 76 operator scavenges some lug nuts off his own car, permitting them to fit the spare. Woefully behind, having lost perhaps two hours, they nevertheless decide to continue to an honorable finish.

(39) PRDA: Make the only stop of the journey in Albuquerque when it is realized that the on-board gas supply will not last. Using two pumps, 78 gallons are added and the portable toilet is emptied. Lose seven minutes.

MIDNIGHT/DAWN. TUESDAY, NOVEMBER 16

(40) FERRARI: Moves into teeth of storm on the eastern slope of Continental Divide. Ice and fog slow pace, but worn rear tires with 40 pounds of air for high-speed running make car nearly uncontrollable. Forced to run over an hour at no more than 55 mph.

(41) CADILLAC: Accidentally leave behind credit card (and unpaid $14 bill) at a gas station in Grants, New Mexico. Arrested by three police cruisers. Officers have drawn their guns. Dragged back to police station where an explanation is given. Back to gas station to sign card. Harsh words for the attendant prompt another pickup by cops who claim crew has threatened the attendant's life. More frantic explanations bring old warning to "Get out of town." Lose 40 minutes.

(42) TANKERS: Left side exhaust pipe comes loose in the storm outside Gallup, New Mexico. Repairs are made with a coat hanger.

(43) AMX: Nearing the halfway point, with the car still performing perfectly, they decide to up the pace.

(44) PRDA: Aware that sedate travel at the beginning of trip was a mistake, they begin to run harder, but bad weather makes speed difficult.

(45) FERRARI: Skittering along on ice, it is passed by the Cadillac. The shocked crew, who figure they are far ahead at this point, chases the Caddy to Arizona-New Mexico border, where they are caught up at a vegetable inspection station.

(46) CADILLAC: Equally shocked at sighting the Ferrari, they suddenly realize they are still in the chase. They press on through the fog, with Ferrari, when forced to stop for gas at Winslow, Arizona.

(47) FERRARI: Gas stop at Flagstaff brings Cadillac even again. Icy road forces both cars to slow to 60 mph. Not wanting Cadillac to follow on Ash Fork, Arizona, turn to route 89, they permit their rival to gain a mile lead. Turn south is made without being spotted by Cadillac crew.

(48) TANKERS: Tom Marbut, who is navigating, is asleep when Ash Fork cut-off is passed. This forces the team to take a more conventional route into California.

(49) FERRARI: Masterful driving by Gurney negotiates the extremely dangerous stretches of Route 89 through the Prescott National Forest and the cliffside highway at Yarnell with relative ease. Yates proves "Ban don't wear off."

TUESDAY FORENOON

(50) MOON TRASH: Arrested for speeding near Ash Fork, Arizona. Lose 15 minutes.

September 1974
Honda Civic

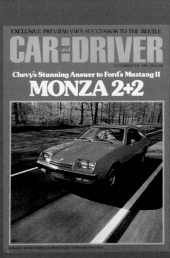
Honda Civics have been arriving on these shores for just over a year now. And in that short time, an impressive array of laurels have been strung around this little sedan's compact neck. First, of course, was a semi-coveted Import Car of the Year award which Honda subsequently spotlighted in its sales promotion efforts. That was followed by an unsolicited (and you have to admit, brilliantly timed) testimonial from our own Environmental Protection Administration proclaiming the Civic as the gas mileage champion of all the cars sold in the U.S. And finally, a no less circumspect bunch than you, our readers, voted the Civic as the Best Economy Sedan in *Car and Driver*'s Eleventh Annual Readers' Choice Poll.

All of which suggests that the current demand for the new Civics might be a whole lot higher than any of us would have guessed when the first one rolled off the dock.

Top speed: 87 mph
0-60 11.9 seconds
50 hp (SAE net), 59 lb-ft of torque
Price: $2,627.40

(51) TANKERS: Arrested for speeding in Kingman, Arizona. Lose 20 minutes.

(52) FERRARI: Arrested for speeding in Quartsite, Arizona. Lose 15 minutes.

(53) CADILLAC: Arrested for speeding near Needles, California. Lose 15 minutes.

(54) TANKERS: Arrested for speeding in Ludlow, California. Lose 15 minutes.

(55) PRDA: Meet up with Cadillac at Needles. The two began a 215-mile battle, passing and repassing, that lasts until San Bernardino, California.

(56) TANKERS: Following their arrest in Ludlow, they are followed for next 100 miles by a patrol car (not the one that had arrested them). They dare not exceed 65 mph.

(57) FERRARI: Convinced they have lost, crew checks Ferrari's top speed (172 mph) on Interstate 10 east of Indio then decide to try to make the run in under 36 hours to salvage at least part of their honor.

(58) CADILLAC: Knowing they are leading the PRDA on elapsed time, an argument erupts over whether or not to follow the PRDA to Portofino, automatically beating them (because PRDA left earlier), or to race onward at the risk that someone else might beat them both.

(59) PRDA: While the Cadillac crew argues, the PRDA hides behind a moving truck, lets the Cadillac run ahead (much as the Ferrari had done earlier), then cuts off to the Riverside Freeway, a shorter, faster route. The Cadillac continues east on the congested San Bernardino Freeway.

(60) FERRARI: After a particularly brisk but inconspicuous run over the Riverside, Newport, Garden Grove, and San Diego Freeways, they reach the Portofino Inn and are surprised to find no other competitors have made it before them. Their time, which seems to be a winner, is 35 hours and 54 minutes.

(61) PRDA: The shorter freeway route makes the difference. They arrive 53 minutes behind the Ferrari, in 36 hours and 47 minutes, a solid second.

(62) CADILLAC: The longer freeway trip costs them 12 minutes and they end up losing second place to the PRDA by 9 minutes. However their time of 36 hours and 56 minutes gives them third and the problem of what to do with the car—its owner isn't expecting delivery for three more days.

(63) AMX: Running strong, they pass the Travco at El Reno, Oklahoma.

(64) TANKERS: They finish fourth, recording a time of 37 hours and 45 minutes.

(65) MG: Minus his car, but having flown in from Columbus, Wes Dawn appears at the Portofino to greet the finishers.

TUESDAY AFTERNOON

(66) MOON TRASH: Bloody but unbowed, the weary team rolls across the finish. Despite their troubles they have recorded an exceptional time of 39 hours and 3 minutes.

TUESDAY EVENING

(67) TRAVCO: While crossing the Continental Divide a swerve by Frasson spills a pan of hot lasagna off the stove and onto the motor home's shag rug. This is probably the most critical moment in the entire running of the Cannonball Baker.

(68) AMX: Finishes in 37 hours and 48 minutes, taking fifth place and losing to the Little Rock Tankers by three minutes, the crew is extremely fatigued.

(69) TRAVCO: Finishes in 57 hours and 25 minutes, surely a record for motor homes and only 21 hours behind the winner. If only they hadn't spilled that lasagna!

December 1975
Lamborghini Countach

Take a run through the gears in a Lamborghini Countach and you eclipse every speed reference on the books. First alone will thrust you well beyond America's statutory speed limit. Third will boost you past all but a couple of modern-day Detroit machines, and fourth will blow off virtually everything made in Europe. For the handful of exoticars that fourth can't manage, the Ferrari Berlinetta Boxer and Porsche Turbo Carrera, to name two—there is the superdeterrent fifth gear. Ease the stiff lever back into its top notch and you begin a gentle battle with the wind from just under 150 mph to well over 180. All challengers gradually fade to inconsequential specks in your rearview mirror. Keep your foot down and the scenery blurs to a continuum of color dissolving any speed reference. The rear-mounted engine thunders through 12 intake throats and four exhaust stacks, all of them inches from your neck. At the other end of the car, there is only silence as the Countach's sharp nose slices a clean hole in the atmosphere.

—*Don Sherman*

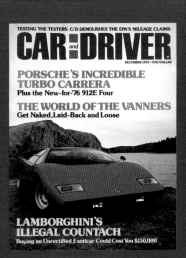

TESTING THE TESTERS: C/D DEMOLISHES THE EPA'S MILEAGE CLAIMS

CAR and DRIVER
DECEMBER 1975 · ONE DOLLAR

PORSCHE'S INCREDIBLE TURBO CARRERA
Plus the New-for-'76 912E Four

THE WORLD OF THE VANNERS
Get Naked, Laid-Back and Loose

LAMBORGHINI'S ILLEGAL COUNTACH
Buying an Uncertified Exoticar Could Cost You $150,000

1985

The Second Coming of David E.

The "me" decade was drawing to its polyester leisure-suit end, but as America stumbled through the aftermath of Vietnam and disco toward the 1980s, there was little consensus on what had happened to the country since the days of Camelot—and what was coming next. What was happening, it turned out, was a move into an altogether more conservative age. It was as if America had been exhausted by wars and sexual revolutions and the insurgency of a rebellious younger generation. The Carter years were the crucible for the coming change: four short years were enough to sour the nation's mood even more than Watergate and the war had been able to.

1978

Three Popes serve in Vatican City. Pope John Paul II begins his rule as pontiff.

Sony introduces its portable Walkman music player

Fleetwood Mac's "Rumours" is the Grammy Album of the Year

Test-tube baby Louise Brown is born

The economy tanked, inflation spiraled into the double digits, and interest rates hit the highest levels since World War II. Carter sought peace in the Middle East, but even progress there was trumped by the shadow of Soviet intervention in Afghanistan.

The kidnapping of American hostages during the overthrow of the Shah of Iran in 1979 and the failure of a rescue mission was the symbolic nadir of American strength abroad—and when it came time for Americans to register their displeasure at the voting booth, they did. In 1980 the country vividly showed how ready it was to be over the "malaise" that Jimmy Carter himself had diagnosed the country with. His opponent in the presidential race, former Governor of California Ronald Reagan, used Carter's imagery against him in asking the nation if it was better off than it had been when Carter took office. He appealed to a sense of optimism in America, winning a resounding victory in the elections, with 489 electoral votes to Carter's 49.

Reagan's plain-spoken appeal had struck a chord, and long before he promised that it was "Morning in America," the recession that started in the Carter years began to abate. The economy went back to work and Reagan delivered on his election promise to cut taxes and restore America's prestige abroad. Reagan was the center and emblem of America in the 1980s. Those who didn't trust his faith or believe in his intellect were loathe to cross public opinion of him.

His speechwriter and biographer Peggy Noonan said of him: "Ronald Reagan told the truth to a world made weary by lies. He believed truth was the only platform on which a better future could be built. He shocked the world when he called the Soviet Union 'evil,' because it was, and an 'empire,' because it was that,

too. He never stopped bringing his message to the people of the world, to Europe and China and in the end the Soviet Union. And when it was over, the Berlin Wall had been turned into a million concrete souvenirs, and Soviet communism had fallen."

The deep recession Reagan inherited had caused a calamity in Detroit. Ford nearly declared bankruptcy in the early 1980s, General Motors had skated too close to the ice, and Chrysler had to be bailed out by the federal government with loan guarantees. All the while, Honda and Nissan and Toyota were planning to set up factories in the U.S. to meet the steadily rising demand for their cars.

Bruce McCall, a *Car and Driver* contributing editor for 30 years, put Detroit's problems in pointed perspective: "So battered and clueless was Detroit circa 1982 that it's possible General Motors thought the Cadillac Cimarron was a good idea and a fine automobile. It was breathtaking only in the contempt it showed: just slap glasses, a false nose, and a mustache on a compact Chevy and the boobs will shell out big bucks for what they think is a dwarf Cadillac. For cynically exploiting the iconic Caddy name on this mediocre road weasel in search of short-term incremental sales, Roger Smith, who was CEO and chairman of the board at the time, deserves to have to drive one for life. Market demand for a handy sized cargo box was nonexistent until the first Chrysler minivans went on sale and promptly sold out. A tribute to the hidden benefits of adversity if ever there was one. Ford had already brushed off the concept. Does anyone think the minivan

165

would exist today if product-desperate Chrysler hadn't taken a fling? You can tell your grandchildren that in 1981 in America a free people in great numbers actually chose to buy and drive Chrysler K-cars. They were ugly, raspy, flimsy, and underpowered. Tell your grandkids of federal bailout loans, of an innate sympathy for even the corporate underdog that Lee Iacocca's TV rabble-rousing tapped and unleashed until it swept the nation and made K-car buyers feel themselves actors in a real-world replay of *It's a Wonderful Life*. When that doesn't work—and it won't—tell them, well, you had to be there."

The 1982 Mercedes-Benz 300SD Turbodiesel sedan became a symbol of the weird era that was the early 1980s: a two-ton, five-cylinder, 120-hp slug of a tub that crawled from 0 to 60 mph on its hands and knees, clacked like a sackful of castanets, outpriced almost everything in the U.S. high-luxury market, and ruled it. It made exquisite sense at the time. Indeed, among luxury buyers torn between memories of the recent fuel crisis and the flash-your-cash seductions of the Reagan years, what more pluperfect choice than a diesel-powered Benz? Dealing with the onset of safety and emissions rules had crippled the industry, but by the time Reagan entered his second term there were signs that a turnaround was at hand. It was particularly true at Ford, where a new generation of vehicles like the 1983 Thunderbird and 1986 Taurus would emphatically state that the company was looking toward the future. General Motors had made it through the recession and had interesting cars with the Corvette and Fiero. And Chrysler had Lee Iacocca and one sturdy platform that would spawn a whole fleet of cars ready to be marketed with the Made in America label.

At *Car and Driver*, the transition into the 1980s had started with a sea change, leaving the East Coast for the Midwest. After 23 years in Manhattan, *Car and Driver* moved to Michigan to be closer to the epicenter of the auto industry, and to be in a place less hostile to driving and to cars: "*Car and Driver* magazine and I will be moving to Ann Arbor, Michigan this spring," prodigal editor Davis announced in his column to readers in 1978. "This is a wonderful thing for the magazine, complicated and in some ways traumatic to be sure, but a wonderful thing nonetheless. I just bought a nutball house with a three-dog kennel and a four-car garage, and now I face the car enthusiast's eternal dilemma: What kind of wheels am I going to buy?

"Some of you, fearing the worst, have written to express your concern about the move. 'Are we selling out to Detroit?' 'Will the magazine lose its journalistic sting out there in the bucolic heartland?' The answer to both questions, and a variety of similar ones, is an emphatic No! New York is a silly place to put out a car magazine. Our parent company does well here, and this is the publishing center of the world, but our bill at the Red Ball Garage does run us about two grand per month, and New York is an exasperating place from which to escape by car during the rush hour—which sometimes lasts all day.

"In Ann Arbor, when one of the guys sticks his head into my office and says, 'I just picked up the new Turbo-Whatever and it'll flat knock your hat in the creek,' I'll get up, walk a few yards to the parking lot, drive it away, and be on peaceful country roads in less than ten minutes. Next to that, even move-related benefits like better access to the University of Michigan and the domestic automobile industry take second place, important as they are."

Davis acknowledged the tremendous pressure the auto industry had been under since his last tenure as editor. But unlike many car writers, Davis gave credit to the government for enforcing changes in the way cars were designed—if only

Mercedes 300 SD.

1981   Sandra Day O'Connor is nominated to become the first female Supreme Court justice

MTV goes on the air   **1982**   Princess Grace of Monaco dies in auto accident in Monaco

halfheartedly. "Cars have gotten dramatically better in the past five years, which means that we have more of them to test, more in which we think you'll be interested. The government must get its fair share of credit for the improvement, but governments are by definition not to be trusted, and we must never let our editorial eye wander too far from the activities of those who'd protect the car enthusiast out of existence. The vitality of the market for magazines like this one, and the continuing improvement in the cars we drive make us optimistic."

The optimism Davis and the magazine staffers shared came out in print as well as in the office. The move to Ann Arbor would remove the magazine from the literary circles in which it traveled in New York. It would trade the 24-hour appeal of the Big Apple for the leafy suburbia of a big college town. For most of the staff, the location didn't much matter. Working at *Car and Driver* did.

Rich Ceppos was one of the newer editors hired while plans were forming to move the magazine. "I didn't care if we were moving to Boise," Ceppos, who later became the executive editor, recalls. "The move to Ann Arbor created a tight-knit group, we only knew each other, and we were all young and single. It was just a really cool time—we hung out a lot together, we raced at Nelson Ledges together. It was a great atmosphere for talking about cars. Of course, we thought we were a lot smarter than guys at the car companies. In Detroit, the light was beginning to go on about what good cars were about."

Visitors to the magazine's new offices got the same whiff of camaraderie, as did editor-at-large Gordon Baxter during a trip to the magazine after it had been repotted in Michigan. Michigan and the auto industry, he realized from the moment he touched down, was a different world than New York publishing. "People start talking cars just as soon as you get off the airplane in Detroit.

'You won't see any foreign cars here,' said the old crackpot in the coffee shop. 'You rent a foreign car here and leave it in the hotel lot and somebody will trash it for you.'"

Baxter found the *Car and Driver*'s offices, where they're still located today, with surprise, as most guests find the humble digs. "I found '2002' in big white letters on a modest, two-story office building, a low, brown structure sitting well back between two identical units. No banners said this was the home of *Car and Driver*. No flags. The big, smooth asphalt lot in the rear had no Rolls Royces or rocket ships, just the random pickins of what office workers drive. Our name was only in little black letters on the building directory in the small foyer. The building is a rectangle, the offices built around casual tables and chairs in the atrium. Lots of warm wood, but no catering by Romanoff's. The folks sitting there seemed to be brown-bagging it. I walked by the *Car and Driver* door twice before I found it."

Past the vanguard of receptionist Mary Ann Pickney, Baxter got the whirlwind tour. "All the women were beautiful; the men looked brave," he thought as he lunched with new technical editor Csaba Csere, who had joined the magazine in 1981. Then 29, Csere was a bachelor, a graduate of MIT, and an engineer in Ford's Advanced Engine Engineering group.

Baxter also met editor Jean Lindamood, another Davis hire with unusual car experience and a storyteller's brain. "Associate editor Jean Lindamood is the daughter of Bob Lienert, editor of *Automotive News*, and the sister of Paul Lienert, managing editor of *Autoweek*. She came to see me, at her brother's suggestion, when she was laid off as a mechanic-test driver at the Chrysler proving grounds. She only had in her portfolio at that interview several copies of the proving ground local's UAW newsletter, which she edited, and a yeasty stream-of-consciousness essay

she'd written for a local literary magazine when she was driving her own cab on the streets of Ann Arbor. I decided to hire her on the strength of that essay and her ebullient good humor, and Sherman found her irresistible because she can weld. The other day I asked her if she was impressed by Csaba Csere's first appearance, for us, at a press conference, and she said, 'Listen, he made those other guys look like base nosepickers, man.' All this, plus welding experience. My cup runneth over."

Baxter came away with a sense that anyone who stops by 2002 Hogback comes away with, whether they're working for *Car and Driver* or not. "Our personalities are allowed to surface in the magazine. And that is rare. Yes, there is some near arrogance in the cocky humor in that little building at 2002 Hogback Road. It's the sureness of a group of men and women doing something well. I've only seen it once before, briefly as a reporter in Washington. Inside the Kennedy White House was like that."

In 1980 the magazine had celebrated 25 years on the road. And as the industry struggled to meet the standards of a new generation, the editors of what had become the most influential car magazine in America were impressed. "Our own national automobile industry has proved the last to understand how the government helps. They have railed and complained about government regulation strangling the industry and shutting down automotive progress, but cars have improved more in the years since the government intervened than at any other time in the past half century. Who would have believed it?" Davis asked.

Davis's way of rewarding the car makers that showed real signs of progress evolved into a new *Car and Driver* tradition: 10 Best. The annual issue would showcase the best cars of the year, voted on by the editors. In the first competition, five domestics and five imports were voted in: the AMC/Renault Alliance; Chevrolet Caprice Classic; Ford Mustang GT 5.0; Honda Accord; Mazda RX-7; Mercedes-Benz 380SEL; Pontiac 6000STE; Porsche 944; Toyota Celica Supra; and Volkswagen Rabbit GTI.

By 1985 the most dramatic changes in the American auto industry since the consolidation of hundreds of companies into the Big Three had been set into motion. The Japanese competition was coming on strong with American-made Hondas and soon, Toyotas and Nissans. And in 1985, *Car and Driver* would find out what wrenching change could mean yet again. Only this time it would mean the final departure of David E. Davis, Jr. In that year, Ziff-Davis, the owners of the magazine since it had been *Sports Cars Illustrated*, sold its interest in *Car and Driver* and other magazines to CBS as that company tried to build a publishing empire to match its television holdings. On January 4, 1985, *Car and Driver* became part of the CBS empire, alongside *Road & Track*, which has been a CBS magazine for 13 years.

By the summer, it was clear that CBS and Davis were at odds over the direction of the magazine. Quietly, in the October issue, Davis let the bomb drop. "Happy trails. This is the last time I'll write this column for this magazine. I came back to *Car and Driver* nine years ago to the day. I had planned to stay at this typewriter writing these notes to you my friends until they carried me out. Unfortunately, things don't always work out as we'd like them to. I love all of you as I love this magazine, and I'll miss you, as I'll miss *Car and Driver*. See you somewhere down the road."

Within a few months it would be announced that Davis was starting a new car magazine, *Automobile*. A chunk of the *Car and Driver* staff would decamp from Hogback Road to the other side of Ann Arbor to join Davis and Jean Lindamood in the startup. And *Car and Driver* would go through a few months of hard work filling the void left behind.

M*A*S*H signs off the air

<

1984

"The Cosby Show" debuts on NBC

Vanessa Williams gives up the title of Miss America after nude pictures of her surface in "Playboy"

May 1978
Mazda RX-7
At last the rotary engine has a sporting chance

Dreary days are over for the rotary engine. After eight years of yeoman service pulling around frumpy sedans and mini pickup trucks, Felix Wankel's wondermobotor has earned a special reward. Mazda has promoted its fine-tuned rotary to sports car duty. This two-place rotary rocket has more sex appeal than *Charlie's Angels*, and yet purists will surely flinch over the chassis layout. Just like the RX-3, the engine is front-mounted, the suspension includes plain old MacPherson struts and a rigid axle, the steering is recirculating ball, the wheels are 13 inches in diameter and the brakes are a mix of discs and drums. Hardly what you'd check off on your sports-car dream sheet. And yet you'd gladly trade your favorite fantasy for an RX-7 after one quick test drive. A rotary engine humming eagerly through the gears is absolutely charismatic, and, if this doesn't ring your chimes, you'll be pleased to find the rest of the car in harmony with the melody under the hood.

—*Don Sherman*

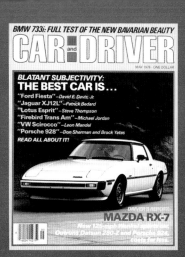

October 1978
Driver's Seat

By David E. Davis, Jr

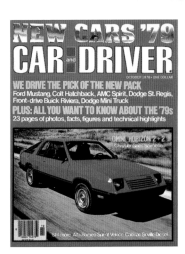

I probably shouldn't be writing this in *Car and Driver*, but since *Car and Driver* is the only magazine for which I write on a regular basis, and since I feel obliged to get it down for somebody to read, here goes...

I never cried for a dead race driver, even though 30 or 40 dead race drivers used to be friends of mine. God knows it's not because I can't cry. I've wept as I left the Nürburgring, because the race was over and I was leaving my summer friends and going back to New York, and because the Eifel Mountains and the Ahr River and the morning were all so beautiful. As a 19-year-old boot at Great Lakes I got all choked up in my first big review when those thousands of guys came to attention and the band struck up "Anchors Aweigh." Women have made me cry, and I cried in 1955 when I first saw what the Sacramento racetrack and my own imprudence had done to my face. As I've gotten older, though, tears have come harder, and at greater intervals.

Yesterday it happened to me again. I was flogging our Volvo Boss Wagon across the back roads of Ashland County, Ohio, crying like a baby, while my wife and a Brittany spaniel pup tried in vain to comfort me. Driving hard and fast seemed like the only cure, so I kept it on the wood until my eyes dried and I could breathe normally. It had finally come to me, in a rush, that my father, who'd died a few days before, was really dead.

I knew he was going to die because they'd all said there was nothing to be done for the cancer they'd discovered only two weeks earlier, but I'd allowed myself to believe that he'd last long enough for one more deer season, even if I had to help him into the woods and sit with him. Maybe I needed that more than he did, but I wanted very badly for him to see the sun rise in deep snowy woods again, and maybe scare up a grouse, or sit silent while a cedar squirrel crept up to sniff his boot sole. But with 73 years and probably four dozen hunting seasons on him he dozed off one Sunday morning and his heart just stopped.

He wasn't a car enthusiast, not in the sense that you and I are car enthusiasts anyway, but he did love cars and he was an automotive person. He drove fast and well, most of the time, although he occasionally suffered the same kind of lapses we all do. When he was young he hit a mule with an open Buick touring car, said mule landing inside the car with him and nearly kicking him senseless. Another time in the same car, he and a couple of drunken friends were on their way to a dance, having stopped for a jug of what he called "Who Shot John," and got stuck in some trackless waste near Hazard, Kentucky. He blearily announced that he'd get out to see what was wrong, opened the door, stepped off the running board, and fell 20 feet into a rocky creek bed.

I remember a 1934 Ford, a 1937 Plymouth, a 1940 Oldsmobile (that saw us through the war), then a 1946 Olds that got rolled, and a 1947 Olds that he stuffed into the center of a railway abutment, maiming himself for life and very nearly ending it all right there. Most of my earliest memories involve night rides, often in the rain, sleeping on the back seat with the harsh mohair upholstery abrading every exposed surface on my body. I was enveloped in car smell and car noise and I'd wake fitfully from time to time, hear the sound of my parents' voices or the rowr-rowr snick-snick of inefficient old windshield wipers, and feel uniquely safe and secure. We drove everywhere, sometimes hundreds of miles at a crack, and he never surrendered the wheel. My mother claims that I got my automotive start earlier, as a baby, when I used to sleep on the parcel shelf of a Model A Ford coupe with our Boston bulldog, Bozo. My favorite toy, she tells me, and my best-loved teething device, was the hard rubber shift knob from that Model A. When my dad sold the car, he had to come home and retrieve the gnawed shift knob from my playpen and my mother got the sniffles.

When he died last week he had an aged but sound Dodge van, which he called "The Bluebird," and a pristine Nova coupe. He and my mother covered most of the eastern United States and Canada in that van, buying antiques for their shop, and it was treated like a member of the family. On the way to the funeral she said that he'd have given a lot to be riding in our trick Volvo instead of the hearse to which they'd consigned him, and she was certain that he'd have been impatient with our crawling pace going to the cemetery.

I know that I got involved with racing because of him. He'd been a fine athlete in his youth, played college football with Bo McMillin at 152 pounds, played semi-pro baseball in a coal miners' league in Welch, West Virginia, and done a fair bit of boxing and pool hustling. All his life he was that same athlete, arm wrestler, wise guy, storyteller, needler, and headstrong adventurer. I needed to prove myself his son and heir, yet I was intimidated by his prowess in all the standard games. After' a lackluster and halfhearted athletic career, I stumbled onto motorsport and never looked back. He never saw me race, but I think he got a kick out of the idea, and I know that he was pleased when I drifted into writing by way of *Road & Track*

magazine. One of his own dreams was a career in journalism.

He taught me about jazz, and the big bands of the 1920s. He taught me about good furniture, and Bennington pottery, and mercury glass. He taught me about laughter. He taught me to drive his way, fast and aggressively, and imprinted me with his Kentuckian's distrust of governments and do-gooders. I got his love of hunting and fishing with my genes and, like him, I'd rather be outdoors than in, going somewhere rather than sitting still. He knew the woods as most suburbanites know their lawns. He was a natural shot, a hunter who never missed—as near as an awestruck adolescent could tell—and he did not suffer fools gladly.

For the first 20 years of my life I was under the impression that he was trying to kill me. At his direction I once backed a Ford Okiebox camper off a six-foot clay embankment, and when my mother and I went through his things we found the very Pflueger Supreme casting rod with which he buried all the treble hooks of a six-inch Bass-Oreno in my 14-year-old shoulder one night on Pontiac Lake.

For the past 28 years he was in pain, yet he stumped through life on his bad leg and had more fun than any three healthy people I know. He brought beauty into a lot of households—building beautiful furniture and restoring battered and broken antiques that lesser craftsmen might have discarded—and his own household was one of the happiest and most entertaining places I've ever been. As I drove away with his lovingly maintained hunting and fishing gear in the back, I suddenly choked on the realization that he really wouldn't be using it anymore, and I just couldn't handle that. He was David E. Davis, Jr., until his father died, and then he dropped the Junior. I can't do it though. For me, he'll always be the original.

June 1980
Puff, the Dangerous Driver

The *Car and Driver* team reprises its impaired driving story from a few years back with a new variable—marijuana, rather than alcohol. The results are similar: giggles, crunched cones, and the realization that one drug acts on drivers in just as nefarious a way as the other. Ceppos wrote: "What I realized from our afternoon trip to nirvana is that marijuana erodes driving skills in a far more subtle way than alcohol. No matter how much I smoked—and by my last run I had ingested far more than I would at a party—my hand-eye coordination suffered hardly at all. In fact, I'd venture to say that I performed our driving tests no worse than if I had been very tired. No matter how mellowed-out I was, I was still able to screw down my attention long enough to handle the two short driving tasks adequately. Only once did I almost flub the lane-change maneuver but I managed to catch my mistake and hit only one cone. And the problem wasn't one of execution so much as simple lapse of concentration. That incident, in fact, was the only indication the tests gave of what was really happening to me out there. It started subtly enough. After the first regulation two-hit toke-up, I began ascending ever so gently, a warm inner glow just tugging at the fabric of my consciousness. On the whole, it was pleasant and no too distracting. But marijuana affects me strongly, and the next three one-toke rounds took me from being mildly high to thoroughly stoned to completely wrecked. The higher I got, the more my normal state of mind receded. As I waited on the bus for my turn, time dragged. Someone would talk while I was taking notes and I'd forget what I was jotting down, right there in mid-sentence."

Sherman concurred: "I learned that I can control a car under the influence of marijuana. I also realized that the really impossible task is staying awake to do so. This is the most important finding in the whole experiment—dope may not hamper your driving ability, but it will kill your long-term concentration… and probably you too, if you're foolish enough to dope and drive."

—*Mike Knepper*

May 1982
Road Research Report: Porsche 944

By Michael Jordan

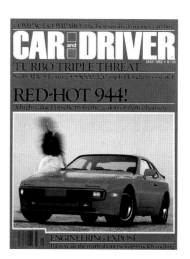

The Porsche 944 is a great car. It renews your faith in Porsche, because the men who made the 944 put into it everything they know about fast cars.

I t renews your faith in fast cars, fast living, and fast women, because it brings you these things at a reasonable price and with fuel efficiency besides. From now on, Porsche performance is no longer restricted to those entertainment lawyers in Los Angeles who scuttle through Coldwater Canyon in their 911s and 928s on their way from their homes in Studio City to their warrens in Century City. The rest of us can finally have a piece of the action.

    The thing that really makes the 944 a terrific car, though, is the conviction of the engineers who made it that only performance matters. Not market position, not price, just performance. And as so often happens, dedication to a simple ideal has improved both market position and value. The result is the best combination of performance and economy that money can buy—a serious car that advances the state of the automotive art.

    After all, that's what we expect from Porsche.

The most seductive combination of economy and performance money can buy.

January 1983
10 Best Cars

Without as much fanfare as it now receives, 10 Best begins with a first slate of vehicles. The first time around, five domestics and five imports are allowed, with the sole requirement that they be series-production models available through normal dealership channels. And the winners are:

1. AMC/Renault Alliance
2. Chevrolet Caprice Classic
3. Ford Mustang GT 5.0
4. Honda Accord
5. Mazda RX-7
6. Mercedes-Benz 380SEL
7. Pontiac 6000STE
8. Porsche 944
9. Toyota Celica Supra
10. Volkswagen Rabbit GTI

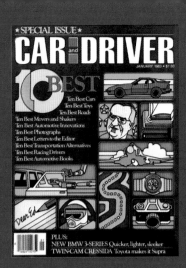

10

7

8

9

January 1983
10 Best Roads
The automobile is the greatest single mode yet invented to travel to more places than even God and Mother Nature could have foreseen. The automobile requires not that you go slow or fast, but merely, if you are constituted as we are, that you go. Travel will never be less expensive and the roads will never be more rewarding than they are now:

1. **Arizona and New Mexico: U.S. 60**
2. **Arkansas: Arkansas 7**
3. *California: California 1*
4. *California: California 49*
5. **New York: New York 17**
6. **New York: New York 97**
7. **Ohio: Ohio 83**
8. **Vermont: I-89 and I-91**
9. **Vermont: Vermont 100**
10. **Virginia and West Virginia: U.S. 250**
11. *The 200-mph Highway (undivulged)*

—Larry Griffin

10 BEST Roads

Don't let the garage door hit you on the way out.

BY LARRY GRIFFIN

• A nonsensical rumor has achieved inexplicable perpetuation over the years, and it deserves a quick if tardy death. This rumor resolutely holds that there is no place left in this day and age to have fun driving a car.

Whom is this rumor kidding?

God and Mother Nature have made quite a couple for some time now, and the prodigious fruits of their fooling around are laid out in infinite variety, whooping-good chunks of feistily textured landscape set down willy-nilly to confound the dullard flatlands. Laced interval by wide interval across the intricacy of this landscape is pavement. From the mildest to the wildest, it is all laid down for our good uses, and we are here to celebrate the best of it.

The automobile is the greatest single mode yet invented to travel to more places than even God and Mother Nature could have foreseen. The automobile requires not that you go slow or fast, but merely, if you are constituted as we are, that you go. Travel will never be less expensive, and the roads will never be more rewarding than they are now. The sun rises every day on the op-

mph), U.S. 60 slices across the Apache reservation, dips into Salt River Canyon, then climbs through the mountaintops north of Fort Apache. The tribe runs huge lumber, cattle, and recreational enterprises. DED, Jr., says, "Out past Springerville, you're on top of a high mesa and, God, it's spectacular for fast driving at night. Headlights pop over a rise and you dim your lights ten minutes too soon!" Mr. Davis also espouses affection for the wendings of U.S. 60 across Missouri's Ozark region ("There isn't a bad road in there!").

Arkansas: Arkansas 7

Highway 7 is one of the best-kept secrets in the country. Once anointed one of America's ten most beautiful roads by *National Geographic*, it is tucked into the folds of the Ozark National Forest and the Ouachita Mountains. Its best

California: California 1

So there won't be any question, let's just go ahead and coronate Highway 1 as the single greatest driving road in the United States. Hell, maybe the world. From Las Cruces, north of Santa Barba-

stretches link Harrison up north and Arkadelphia, south of the newlywed and horse-racing center of Hot Springs. The bonus beauties of 7 are its shortages of both traffic and interruption (30-mile legs without settlements) and a length of 250 miles. This is a road mixing elemental and advanced challenges in well-balanced proportions. Avoid it like the plague in icy weather, but make a beeline for it any other time. Guaranteed to knock your socks off and turn you into a seriously addicted repeat offender.

rocky coast rushes up to meet you, don't come around haunting us. At least you'll have savored every moment right up to the last.

California: California 49

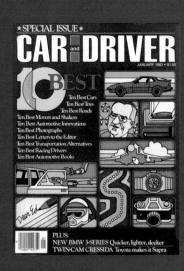

forty-niners' towns survived their decline and got paved. Packed with the crumbling history of harum-scarum treasure seekers, 49 graces tangled hills in the north and clings tensely to immense fallaways (*sans* guardrails) near magnificent Yosemite Park. This area is sure to get your heart's attention one way or another. Your passenger will want to alternate between blindfold and binoculars.

New York: New York 17

The stretch of Highway 17 we're voting for here is four-lane road. While it's anything but typical of the highly athletic driving environments we normally seek out, it has two unassailable strengths—beautiful pastoral scenery and a freewheeling character that reels

LARRY GRIFFIN

out across the majestic rolling hills of western New York State in exactly the same flawless way that Germany's autobahns reach out their high-speed tentacles across broad belts of dark forest

tan's steel-trellised window on the Unwashed West. Like almost everything that lies beyond the G.W. Bridge, Highway 97 is sure to petrify normally pedestrian types with its vicious esses carved

Ohio: Ohio 83

All who labor under the misapprehension that Ohio is ruled by radar robots with machine pistols and mirrored sunglasses, sit down. Everybody else, form up at Millersburg for a 93-mile recce run down Highway 83 to Beverly. The occasional county mountie who ventures out is *extremely* occasional, and 83 is fully equipped with all the great, convoluted, large-scale elements of a Grand Touring road, yet it brings you intimately alongside and into and through dozens of working farms without throwing you unexpectedly into the war of nerves that exists nearby between drivers and the Amish, whose

Vermont: I-89 and I-91

Top speed is something every car has. Some have it more emphatically than others, and these are the cars that will be the happiest on the far reaches of Vermont's two Interstates, both of which charge north all the way to Quebec, providing the quickest and most breathtaking routes to the gemlike city of Montreal. Moreover, if Montreal is one of the most nearly European cities

out of river bluffs and its mean dogleg anglings and blind crests over humpbacks. If you've got an extra day or two, jog up to N.Y. 30 and set a course for the Adirondacks.

LARRY GRIFFIN

black, horse-drawn buggies are exquisitely picturesque but spend most of their time cluttering up the far side of every steep rise. Not on 83, somehow.

in North America, then I-89 and I-91 are unquestionably North America's carbon-copy autobahns, replete with all the potential swiftness that anything on wheels can provide. The roads streak north with an intensity that far busier Interstates only hint at. There's nothing to do but be blown away by the awesome reaches of forest and mash your motor before the Bear Force lifts off.

July 1983
Escape From Baja

By Brock Yates

Ten gringos face floods, frijoles, and federales . . . and live to tell.

This affair began as an honest attempt to evaluate eight sedans in the European idiom over a 2,300-mile route between Southern California and the tip of Baja California in Mexico. Decent, responsible automotive journalism, *Road & Track* does this high-adventure stuff all the time. On more than one occasion, they have encountered overcooked cheeseburgers and canceled motel reservations.

It even rained once. As for us, it got a little more complicated. In retrospect, that was to be anticipated, when you consider that our widely esteemed technical director, Donald Sherman, organized the campaign.

Before the mission was completed, the hapless followers of Sherman faced bouts of the turista, numerous encounters with the Mexican federales, a high-speed collision with a cow, floods, maroonings, the deep-sixing of a Datsun Maxima, and the consumption of more high-octane tequila and stomach-scouring Mexican food than any collection of Americans since Black Jack Pershing chased Pancho Villa.

But let's not carry this military analogy too far. If our Sherman, and not William Tecumseh, had devised the original March to the Sea, Richmond, Virginia, would be the capital of the United States and Jesse Helms would be president. So be warned that what follows is no normal meander over the byways in search of automotive truth. This, Bucky, was a freaking war....

Sunday: We leave Newport Beach (yes, yes, we know, we know) in the midst of the 49th monsoon to hit Southern California this year. Ugly nimbus clouds roll in off the sea.

There are ten of us, high-type professionals all. There are eight automobiles: two American (a Pontiac 6000STE and a Dodge 600ES); two Japanese (a Datsun Maxima and a Toyota Cressida); and four from Europe, where this brand of machine was born (a new Audi 5000S, a VW Quantum, a Saab 900 Turbo, and a Volvo 760GLE). Euro-sedans. Four-doors. Priced between $10,000 and $20,000, bracketed by the likes of the Honda Accord on the low side and the BMW 528e on the high.

The mission: a two-day, 1,150-mile, America-versus-the-world run to Cabo San Lucas at the tip of Baja, then a one-day layover in the sunshine and two days back. Our destination today is an oasis in the central Baja desert called San Ignacio.

Reaching the border is simple. Our one nod to preparation is a supermarket stop to grab some bottled water. Otherwise, we exit the United States with the same level of preparation one might employ for a trip to the Kmart: no tools, lights, or first-aid kits. When other magazines go to Baja, they're outfitted like the Afrika Korps. But we have one trump card: a childlike faith that our leader will bring us through.

A chunky guard waves us into Mexico at Tijuana. The four-lane to Ensenada is pocked with tightly radiused curves. An ancient Volvo wagon with California plates races us at 80 to 90 mph all the way to Ensenada, but none of our eight cars is even breathing hard as we stop for lunch. Our next encounter with Mexican officialdom comes in the parking lot of Hussong's Cantina, where one of the least civilized

members of our group [Yates-Ed.] is arrested for recycling several liters of Dos Equis against a wall. Lindamood, the only one among us who speaks any Spanish, gets the culprit off with a $10 fine by denouncing him to the cops as a pig.

We plunge into fast, twisty two-lanes south of Ensenada. Route 1 rides high along some splendid seacoast vistas toward San Quintín and then bores inland to the mountains at El Rosario. We wonder but say nothing about customs. Having blasted past the place where the Maneadero checking station was supposed to be, we may be operating as Yanqui wetbacks, without the faintest authorization to penetrate so deeply into the nation. No matter: The cars are running well, the night is cloudless, and the road is clear, save for an occasional bus and the odd battered pickup.

Our only glitch comes when we switch cars in the darkness. Several of the party, seeking naps, double up. We drive away, leaving the Maxima and the Quantum at the roadside, and have to race back 15 miles to retrieve them. The fact that Sherman detected the error so quickly means his plan is working to perfection.

Monday: Is B. Traven running a haberdashery in San Ignacio? Mr. Davis Jr. is wearing a snap-brim felt hat, last seen on Walter Huston in *The Treasure of the Sierra Madre*. The tiny dust-caked village sits in a basin clustered with date palms planted by the Spaniards when the Jesuits started their mission here in 1728. We take a leisurely tour of the ancient stone church before rolling south. Empty roads beckon. Speeds rise. Large signs warn, "Designed to Promote Economic Development, Not for High-Speed Driving," but make little impression.

Nor are we slowed by the "curvas peligrosas," which are generally punctuated by burned-out car hulks, rumpled guardrails, and coveys of handmade crosses.

Stray cattle begin to appear at the roadside, spavined beasts that pay no heed to the passing vehicles. The immense steel bumpers on the big Dina trucks we pass begin to assume a meaningful function.

We switch cars, and impressions begin to gel. Sherman, Csere, Ceppos, and Griffin are delighted with the new Audi, despite its slightly sterile aura. Committed traditionalist P.J. O'Rourke reveals a quiet loathing for front-drive cars and extols the rather zany handling of the amply powered Cressida, a schoolmarm with a harlot's heart. The Pontiac and the Dodge are pleasant surprises.

Who can remember a Detroiter that would absorb such extended hard driving without frying its brakes, boiling its coolant, and loosening up like a Hong Kong toy? The Volvo, which appears to have been styled from an old Amana upright freezer, may entice Electra 225 devotees. The Saab and the Maxima charge along with terrier-like enthusiasm, while the Quantum, for all its quiet competence, becomes the wallflower of the group.

We are ambushed by the cops in La Paz. They want a closer look at our new cars. Lindamood is brilliant as she aborts impending arrest by demonstrating the Datsun's idiotic synthesized voice to the awestruck lawmen.

It is a black night in the mountains. Our little convoy is rushing the final miles to Cabo San Lucas when Csere nails a cow. He center-punches a 500-pound black steer, at maybe 60 mph. Protein for the people! One wounded Dodge 600ES, but thankfully, no other injuries. We grope in the lonely darkness to assess the damage. The hood is shredded. The roof is dented. The car runs happily, but the radiator is ruptured. We push the car 60 miles—primarily with the purposeful Audi—to our hotel. Angry guests blunt our beachfront attempt to celebrate our arrival.

Tuesday: Too much sun, too many piña coladas, but good news: the Dodge survives. Sans hood, it is ready for the run back home. Lindamood and Ceppos fall to the dreaded turista.

Wednesday: On the road before dawn, heading back to San Ignacio. The Dodge is gaining fans by the hour. Hard driving in the mountains reveals an interesting fact: the automatic-transmission cars—the Volvo, the VW, and the Pontiac—can be driven as quickly and more easily than the five-speeds. Ominous clouds build in the north.

The federales nail us north of Loreto. Suspicion about the Dodge's missing hood is our downfall. The cop is a young, round-faced kid in a clapped-out Dodge cruiser with bald tires. His girlfriend is riding shotgun. The cop wants to see a report on the cow collision, but we have none. This is not a good situation. We deploy Sherman and Lindamood in the 600ES for the drive back to Loreto with the federale. The rest of us head north to a rendezvous at San Ignacio.

It is raining seriously now, and the "vados" (low spots in the road meant to allow flash floods to run off) are beginning to puddle. The storm hits as we arrive at La Pinta Hotel in San Ignacio. The wind pounds at the palm trees, the rain hammers on the roof. We toast to our lost comrades— who may be rotting in a Loreto calabozo by now—with numerous tequilas and beers.

Sherman and Lindamood arrive late. Because of power

outages, they have had to scavenge gas twice to get the Dodge home. The federale adventure turned to comedy: Lindamood ended up driving the patrol car and manicuring the cop's girlfriend's nails, while Sherman repaired a copy machine for the cop. Weirdness in the Mexican desert has cost a meager $50 fine.

Thursday: A predawn escape is attempted. It is still raining. Sherman is back in command. He should have tried U-boats. Fifteen miles north of town, he crests a hill and skates into a storm-swollen "vado." We arrive a few moments later. Our headlights probe into the darkness to reveal the Maxima awash in the turbulent water. Sherman has slogged ashore mumbling about a lack of channel buoys.

We are marooned in San Ignacio. "Vados" have flooded on both sides of the town.

Aaron Kiley is briefly stranded between two gulley washes while taking pictures. The poor Maxima is hauled out of the water and towed back to the hotel. A dry-out will be attempted, but the fuel injection's brain has gurgled its last. Our only alternative is more food and drink in a terrific little restaurant called Quichule while we wait for the creeks to quit rising.

Friday: The parking lot floods, and we move the cars. Save for the drowned Maxima, they are running well. The Pontiac has developed an antipathy to the urine-quality Mexican gasoline and the Cressida's dash has a faint tick, but otherwise the machines have resisted every sort of abuse we could heap on them.

More may be demanded, however. Word filters in that the road north is devastated. Weeks may pass before we can escape. Pass the tequila.

Saturday: We devise a crafty plan. There is a back-country trail out of town. It meanders through the garbage dump and over the desert to join the highway.

We will double back south to La Paz and evacuate by airplane. Our refugee party is joined by Dick Ryan, Baja veteran, ace dove hunter, and retired Northwest Airlines pilot, who, with his wife, Jody, is trying to return to Santa Barbara. An old Mexican named Luis, who wants to get to Santa Rosalía, is our guide. The seven remaining cars (the Maxima is left behind) scramble tentatively over the rocky trails.

Finally, we are free of San Ignacio, and the road is clear and dry. The federales run us down one more time, threatening a two-day impoundment, arrests for our 100-mph daisy chain, and big fines, but Jody Ryan, who is fluent in Spanish and one salty lady, hectors them down to 2,000 pesos (about $14). Let's hear it for police corruption. After a shower at Los Arcos Hotel and one last assault on Mexican cuisine, we make a lucky feint past the customs officials and board an Aeromexico flight to Los Angeles.

Now all we've got to do is figure out what to do with eight stranded automobiles.

Epilogue: Ten days later, Sherman and six assistants flew back to La Paz to liberate the cars. The flood tide had subsided, and the roads were generally in excellent shape. Two days of driving put the survivors back on American soil. (The ill-fated Maxima was trailered to civilization.)

There was no further contact with the federales, and the feared confrontation at the border failed to materialize.

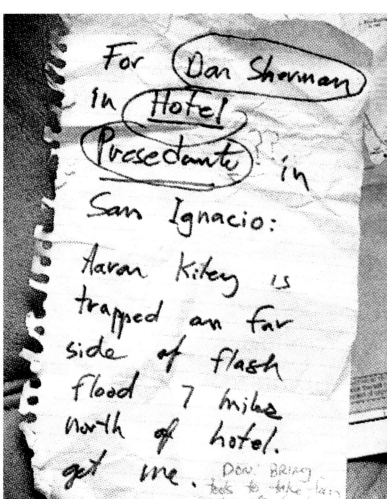

July 1983
Driver's Seat

By David E. Davis, Jr

Baja diary: Maybe truth is stranger than fiction. From the *Detroit Free Press*: GM execs get all hot and bothered

High-level execs at the Pontiac division of General Motors are said to be fuming over a recent incident involving one of their prototype sports cars and two *Car & Driver* [sic] magazine employes [sic] who borrowed the car for a test drive. The car, a fiberglass two-seater sports model, is known to insiders as the P-car and will most likely be marketed under the name "Fiero" (Italian for pride). It seems the *Car & Driver* [sic] duo was taking the prototype for a spin along California's Baha Peninsula [sic, ad nauseam] and decided to drive on into Mexico. As luck would have it, they were detained by Mexican federales who hauled one of them into the pokey for a little questioning. The P-car and the intrepid automotive correspondents made it back to the land of the free and the home of the brave after quite a hassle. But when Pontiac officials found out that their prototype, which had neither license plate, registration, nor insurance papers, went south of the border, there were mucho corporate fits.

The item, penned by somebody called "Judy Diebolt," was virtually a complete fabrication. Where Ms. Diebolt gets her information no one knows, but suffice it to say she ought to get kicked in the slats and sent back to work in the cannery where she belongs. Next, some drunk got hold of the Diebolt story and slipped it past the editors of *Autoweek*, where it ran in just about the same form. This is the sort of thing that makes journalism professors wonder if they shouldn't have joined their brothers-in-law in the cement business when they had the chance.

Here's what really happened...

We took eight test cars into Baja California, none of these eight being a Pontiac P-car. Our plan was to drive all the way down to Cabo San Lucas at the very tip of the Baja Peninsula, spend a day there relaxing in the sun, and then drive back to Newport Beach and *Car and Driver*'s winter testing headquarters.

The full story of this 2,300-mile adventure is later in this issue, but I feel compelled to fill in details of a couple of the more colorful episodes that may have led to Ms. Diebolt's and *Autoweek*'s lapses in journalistic fundamentals.

The trip was absolutely uneventful until the end of our first hour in Mexico, when Yates got arrested in the parking lot of a cantina in Ensenada. Jean Lindamood sprang to his defense, explaining to the arresting officers that Yates was a pig and paying a "mordida" of $10. We all got separated as we left Ensenada and somehow completely missed the checkpoint to the south where aliens are supposed to have their tourist cards validated. An old Baja hand later told us there probably wouldn't have been anyone there anyway. "Mañana," and all that.

We were next stopped by the federales as we left La Paz, on the final leg down to Cabo San Lucas. This time they'd seen eight shiny new cars going by in convoy and couldn't resist the childlike curiosity of cops throughout the Third World. No "mordida" was necessary here. They were content simply to listen to the electronic voice in the Datsun Maxima, telling them that the door was open, the lights were on, the key was in the ignition, et cetera. All very cheery, thanks to Jean Lindamood, all very hands-across-the-border.

It was full dark when we left La Paz—much to my regret, I might add, because I dearly love La Paz, which reminds me of the beginning of *The Treasure of the Sierra Madre.* Nobody drives at night in Baja California except idiots and bad guys, and we're not bad guys. We were 50 miles from Cabo San Lucas when Csabe Csere hit a young steer with the Dodge. The Dodge suffered a broken radiator connection, a crushed grille and hood, and a pair of neat little dents in the roof where the steer performed a hornstand as he cartwheeled into the ravine across the road. The steer suffered a ton of hurt, but only for a couple of milliseconds. He was dead before he hit the ground.

There are two reasons for not driving at night in Baja. One is all the cattle that cross the roads at random, and the other is the off chance that one might encounter the bad guys. I would have felt better about the whole affair if Csaba had mailed some bad guy off into that ravine. Sherman, first at the wheel of the Audi, then in the Toyota, pushed Csaba through the mountains, all the way to our hotel in Cabo. The technical department spent our day of leisure removing the Dodge's hood and repairing its radiator, while the rest of us lolled around the pool and consumed epic quantities of piña colada.

We started back north the following day. Just north of La Paz, I ran over a four-foot rattlesnake as I was passing an isolated farmhouse. I felt bad because I was certain it was the family pet, but I hurried on, leading our caravan, while Sherman and Aaron Kiley drove along on the wrong side of the road taking our respective photographs.

Just south of Mulegé, no longer leading, I came over a hill to find a federale in the midst of an urgent U-turn, about to take up pursuit of the other cars in our little fleet. I passed him, then he passed me, and we were all pulled over. He wanted to know about our hoodless Dodge. Did we have an official accident report? No? His girlfriend was riding shotgun in the beat-up police car, and she said it would be better if the rest of us vamoosed. "If you all go back to Loreto with him, it will be more trouble," she said, so Sherman and Lindamood—our official interpreter—drove the Dodge back to Loreto, escorted by Angel, the federale, and his lovely girlfriend, Florencia.

The reason for the return to Loreto was less ominous than it seemed at the outset. Angel was down to his last official accident-report blank, and he needed to get back to Loreto and a copy machine to copy it. But the supermarket copy machine was busted and the copy center was on siesta when they got there, so they went to yet another store with a busted copy machine, which Sherman set about fixing.

While the copier was being repaired, Lindamood did Florencia's nails, and while the polish was drying, or something, she and Florencia decided to take the cop car for a ride through town. How the citizens of Loreto reacted to this mobile symbol of law and order cruising their streets with a couple of babes inside has not been recorded. In any case, Angel took it well and did not withdraw his enormous .45 from its holster and shoot Lindamood, perhaps because he knew that Mrs. Lindamood had his official federale shotgun in the police car, perhaps because he didn't want to get any messy fragments of Mrs. Lindamood all over the remarkable collection of Twinkies and other items of junk food that he had piled in the back seat. Anyway, the necessary form was filled out—Angel graciously agreeing to describe the location of the smiting of the steer as somewhere within his jurisdiction—$50 changed hands, and our friends were on their way.

On their way, but out of gas. They arrived in Mulegé to find that the power was out, so the gas pumps weren't working. They headed for Santa Rosalía but ran out of gas before they made it. Seeing bright lights down the road, they coasted in that direction. What they found was a brilliantly illuminated slaughterhouse, with a bloody steer's horn in the middle of a bloody floor, but no people. Eerie. They set off on foot, a little scared in the dark, walking right down the center line to avoid any Indescribable Awful that might suddenly leap at them from the scrub at the sides of the highway.

Then, eerier still, they heard keening little voices singing somewhere up the mountainside. Gulping, they headed that way. Amid a collection of darkened hovels they found the source of the voices. They banged on the door, it was jerked open from within, and they found themselves staring in at a rural Baptist church service. "Ask 'em if they've got any gas," Sherman muttered. "Ease off, man, it's a church service," Lindamood whispered. The man who opened the door showed them to seats, and with Sherman nervously shaking the coins in his pants pocket, the service resumed. Lindamood claims nothing will ever top the sight and sound of Sherman, surrounded by the "niños" and "niñitas" of the Santa Rosalía Baptist congregation, singing "How Great Thou Art" in Spanish.

When the service was over, the minister asked his flock to wait while he and some of the kids took our pals into town in the church bus to pick up some fuel. Unfortunately, the power was out in Santa Rosalía, just as in Mulegé, and there was no gas. The Baptists helped siphon a little out of the church bus—enough to get the Dodge started, but not enough to reach the rest of us, 50 miles away in San Ignacio. Sherman made a handsome contribution to the collection plate.

Our brave duo stopped at a motel and asked the proprietor for fuel. A moderately drunk couple from Texas volunteered to help, but in vain. Four young geologists from Mexico City tried to siphon gas from their own truck, but its tank location prevented that. Finally, with the help of the geologists, they did what any right-thinking street urchin would do. They siphoned what they needed out of cars sitting in the motel lot. In the interest of the Yankee image south of the border, they only stole gas from cars with gringo license plates. It was after midnight when they straggled into the hotel in San Ignacio.

Next morning, the Dodge was again dangerously low on fuel, so Sherman set out with Csaba to get it filled at an all-night station about 40 miles up the highway. Our Don was by now in a state not unlike that of some crazed Victorian bwana, pushing his protesting porters and gun bearers ever deeper into the trackless waste. Thus, his attention was evidently elsewhere when he topped the rise north of San Ignacio in the Datsun and hit the flooded vado at God-knows-what-terrible-rate-of-knots. He aquaplaned over the surface for about 75 feet, then sank like a stone. He does not recall what the Datsun's electronic voice said at the moment of its immersion, but we like to think that those poor, hard-scrabble Baptists back at Santa Rosalía would have interpreted his folly as an act of religious observance. Who knows, maybe it was.

Our Trip

1. Yates exposes self. Mexicans award citation.

2. Hey, what happened to the two other cars?

3. Datsun talks to federales,who decide gringos are too dumb for jail.

4. Hungarian sacrifices Dodge to ancient Mexican god of large things in the road at night.

5. Lots of sun. Lots of sick.

6. P.J. discovers restaurant with clean bathrooms. Davis searches for place supposed to have terrific diphtheria burritos.

7. Lindamood and Sherman go off with federales. Rest of us compose likely story for next of kin.

8. Trapped by floods, rendered inarticulate by crank-operated communal phone.

9. Technical director conducts underwater testing of Japanese computer technology. Found wanting. Subsequently attempts to clean computer with toothbrush, but to no avail.

10. Tour of dump shows economy is based on beer and old Chevrolet doors.

11. Emergency airlift to America.

September 1984 Column

By Brock Yates

It's high time we stopped all this naysaying about John Z. DeLorean. Because America's reigning automotive genius has been briefly sidetracked by such matters as the recreational use of 55 pounds of pure Colombian cocaine and a $17 million bookkeeping error, we tend to let the short-term negatives blight the heady contributions this visionary has made to the world of automobiles.

For example, had it not been for John Z. DeLorean, Ronny & the Daytonas would never have entered the pantheon of pop immortals with their unforgettable "GTO." It was John Z. DeLorean who introduced Italian-cut suits to the General Motors executive suite and blazed the trail with the first face job within those hallowed precincts. Not enough, you say, to offset this misunderstanding between him and the FBI, the DEA, the FTC, the SEC, the Northern Ireland Development Agency, the British government, and enough creditors to make Bernie Cornfeld look like David Rockefeller? You want more proof?

It was none other than John Z. DeLorean who brought you such wondrous devices from GM as the Pontiac Judge and the Chevy Vega, the latter an automobile that set standards for small-car quality, performance, and overall excellence that still generate awe among all but the most discerning junkyard operators. Ask yourself: where would companies like Ziebart and Rusty Jones be today without the Vega? Who was the first food faddist among ranking auto execs? Who but John Z. DeLorean had the courage to tune into the good vibes from the trendies and name a small pickup "LUV"? Did Roger Smith or Lee Iacocca have the cojones to distribute a bare-chested wall poster for his adoring public, as JZD did? Whose office in the car business was better decorated than his? Most automobile magnates' wives are leathery matrons who look as if they've been shackled to a bridge table on a Scottsdale, Arizona, patio for the past three decades, but John Z. hooked himself a pair of real beauties on his last two forays into the marriage game. Centerfold stuff. Real eyeball poppers, which ain't all bad.

But his greatest accomplishment centers on his ethical sports car—a machine so brilliant that it could be driven at blinding speeds and still make the driver and any passenger impervious to injury. Not only was it unbelievably safe, according to its maker, but what other manufacturer had the courage to sell his car with a lifetime supply of Brillo pads? Who else possessed the nostalgic sensitivity and good humor to design an essentially outdated machine, with the engine comically hung out the back, and then wait six years until this vintage concoction had fermented into pure vinegar before heaving it onto the market? Sure, there were smart-asses around who felt the DMC should rather have been called the DOA, but they were only jealous because they hadn't been able to dupe legions of private investors and governments out of millions for their own pet projects.

Now the poor fellow is in the dock, fighting for his freedom and his reputation. His attorney, the hard-driving Howard Weitzman, is trying to convince the jury that JZD was the victim of a sleazy con by Ed Meese and his Reaganite pals in order to

hook a big name to shore up their sagging anti-drug campaign. A witless player was our hero, says Weitzman, in a ruthless game being manipulated by the feds' chief witness, James Timothy Hoffman, himself a former importer of South American agricultural derivatives.

We'll go even further: not only was poor John Z. probably innocent of even considering a deal with the evil powder, but it is likely he was just playing along, perhaps himself on the verge of leaping off the couch in that Los Angeles Sheraton Hotel and making a citizen's arrest at the moment the feds barreled into the room and read him his rights. All the worse luck that our man was so convincing as an undercover operator that the G-men videotaped him rhapsodizing over a bag of coke and describing it to be "like gold." But then based on his abilities to pose as a novelist, an all-pro sports-car driver, horseman, lover, financier, golfer, and general Renaissance man, this gift of acting came back to haunt him at a bad time.

His lovely wife, Cristina, has an interesting point: she keeps talking about a dark plot to knock John out of the car business. Probably the CIA (they're behind everything like this). Our speculations go this way: the Company guys from Langley no doubt got one look at the DMC-12 and decided it was so advanced that if one fell into the hands of the Russians it would be worse than having a Soviet death star hovering over Bloomingdale's. If it wasn't the CIA, it was surely a cabal of the big oil companies and General Motors, working in concert with the Trilateral Commission. The motive was simple: the appearance of the DeLorean in the American market would trigger such a consumer revolution that General Motors and at least a couple of the younger Seven Sisters would be run out of business. You want more proof?

Just ask Cristina about what happened to the Fish carburetor.

Now there is also the matter of the missing $17 million. Sure, John and his guys are having a little trouble accounting for that. But remember, when you're dealing with really big numbers, it's easy to misplace a few bucks now and again. A million here, a million there, and pretty soon you're talking about real money. Be confident that when the authorities do a thorough audit they'll find that the Friends of the Earth, Mother Teresa, and other of John's favorite charities will have been the prime beneficiaries of the absent funds.

The hard fact is that the American media, as always, has it right. They incessantly describe John Z. DeLorean as a desperate man "struggling to save his sinking car company." That is perfectly correct, and a pox on those who snort (whoops, perhaps "scoff" would be a better choice) that JZD was so worried about saving his company, why did he loot it in the first place? No matter, it will all come out in the laundry, as we say. Surely this America martyr will be declared innocent, thanks in part to his born-again Christianity (worked for Charlie Colson) and in part to the wisdom of the jurors, who will know a setup when they see one.

And if the worst should happen? The unthinkable guilty verdict? Don't despair. After all, Spiro Agnew might have an extra post for JZD in the international lobbying biz, or John Ehrlichman could put him in touch with his literary agent. Cristina might even make a few bucks with *Playboy*. Remember, it worked for Rita Jenrette.

And, if all else fails, there's always Bob Vesco, now said to be in Cuba, trying to aid the Castro government with its nagging balance-of-trade problems. It is said that he's in the market for good men—with experience.

September 1984
Indy 500

By Patrick Bedard

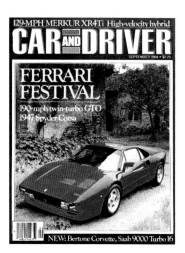

They tell me that on the 59th lap of the 68th running of the Indianapolis 500, I was involved in an accident that lacked only a mushroom cloud for being truly spectacular. Frankly, I don't remember anything about it.

I recall quite vividly the pre-race panic over my lap-belt. In Indy cars, belts are not easily adjustable. Several days before, I'd asked that mine be tightened a fraction, which meant loosening some bolts down inside the tub; and afterward, we'd never checked the fit. On the grid, seconds from "Gentlemen, start your engines," there seemed a very real likelihood that the two ends wouldn't close around me. Chuck was the one who always buckled me in, and he couldn't make them reach. Can you imagine a car being pushed off the starting grid of the Indianapolis 500 because the belts won't fit? The ignominy of it. The all-time high-water mark in screw-ups. Try explaining that to your sponsor: "Well, Escort, we had it all figured, except..." I could sense Chuck's fighting the possibility and slowly being pulled beneath the surface of it. Then someone else, I think it was Ron, joined the struggle. They both bent over the cockpit, and I could feel them strain. The car quivered with their wrestling.

Then there was a click. The lap strap was tight as a steel packing band, but it felt just right to me.

I remember the start of the race, the disorder of it. The cars are bunched up, in the first turn, and I have to lean hard on the brakes to avoid running over the one just ahead. I am ready for anything but such a slowdown. The capability of the car at Indy is such that the brakes are merely ballast on the track: the driver's mission is to take each corner as close as possible to full power. The contest, when triple-distilled, boils down to this essence, and the evolution of drivers is such that only the ones who excel at holding the power down make the next cut. Still, survival is its own reward. The start at Indianapolis—three cars wide, leading to a one-lane turn—is bizarre enough on the face of it that any special warning would only be redundant. Mentally, I may not have given much consideration to a jam-up in Turn One, but I notice that my braking foot is ready with a survival plan of its own.

Everything mentioned thus far is merely prologue. How will the car handle? I've thought of nothing else since carburetion day. That was our last chance to try the car before the race and it was nasty. The rear kept taunting me, threatening to leap wide, bolt out of control in a crazy rush toward self-immolation. We could change the overall balance—dial in push or neutral or loose—but the demonic hip feints remained, daring me to adjust 1 mph to the cornering speed.

Race cars occasionally get unruly like this. It's usually a loose bolt or a stripped thread or a cracked bracket. Someone has to go through and find the needle in the haystack. Jim Wright is the chief mechanic, and I've never seen a needle elude him. When his inspection of the car is complete, he produces a list of things that don't meet his specifications. He and I have been through these investigations before and when he is satisfied I always am. Still, drivers are skeptics. In this they are indulged because it is understood that when the race starts they drive the car anyway, like it or not. I wonder if the 500 will be a joyous dance at the edge of physics or a duel with a demented machine. The answer is in by Turn Two. The driver will have to watch his ass today. The car is ornery, on edge, always looking for an opening. Obviously, there is a contingency plan. They know it in the pits. Back off a discreet amount and try to get to the end. There is no other choice. Racing seems very glamorous on the outside, but much of it is merely endurance.

I know the leaders will be by soon. It's just a matter of time. But who? And by what margin? I have the curiosity of a spectator. The mind has apparently already compensated for being off the pace. It's Mears! And after a short interval, Sneva. They are fantastic to watch, so fast yet human, the drivers working away at the steering. I can tell by the front wheels, ceaselessly being reangled to maintain that essential balance at the limit. Their speed reminds me of my lack. The difference between me and a spectator is the level of frustration.

Uh-oh, the engine, it's softening. Will it seize? No, just lost a cylinder. I feel it stagger, hear its syncopated breathing. With Cosworth, we'd shut it off, try to save the pieces, but the Buick is cheaper. I radio the pits. They say, "Stay out." This would be a good excuse to come in—if we were the kind of guys who quit. But if we were the kind, I suppose we wouldn't be at Indianapolis. The oil pressure is fine. Temp is okay. But the revs are way down, and the manifold pressure is off.
I turn up the boost. The racket from the engine gets worse.
I don't know how to play this.

More cars are coming by now, four, five for every one that I can pass. One will slip beneath me just as I set up for a turn. A damn nuisance is what it is. I have to make sure there is nose room as we merge in the same arc—sometimes even back off, sacrifice precious speed, then follow in his wake. The car hates turbulent air interrupted by someone else, air not lying perfectly still in wait for its aerodynamic planes. It slues its tail, a threat,

like a fist shaken across a barroom. How much can I get by with? I don't know, but at least the decision will be made by somebody I trust, namely me. That's the deal in racing. No executive board is calling down moves from the 23rd floor.

Yellow! First of the race. I go on full alert, in anticipation of a disaster that would block the track. Nothing major, though. At least this pit stop will be a cheap one. If, that is, they signal me in. They do. Okay, look for the board marking the pit. There'sChuck. Stop on the marks. Good. Car is on the jacks. They're changing rights, maybe left rear, too, I can't see in the mirror. Hold the brakes while they run the wrenches. Look for Chuck again. He'll give the signal to go. Car's down. Go! God, what a mess the engine is. Five cylinders. Full throttle, and it won't spin a wheel.

I'm way back in the line. When I'm in Turn Two, the pace car is almost down the back straight to Turn Three. From directly behind, it's hard to see the flashing lights on top, but as it bends into Turn Three, I can see easily. When the lights go out, get ready for a start. With this V-5, I'm going to have to be one ready buckaroo or the whole train will go by. Ah, there go the lights. Green! A few cars edge by, but not many, not the massacre you'd expect. I remember congratulating myself.

Then the race kinda runs out, as if the memory player were sucking air. My first recollection after that was of a green field, view angled from overhead, with a darker green structure in the corner, maybe a tent. Everything was still, like a photograph, but the depth was too much, too real. I commented on it.

A voice said there had been an accident in the Indy 500. I was alive. Not to worry. Worry? What is there to worry about. Right now I'm sort of lost. But nothing hurts. And the car isn't trying to kill me anymore.

Patrick Bedard's race came to a horrific end on lap 59. The exact cause is unknown, though suspension failure has not been ruled out. The escort Radar Warning Special left the racing groove well past the Turn Three apex, looped through 270 degrees and then crashed tail first into the north-end infield barrier. There was a flash of burning oil, but virtually no fuel spillage or fire.

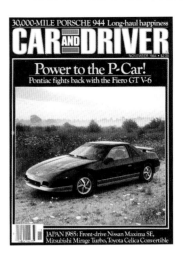

November 1984
All Bow Down

By Larry Griffin

What happens when you take a $105,000, umpteen-quadzillion-mph, so-red-it-can-make-your-eyes-hurt Porsche DP 935 to your high school reunion in Kansas.

Any excuse is good enough to drive a Porsche DP 935. My high school reunion would do just fine. Actually, it would be perfect. It was fast approaching, and I wanted to approach it even faster. Yesterday couldn't be soon enough for Kansas to be struck by a lightning bolt from Germany. No holds barred, I wanted to show up for the reunion in the most brutal-looking, most hideously fast car ever seen in southeastern Kansas, juvenile, but fun.

I had toyed with the idea of the 20-year get-together for some time. I liked what I was doing with my life, and I wanted to see what everybody else in the Class of 1964 was up to. So it was down to basics: A Ferrari might be good to arrive in, or perhaps a Rolls Royce. A Lamborghini—ah, now that would be a statement! How about the most rewarding of exotic cars, a BMW M1? One by one, I toyed with and eliminated candidates. Too common, too sedate, too ridiculous, too understated. Then we tested a Porsche DP 935 (*Car and Driver*, May 1983), and it became one of perhaps five cars in the world I would kill for.

With a price tag of $105,000, a shape straight off the Mulsanne Straight, and a top speed sufficient to rearrange the earth's rotational forces, the DP 935 is a street-performance benchmark at *Car and Driver*. Even with the big boost knob between its wraparound seats twisted to the minimum setting (which was highly recommended in view of a rumored appetite for expensive Mahle pistons), the original DP 935 defied common experience by posting a 0-to-60 time of 4.6 seconds, a 0-to-100 time of 10.5 seconds, a 0-to-130 time of 19.3.seconds, a 70-to-0 braking distance of 179 feet with flawless control, and an all-time Porsche skidpad record of 0.84-g lateral acceleration. Clearly the car for me and the Independence High School Class of 1964.

In 1964, Independence was a town of about 11,000, and it was shrinking. The problem was classic—small town, limited chances, dull atmosphere, television's outside world beckoning. We all knew what stupendous possibilities lay beyond the city limits. Far beyond.

The Class of 1964 counted a number of horrifying circumstances sifting through the neck of its yearglass. John Kennedy was assassinated in the fall of our senior year. Vietnam was already big news, and those who were less than eager to go were ripped by thoughts of the draft. Those who weren't tangling with the ugly reality of trooping off to star in television's war were fitting themselves willy-nilly into colleges or careers, but in almost every case the common denominator was that the solution lay somewhere beyond Independence, Kansas.

My mother was long since divorced and had stuck with the locally headquartered Arco Pipeline Company, which is still centered in Independence, its 500 or so employees the biggest working body in a town that's now shrunk to 10,000. Until she retired a few years ago, she was the executive secretary to each successive pipeline president, for 30 years putting to use her writing, diplomatic, and organizational skills.

197

What I got out of the deal were some of her writing skills, a little diplomatic rub-off, a good upbringing, and the wonderful feeling that I could do almost anything. What I didn't get were all of her organizational skills, but I could at least organize her car for a drive. First it was a 1957 Ford two-door six. I'd drive it around and around the huge elm tree in the backyard until (a) the car overheated, (b) the transmission barfed all its fluid, (c) the gas tank emptied, or (d) the grass under the tree died.

Flying into Tulsa, Oklahoma, to pick up the 935, I thought of all these things. Even the in-flight music program had a special 1964 selection—"Hello, Dolly!," "My Guy," "Under the Boardwalk," "I Want to Hold Your Hand"....

The DP 935 has been delivered to Tulsa on a flatbed from Richard Buxbaum's Classic Motors in Chicago. I am ready (foaming at the mouth, even), and the car looks to be ready, too. Red? You want to talk red!? Stevie Wonder could see this car! The fine fiberglass bodywork is by Germany's Designer Plastics (DP) Automobilbau, which has supplied molded-fiberglass parts to Porsche for at least one low-volume production car.

The car Buxbaum has sent is the really wild new DP 935. It makes the original look like Grandma's shoe. The nose is now virtually identical to the racing 935's, scooping low, laving up everything in its path—air, chipmunks, other traffic. Flip-up headlights have been mounted in the lenders, though the original air-dam high-beams have been retained. A large oil cooler sits behind a distended oval snout, and huge inlets duct air to the front disc brakes. The OP's big alloy wheels have been upsized to 9.0-by-15s at the front and earth-flattening 13.0-by-15s at the rear. They carry Pirelli P7

225/50VRs beneath the steep nose and 345/35VRs beneath the looming whale tail.

Buxbaum claims that this engine dynoed at 393 DIN horsepower before emissionizing, a transformation accomplished with the usual aftermarket add-ons and a sharp drop in compression ratio. This is said to be necessary to make this engine live with everyday super unleaded. With this thought vaguely playing in the back of my mind as I ease Germany's Atomic Cockroach out of the dealership's mildly sloped entrance, I set off in the approximate direction of U.S. 75. The air temperature is well up into the 90s, as is the humidity. The engine is cobby, but I figure it's just the highly tuned start-up blues.

A block and a half and it quits dead. After a few expletives, I abandon the car, flashers aflicker, and sprint back to the dealership. A fellow with a cooler head than mine queries rather loudly, "Not out of gas, is it?"

Indeed, the tank is bone dry. One sip from a gas can and a guzzle from self-serve and the DP 935 sets its nose into northeast Oklahoma's heat, swallowing bursts of two-lane and farting mirrored munchkin motorcars out from under its whale tail.

The car drives beautifully. Like the last DP 935, it steers lightly despite the huge tires. The DP tracks cleaner than a standard Porsche Turbo, turns in better and much more willingly, and shifts around less on its stubby wheelbase under fore, aft, and lateral loading. DP moves the engine 1.5 inches forward to reduce the car's tail—heavy tail—happiness. The four-speed shifter is crisp, and the ventilated and crossdrilled four-wheel disc brakes demonstrate enormous stopping capacity.

At low revs, the de-smogged motor feels distinctly flat. When you knock on the door for big boost, there's nobody home, but at least there's no knocking back from inside. Our last DP was uncertified, drank the highest octane it could get, and liked regular gurglings of octane booster best of all. That was a nuisance, and the car was almost certainly a stronger polluter than this new and legalized car, but holy tewawas did it go! ("The moon, Herr Driver? Of course!") The new car is dead from the neck down until 4,500 rpm, when things begin to circulate back there. At 5,500, you'd better have your prayer beads out, because there's no reaching for them. This car comes with stock seatbelts and no inclination whatsoever toward emotional restraint. Fifty feet of rope, a few tubes of epoxy, and a speaking acquaintance with Billy Graham would do better. Lash yourself to it as if to Moby Dick.

The car swallows ground like sunshine racing the horizon. People in Oklahoma and Kansas are stunned by this riotous sight. The mouths of Z28, Trans Am, and Corvette drivers drop open in the first syllables of babble. People afoot suddenly forget how to walk. Feet perambulate unattended. No one mistakes this car for a toy.

It is so fast that I have so far held off full revs in traffic. Passing maneuvers are ripped off like paper towels, albeit with a lot more noise. Nearing Independence (wait till you see this, home-towners!), I decide to sample the big rush. Just how fast is fast today? A downshift to third for maximum warp pastes the human pudding into the seat like sealer into a bathtub joint. The telltale needle on the big boost gauge is rammed steady at a bit more than 1.25 bars (18 psi)—more than 50 percent greater boost than a stock 930 Turbo. Wa-haa!! Can't hold me now! Uhhhh... Maybe

you can't hold me, but something's got me! Holymoly, the throttle is stuck wide open!! Can't lift it! Flat in fourth, 130 and soaring, 90-degree corner rushing in, but plenty of time, just gently cut key...eeeasy, not enough to lock steering...engine off, now clutch it quick to coast half-mile into next farmyard.

I came into this project knowing that this was the car Buxbaum's pal Borjan had crashed on an autobahn ice patch at 160 in the dead of a winter's night. I knew that now, after a total rebuild, the car was intended mostly for display purposes. But then I came along, wanting to pull in the hometown folks. Still, I didn't have in mind pulling them to a wake.

And now, what of the reunion? My story? Will the Class of 1964 never see the Atomic Cockroach? A quick call to me mum's house, a scant four miles away. She arrives in her Mazda 626. Since the DP's engine will run at only 800 rpm in first, second, or third gear, I lead the way around the fringes of town at a gurgling 20 mph the 626 following protectively. The ignominy!

Tomorrow, Friday evening, is the opening picnic at the park. I have obviously been all wrong for years: God does not want me to have fun.

Friday, dawn, sunny, humid. Stuck in my own hometown in outback Kansas with a broken DP 935. But all will not be lost. I idle the car over to Kendrick's Conoco at Penn and Oak as soon as it's open. For a paltry five bucks they let me use their tools and walk-under bay. I can see that a spherical rod end connected to the throttle linkage's bell crank has ruptured because the bell crank itself (possibly crash-damaged) was distorted by my heavy foot. Damn! A call

to Chicago: Buxbaum will strip the right pieces out of the DP 935 in his showroom and air-freight them. All I need is a flatbed truck to take the car to a dealer in Tulsa, where the parts should arrive by mid-afternoon. The Conoco guys tell me there's only one flatbed outfit in the area for a lowrider like mine—Dale's Body Shop on West Main. A half-hour later, Dale's flatbed arrives, and we begin an endless series of ramp buildups with two-by-fours to get the DP onto the steeply tilting bed. Photographer David Hutson arrives from the Kansas City area. Finally, we get the car to Tulsa and offload it directly onto a lift at Precision Imports Porsche-Audi-Mazda.

I remember these guys now: they serviced a 928S test car for me last year. Service manager Berry Berryman and Porsche technician Tom Charlesworth peer at the DP and start clucking, partly in awe (actually, there are two or three DPs in Tulsa), partly in worry. But once the pieces come in, Charlesworth buttons up the car in a mere 45 minutes, also replacing a leaking oil line. Thanks, guys.

Back to Kansas. Hot, filthy, sweaty in the worst way, we have no choice but to make straight for the picnic. It's at Riverside Park, a longtime joy for Independence, full of greenery, open spaces, pools, a locomotive, a jet fighter, a band shell, a zoo, a river, and. the football stadium where our Bulldogs worked on their 50-game winning streak back in the 1960s.

Class member Pat Tucker Alexander has reorganized the Class of 1964, and the group is wedged between two of the Four-H buildings for a barbecue. Hutson and I take one look at this arrangement and take matters into our own grubby hands. I motor the Atomic Cockroach right into the middle of

the picnic, and everyone falls down in full quiver, especially the kids. But who are these adults? For me, the crowd is broken into thirds—one-third I recognize immediately, one-third I recognize after a little mental homework, and one-third I can't recognize even after they've said hello. And more than two-thirds of the alumni have moved away for good.

Larry Walling! Robert Velsir! Terry Wood and wife Tina Williams Wood! Dennis Messenger! Barry Polston! Mary Lou Pouncil Washington! Karen Simpson Fiske! Jim Boomis! Kathryn Troutman Sack! Kay Wren Ackerson! Cindi Pattin Burns! And dozens more.

Amazing. And here's a short, bearded, partly bald guy, leaning into the Porsche, saying, "Do you know me?" I look around for the hidden American Express camera.

Jeez, he's changed, but he's still Bill Self, neat Bill, our class VP, and he's bananas over the 935. "Holy cow, I thought it was just an imitation when I drove up!" he's hollering. "How are ya?... I live in Ogden, Utah, now, but I take my kids to the Vegas Grand Prix every year. Listen, I've got two old Jags, and I was gonna trailer the Mark II 3.8 back here, figuring that nobody would be able to top that. My God, am I glad I saved the gas money! Can I have a ride!?"

First victim. Heh-heh-heh. More hellos first, though. I feel Something Warm and Very Female pressing into my ribs. I turn to see an enormous pair of Blue Eyes looking up, Pouting Lips saying, "Lawrence. You don't remember me, do you?" "Oh, yes, I do." "You came over to my house in the third grade, and we went down into the basement. You spit on the carpet!" Well, listen, it wasn't easy being tough back then. I look into Blue Eyes again

200

and fear for my singleness now, I feel some heat here but spot a name tag with marriage-type nomenclature on it.

I feign a lack of interest and spot Steve Ahmann. . .Steve Ahmann! His mother used to own a flower shop, where we worked. We used to take turns delivering flowers in the shop's Fairlane wagon. I'd stick all those arrangements in there, race around town spilling them all over the back of the car, rearrange them vaguely on the way up the walk, and wonder why I never got any tips. Steve was almost as bad. Now he's landscaping in Phoenix.

Our partner in crime was Ralph Earhart, Jr., and he and his wife, the former Kay Price, are here, too.

"Ralph!"

"Lawrence!"

I look quickly around. It's been a long time since anybody but my mother and the Blue-Eyed Heat-Bringer have called me that. Ralph and Kay and I leap into whatuvyabeenuptos? and I discover that Ralph has gotten almost entirely away from cars. His dad was once the best Ford salesman in town. We bought our second Ford, a new 1963, from him. I hot-rodded that Galaxie as well as I could, aiming it as much toward handling as acceleration (at 17, I already dreamed of working for *Car and Driver* someday). Ralph, Jr., raced the flower-shop Fairlane, carrying funeral sprays from the funeral homes out to Mount Hope Cemetery. Good duty. His greatest pleasure was bottoming out under the Park Boulevard railroad overpass at 90 in a 30 zone to see how far the car and the flowers could rebound up the hill toward the waiting plot. The women at the flower shop were forever puzzled as to why that car always needed shocks, but Ralph says he never failed to arrive well before the funeral procession. No surprise there.

Ralph will go for a ride in the DP 935, too. And tomorrow, I'll select the best-looking woman in the class for the ride of her life. I am overwhelmed by the response to the car. It is beyond all expectations. An amazing number of people know what this car is. Or think they do.

Bill Self is about to find out for sure. Ralph's wife, Kay, who is very tall, was once asked to a dance by very short Bill, but he called back two days later to say that he couldn't take her. Suspecting he'd found somebody more to his liking, Kay asked why, and Bill said simply, "I've decided you're just too tall," and hung up. Tonight, he has no cold feet. I am surprised to see that his wife, Liana, seems unconcerned as he straps into the DP's passenger seat. If only she knew.

We burble away and around and down past the glow of the woodsy Little League diamonds. I'm trying hard not to give Bill a preview. We clear town, and I ease the speed up, letting the big turbo run easy as it warms to its task. Yes... it's about ready... now!!! Wham, bam, thank you, ma'am! It's the full-boost boogie!!

Have you ever seen a skull burst through skin? Self whoops and hollers, the boost pasting him back, the car slithering brutally through a series of ever faster corners then feed into a snakings that wings up and over a blind crest, where we encounter traffic monoliths. Despite his harness, Bill lunges to brace himself against the dash as the webbing bites his chest. The DP's phenomenal brakes grunt the car down to a virtual standstill in nothing flat. It's not even close. Bill's expression changes from grim to grin, and he blurts, "Oh, my God!! This is the high point of my car days! I don't believe it! I didn't know cars could do things like this! Wow!!"

September 1985
Ferrari Testarossa

The Testarossa is the first Ferrari in my experience that drives as well as it looks. If you like the photos, you'll love the red beast in real life; and if you're lucky enough to see and drive one, you'll think about calling the devil for a hot deal on your afterlife. Yes, the TR fits, sticks, goes, and slows with the best of them. It's everything a Ferrari should be and at the same time exactly what Ferraris haven't been for at least a decade in America. I'll admit the package is bulky and heavy, but in this case the width and the weight are almost justified. I wouldn't settle for one fewer cam, valve, or horse even if I had to add lamps and wave red flags to clear the way for the wide one. In my book, this is the ultimate in speed with style. What's more surprising, though, is that the Testarossa is also a remarkably comfortable Ferrari. It has excellent seats, well-situated controls, tolerable interior noise levels, and an actual ventilation system. "Hello, AT&T? May I please have the area code for Hades?"

Top speed: 181 mph (estimated)
0-60 5.0 seconds
370 hp, 348 lb-ft of torque
Price: $115,000

—*Larry Griffin*

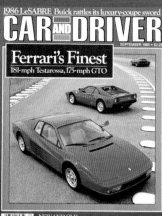

NO PARKING

NO PARKING

BELOW, TOP TO BOTTOM:
Old pal Ralph Earhart enjoyed
the ride. Griffins and Radar,
vaguely cooperative dog.

We have before us your standard 37 year-old male child. Just like me.

Saturday morning is for pictures a mile or two outside of town, action of the DP 935 around the hilly, wooded, far-reaching environs of Elk City Lake (which is managed by 1964's Terry Wood). This part of Kansas edges into the famed Ozark character varied and crookedly raked with a scattering of asphalt threads. This Kansas is not related to the better-known Kansas wheatscapes to the west (although Laura Ingalls Wilder's true *Little House on the Prairie* was only ten miles west of Independence). Here around the lake, the DP whangs its muscles into action, latching onto the pavement with German tenacity. Afterward, as he stows his lenses, veteran race photographer Hutson eyes the hills and the devious road and says, "I can see where your fantasies of the Nurburgring came from."

Saturday is also the day for Ralph's ride. He is calmer than Bill, but I can feel his eyes rolling. Still, he's calm enough to press the infrared shutter release that Hutson has employed for some dash-mounted fisheye shots; I am too busy driving for that. Ralph presses the button through thick and thin, thin being the first 140-mph burst, thick being the all-slicing-and-dicing slithery squiggles that work your head like a yo-yo—and also the spot where the throttle lodges open again at full boost in fourth. I give it points for consistency. I hope Ralph has noticed my Yeager-like response (oh, to wrestle with the sound barrier!) as I note, "Throttle's broken again and stuck wide open," and reach to cut the ignition. Ralph is helpful but fairly quiet as I effect crowbar-type repairs

204

on the linkage and cruise gently back to town, where he shortly disappears. Bill Self comes around, chuckling that Ralph has confided with a shake of his head that he thinks he saw God for the first time.

The ginchy-throttled DP toodles to the grand-finale dinner dance, where I park it smack in front of two "No Parking" signs in front of the doors. I've always wanted to do that. I step out, as David E. Davis, Jr., would say, dapper beyond your wildest dreams. I am hot tonight—light-brown pleated slacks, bold-striped brown-and-cream shirt with white collar, chocolate-with-white—pinstripes Ferrari tie from Enzo himself, burnt-sienna-and-white Italian wing-tips, and trim, cream-colored sport coat. I feel disgustingly spiffy, but also a little like the Good Humor man. Let's be frank here: I'm hoping one of the ladies will mistake me for a chocolate sundae.

The instant I'm through the doors, Blue Eyes entwines herself in my arm and poses us for a picture. I feel warm. I ask about her past 20 years. (Gad, she looks wonderful.) She replies that she's been mothering (three girls) and just got a divorce. (Jeez, it must be 120 in here.)

The night's emcee, my cousin James Johnson, makes his way to a microphone and announces that the red car out front is, as rumored, a raffle prize and that $100 bids should be deposited with him. There will be no receipts, he'll just remember everybody by serial number.

Class president Mike Jackson, who lived at the opposite end of my block, has failed to appear from his Illinois digs, so an impromptu move ensues to impeach him, to be promptly replaced by class wag and all-around good/bad guy Barry Polston, who wins all hands.

There is also sadness. One woman, barely recognizable from chemotherapy, is wheeled in in a wheelchair. Everyone feels terrible. Some rush to say hello, others can hardly bear to look in her direction.

And I'm told that ever-smiling Andy Economus was killed in the Vietnam War.

Another fellow died of accidental electrocution only a year ago.

And, finally, Ralph Earhart tells me his dad, his wonderful dad, who was the most conscientious car salesman in town, got some improper medication two years ago and and his brain was fried. His 250 pounds have shrunk to the weight of a prisoner of war, and he is enfeebled beyond help. I feel sick at heart. Mr. Earhart often called my mother 20 years ago to check on the Galaxie 500. "I see Lawrence driving that car all the time," his straightforward but kindly voice would say, "but I don't see you driving it very often, Mrs. Griffin. Don't you like it?"

We both liked it fine, Mr. Earhart.

Aside from the inevitable sadnesses that come with the living of every life, the reunion of the Independence High School Class of 1964 is a rush, and I love it despite my high-school trials. Have I mentioned coincidences? Shoot, Jim Boomis, once gangling, grinning kid whose Greek immigrant dad ran a delicious place called the New York Candy Kitchen, is now the broad-beamed manager of a Detroit electronics firm that builds automotive engine-control computers, and it turns out he lives just five miles from my place! Maybe if we take the DP 935 I can talk him into coffee.

Bill Self sends me a thank-you note when he gets back to Utah. I think he's after another ride. Maybe I'll swap him for one in his Jag. His handwriting has steadied now.

205

October 1985
Far From Eden

By Brock Yates

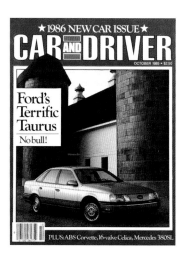

One of James Dean's favorite performances was that of his Porsche Spyder. On September 30, 1955, on a lonely stretch of California two-lane, he drove it to his death.

Welcome the silence. Break for a moment your bonds with time. You'll hear it first—the frantic growl of a four-cam Porsche. Unmuffled. Running hard. Look into the brown-weeded hills, where the old road winds around the edge of the ravine. A tiny silver Spyder squirts into sight, lashing through the apexes, its impudent snout nipping at the wooden guardrails. Stand back as it rushes past, scrabbling for traction on the scarred macadam. Follow its raucous exhaust. The two men in the cockpit—a slight young driver with clip-on sunglasses and a beefy passenger—lean slightly as the Porsche clears the final bend. It powers, clean and straight, speed building, toward the valley. Far off on the western slope, a stand of oaks marks the café at Cholame. But first there is the intersection where State 41 angles toward Fresno. A lone car is approaching, a black Ford two-door. It is slowing, readying for the turn. The Spyder hammers onward, a shiny aluminum pellet aglow in the late afternoon sun. Surely the Ford will stop. Surely the driver will spot the speeding Porsche. Surely the world of heroes and dreamy idols will not be shattered on the road to Cholame....

James Dean opened big and died bigger. In death he had what the movie moguls call "legs"—that mysterious ability to endure in the face of critical assaults, the fevered promotion of rivals, and the notoriously fickle public.

Thirty years ago, at approximately 5:45 p.m. on the 30th of September, 1955, James Byron Dean, a 24-year-old actor with a single major screen role to his credit, crashed at the intersection of California routes 466 and 41, less than a mile east of Cholame. He died minutes later. It was the most famous highway accident in history. It thrust Dean into the pantheon of ritualized cult figures occupied by the likes of Valentino, Monroe, JFK, Elvis, and John Lennon. None of them, not even Kennedy or Presley, was mourned with more sound and fury and endless, hysterical weeping than James Dean.

The keepers of the flame will tell you he dreamed of being a Grand Prix driver and wheeling exotic sports cars from the time he was a surprisingly normal high school kid in Fairmount, Indiana. Perhaps. Paul Newman, who knew Dean casually when both were trying to make it on the New York stage in the early 1950s, remembers no talk about automobiles. "We'd have a few beers and talk about acting," he recalls, "but I didn't care much about racing in those days and haven't any idea if he did or not. If he did, he didn't tell me about it."

What we do know is that Dean did not become a screen idol overnight. In the early 1950s he made a number of appearances in New York television dramas, got small parts in four long-forgotten pictures (*Has Anybody Seen My Gal?*, *Sailor Beware*, *Fixed Bayonets*, and *Trouble Along the Way*), and earned strong reviews for his performance in Gide's *The Immoralist* on Broadway. His first major break in Hollywood came in March 1954 when he was cast as Cal Trask in Elia Kazan's production of John Steinbeck's *East of Eden*.

Although he had owned a couple of motorcycles—an old Harley and a 500 cc Norton—Dean's plunge into the world of

207

California sports cars did not come until a year later. In March 1955, he bought a white Porsche 356 Super Speedster from Johnny von Neumann's Competition Motors on North Vine Street in Hollywood. These were the halcyon days of the West Coast sports-car movement, with races being organized by the Sports Car Club of America and its rival, the California Sports Car Club, at seemingly every vacant airport between San Diego and San Francisco. Natural road circuits like Torrey Pines and Pebble Beach were also active, and plans were being formulated for permanent courses at places like Riverside and Laguna Seca. Everybody raced, or went to the races, or at the very least owned a tiny, two-seat sports car. To do otherwise was to risk social ruin. The serious drivers of the day—Phil Hill, Richie Ginther, Carroll Shelby, Bill Pollack, von Neumann, Ken Miles, Bob Drake, Bob Bondurant, and a blond prodigy from Riverside named Dan Gurney—competed in road races staged by both dubs. Dean joined the SCCA, but he attended few meetings and was known to the membership as just another young actor getting a short-burst publicity push from Warner Brothers.

Less than two weeks after buying the Porsche, he was a star. *East of Eden* opened well, and Dean received eloquent reviews. His introverted, renegade sensuality dominated the screen. One reviewer described this quality as the "innocent grace of a captive panther." Another called it "bastard robustness." Whatever it was, the skinny, slightly bowlegged former bongo player and track star from Fairmount High was the hottest property in show business. Warner Brothers immediately extended his contract and set him to work as the sullen, confused, misunderstood teenager in *Rebel Without a Cause*. Before *Rebel* was completed,

Warner announced that he would star as Jett Rink, the rags-to-riches cowboy in Edna Ferber's *Giant*, then play Rocky Graziano, the fighter, in his screen biography, *Somebody up There Likes Me*. He was dating ravishing starlets like Pier Angeli and Ursula Andress, and he was driving fast. Very fast.

In late March, Dean took the Speedster to the Palm Springs road races and won the novice event. Victory his first time out. He then ran in the main race for small displacement cars and finished third behind the hot MG Specials of Ken Miles and Cy Yedor. When Miles was disqualified on a technicality, he advanced to second overall. Seriously myopic, Dean raced with a hunched, head-down ferocity that was complemented by a substantial talent. Dean was not some twit movie star out to impress his pals; he was ragged and overeager, but he was far from slow. On May 1st he took the Porsche to a Cal Club event at Minter Field in Bakersfield and finished third in the 1300-to-2000 cc Production class, again competing against more experienced drivers. His last race was on Memorial Day, 1955, at Santa Barbara, where he ran in the SCCA Under-1500 cc Production class after starting 18th, he charged all the way to fourth before the Porsche burned a piston.

Then it was over. Director George Stevens had forbidden him to race while the principal shooting of *Giant* was underway, and Dean had to content himself with wild forays through the Los Angeles canyons and on location in the barren west-Texas range around Marfa. It was during this period, when the heady pressures of celebrity were beginning to bear on him, that word passed through the film colony: behind the wheel of his Porsche, James Dean was to be avoided like a subpoena to the House Un-American Activities Committee.

James Dean and Rolf Wütherich (center) check out the "Little Bastard" prior to the Salinas race.

He was a wild man, broadsliding the Speedster through the Hollywood streets like a stunt driver. It was then that he dismissed the 356 as too slow. When his *Giant* constraints were loosened, he would buy a serious race car.

Phil Hill remembers the day of Dean's death. Hill had been maintaining the graphite-gray three-liter Monza that he was driving for von Neumann at the High Hind Avenue Ferrari Agency, but his own rising celebrity status as America's most brilliant road racer had clogged the shop with oglers and hangers-on. Seeking privacy, he and mechanic Henry Pickett had taken the Monza to a small race shop owned by von Neumann on Ventura Boulevard. They were readying the car for a San Francisco region SCCA race, to be staged on October 1st at the airport at Salinas, a dusty town on the northern perimeter of the vast San Joaquin Valley. A produce center, it was best known as the birthplace of John Steinbeck.

Like most of the hard-core racers, Hill looked on Dean as an outsider. Also as an object of mystery, with some faint jealousy, and not a little derision. He recalls Sam Wile, a partner of von Neumann's in the booming Porsche dealership and Volkswagen distributorship, announcing Dean's arrival to an amused office staff: "Here comes the Mickey Mouse Marlon Brando." Says Hill, "I felt he had enormous personal needs to be famous."

On September 17th, Dean made a public-service television spot for the National Safety Council with actor Gig Young, He tagged it with a plea: "And remember, drive safely. The life you save may be mine." Four days later he went to Competition Motors and traded the Speedster for one of five Porsche 550 Spyders that von Neumann had imported directly from the factory. The tiny, aluminum-bodied racer, with a

ladder frame and a midship-mounted four-earn, air-cooled four, was part of a batch of 75 that the factory had built for privateer racers that year. Dean's machine was to become the most famous—and mysterious—of the lot.

At the time, the 550 Spyder was the best small-displacement racer in the world. Not only was it quick and nimble, but its anvil-like reliability helped win many high placings in major endurance races. There was some question whether Dean was experienced enough for the machine, but on September 21st, von Neumann accepted his check for $3,000, plus the 356 Speedster in trade, for Spyder number 550-0055.

Dean took the car to Compton, where the well-known customizer George Barris added a bit of individuality. Stock Spyders were all silver, with only blue or red stripes atop the rear fenders (Dean's had red stripes). Barris painted "Little Bastard" in script across the tail and Dean's racing number, 130, on the doors, the hood, and the rear deck.

Jimmy, as his friends called him, took the Spyder to the streets, driving with customary fierceness. In the days before pollution controls and safety standards, a license could be tacked onto practically anything with four wheels, and so it was with the "Little Bastard." Several days later he had a minor shunt with a lady on Sunset Boulevard and returned the Porsche to Competition Motors for repairs.

At roughly the same time, Dean decided that he would race at Salinas. (It must have been a last-hour decision, because the race program did not bear his name.) He had been there once before, on location for some of *East of Eden*. Dean had established a solid relationship with Rolf Wutherich, a 28-year-old German mechanic who had come to von

Neumann's operation from the factory in Zuffenhausen; it was he who had prepared both the Speedster and the 550 for competition. Because the car was so fresh and the driver so inexperienced, Wutherich recommended that they drive the 300-odd miles to Salinas while someone else ferried Dean's 1953 Ford station wagon and a borrowed trailer for the return trip.

Dean was up early on the 30th, though he'd attended a party in Malibu the night before. He arrived at Competition Motors on North Vine a little after eight, having driven over the hill from his leased home at 14611 Sutton Street in Sherman Oaks. On the way he stopped at the Ventura Boulevard shop, where Hill and Pickett were laboring over the Monza. "It's the only time I ever talked with him, other than a few grunts at the racetrack," recalls Hill. "Generally, he'd show up with this great retinue of hangers-on, and I had no interest in that sort of thing. I needed to be a great racing driver, and that was my sole preoccupation. I'd seen dozens of these so-called godlike creatures from Hollywood, and I'd been inclined to treat him as sort of a mutation. But on that day we talked about racing without all the usual distractions."

Dean had lunch at the Fanner's Market with his father, Winton, and his uncle Charlie Nolan Dean. Shortly after lunch, he met Wutherich at Competition Motors. The Spyder's engine was warming. Three friends were on hand: show-business photographer Sanford Roth, stunt man Bill Hickman (who would make the famed drive for Steve McQueen in *Bullitt*), and Dean's insurance man, Lew Bracker. Roth and Hickman had been enlisted to dead-head the trailer to Salinas.

The route the racers took to the northern-California events was standard: Sepulveda Boulevard to 99 north over the notorious Grapevine and into the San Joaquin Valley; west on Route 166 toward Taft and Maricopa; then north on 33 to Blackwell's Corner. From there it was a flat shot west across the sagebrush-carpeted western end of the valley on old 466 into Paso Robles.

Dean was issued a speeding ticket on Grapevine. He stopped for a soft drink and an apple at a cafe in Blackwell's Corner ("elevation 278 ft., rainfall 8 drops, population 9,002: 9,000 squirrels, 2 humans"), where he chatted with Lance Reventlow, who was on the way to Salinas in a new Mercedes-Benz 300SL gull-wing. They agreed to meet for dinner in Paso Robles.

No one knows how quickly Dean traversed the run from Blackwell's Corner toward Cholame. Some speculate that he was running the deserted road at his customary frantic pace. Others say no, that the fresh race engine that had to be run in, plus the presence of Wutherich, the factory-trained veteran of Le Mans, Reims, and the Mille Miglia, would have imposed restraint. We know this much: he zoomed over the barren Diablo Range, where the San Andreas Fault, looking like the clenched jaws of a half-buried dragon, borders the road, and through what the locals call Polonio Pass. He charged at the valley floor to the east of Cholame far in front of Roth and Hickman in the wagon. As he hit the straight, he was probably loafing the Porsche at 80 to 85 mph.

Heading east was a 23-year-old student from California Polytechnic in San Luis Obispo named Donald Turnupseed. He was driving his 1950 Ford home to Fresno for the weekend. He would have to make a left turn off of 466 where Route 41 angled northeast: a left turn directly in front of the approaching Spyder.

211

According to Wutherich, James Dean's last words were, "He's gotta see us. He's gotta stop."

Turnupseed did not stop. He turned left. At the last second he spotted the tiny car. He spiked the brakes. Dean apparently tried to drive around the Ford and never braked. The Spyder took the full impact of the Ford's blunt grille in the left door. The impact threw Wutherich into the air and clear of the wreck. Dean was crammed against the steering wheel and mauled by the intruding Ford nose. Turnupseed was dazed and bloodied from the impact but essentially unhurt.

A sharp screech of brakes, the hollow report of imploding aluminum, and it was over. James Byron Dean had driven himself into the Valhalla of fallen idols.

Phil Hill was about two hours behind. He came upon the accident site long after the Porsche and the Ford had been hauled to a little Quonset-hut garage in Cholame. Dean's body had been taken to the Kuehl funeral home in Paso Robles while surgeons at the local hospital were deciding whether or not to amputate Wutherich's left leg. Turnupseed told the police he simply had not seen the Porsche, and he was not charged. Hill recalls seeing parked cars and masses of smoking flares and flashing lights arcing in the desert night. After being informed of the crash, he and Pickett drove on to Salinas. Von Neumann and his wife Eleanor had passed through earlier. They had arrived at the moment the Spyder was being hoisted onto the back of a tow truck, and they had asked a policeman if Dean had been hurt. The officer replied, "Yeah, he's been hurt real bad. He's dead." They proceeded to Salinas, unaware that their employee Wutherich had also been in the car.

The coroner's report reveals that Dean suffered a broken neck, coupled with multiple fractures of the jaw and both arms. He clung to life for a few minutes after the crash, then died in the ambulance en route to the hospital in Paso Robles. (One ghoulish footnote: there was not enough blood left to complete a blood-alcohol test, though there was no reason to believe that he had been drinking.)

Within an hour the news was being spread, first by KPRL in Paso Robles, then by word of mouth, and finally by the major media around the world. Considering that his celebrity status could be measured in months, not years, the death of James Dean gained an energy and a mystique unlike any other. Four weeks later, *Rebel Without a Cause* opened in New York. Two weeks after that, *Giant* premiered there. Both pictures were hits, certainly in part because of the pathos surrounding the young star. That was only the beginning. One year following his death, James Dean was listed as the number-one box-office attraction by *Photoplay* magazine and was still the intended recipient of 1,000 fan letters a week. Rumors swirled about his committing suicide after losing Pier Angeli to Vic Damone; about a fortuneteller's prediction of doom; about his surviving the accident and living as a disfigured recluse. All of this was nonsense.

As for Wutherich, he was transported back to Los Angeles by von Neumann, where his leg was saved. However, he never returned to normal. Obsessed with the crash, he continued to work for various West Coast Porsche operations until he became moody and unruly. Finally, the factory returned him to Germany, where he worked with the testing department at Zuffenhausen. On July 28, 1981, he skidded on a wet road in Kupferzell, West Germany, a few miles from his birthplace in Heilbronn, and was killed.

OPPOSITE: This monument
to Dean stands about a mile away
from the crash site in Cholame.
"Death," said Dean, "is the one
inevitable, undeniable truth."

Donald Turnupseed reportedly settled in the Fresno area. No doubt concerned with protecting himself and his family from lunatic avengers, he has refused to discuss the accident publicly.

As for Porsche Spyder 550-0055, this much is known: the wreck was taken to San Luis Obispo, where racing enthusiast Dr. William Eschrich of Burbank removed the undamaged engine and trans axle. The engine was briefly front-mounted in his Lotus 9, without great success, and remains in the doctor's possession. The transaxle is now owned by a collector in Piedmont, California, but the whereabouts of the rest of the car are unknown.

George Barris obtained the wreck shortly after the crash. (Some implied that it was a "jinx" car, citing the case of Dr. Troy McHenry, who used the car's trailing arms on a special in which he crashed fatally at Pomona; but the cause was the failure of a non-Porsche part.) Historians believe that, after some efforts to unkink the frame and bodywork, Barris turned the car over to the Greater Los Angeles Safety Council. It was placed on a nationwide tour, intended to scare young Dean worshipers into driving sensibly.

This gruesome exhibit meandered around the nation for four years, until 1960 when it was put on a train in Florida to be returned to California. The car was stolen somewhere in the Midwest, and it has not been seen since. Some speculate that it was sawed into souvenir bits. Others believe it is in the hands of a private collector. Perhaps it is rotting in some backwater barn. Lee Raskin, a prominent Porsche historian who has extensively researched the subject, wonders whether Dean's family, tiring of the notoriety, had the car stolen and destroyed.

Old Route 466 to Cholame is closed. It lies, weed-pocked and barricaded, to the south of new Highway 46. The intersection has been altered, and there is no sure way of locating the exact point of the crash. On a phone pole is nailed a wind-tattered picture of the "Little Bastard." A mile away, in Cholame (population 65), the scene is essentially unchanged from 1955. Aggie's Restaurant, next to the garage where the Porsche was taken, serves hamburgers and features Hank Williams on the jukebox. A faded poster recounts the life of James Dean. In front of the post office next door, where postmistress Lilly Grant acts as the unofficial curator of the local Dean memorabilia, stands a stainless-steel monument surrounding a tree of heaven. The marker, erected in 1977 by a Tokyo businessman, Seita Ohnishi, who is the proprietor of a Dean souvenir business both here and in Japan, reflects the crash site in its polished surface. Mrs. Grant watches from the door of her tiny post office as dozens of motorists stop each day to visit the memorial. Engraved on its surface is this simple notation: "James Dean, 1931 Feb 8 - 1955 Sep 30 pm 5:59."

Surrounding the monument on a low stone wall is a series of plaques containing sayings by James Dean and by André Gide and others whom Dean is said to have favored. One has been ripped up and carried away. One, which some say was Dean's favorite, is a quotation from *The Little Prince*: "What is essential is invisible to the eye." There is another that seems more appropriate, especially considering that its author was James Byron Dean himself: "Death is the one inevitable, undeniable truth. In it lies the only ultimate nobility for man. Beyond it, through immortality, the only hope."

1993

J550 NKL
Mazda Cars (UK) Ltd.

After David E.

Recent history is the most difficult to judge with an accurate perspective. But no matter what reference points are chosen, it's safe to say that the past 20 years of *Car and Driver* have passed in an era often alarmingly futuristic yet reassuringly familiar. As the U.S. moved from the 1980s into the 1990s, much of the world tried to emulate the country's success with stable democracy. From the fall of the Berlin Wall and the end of the Warsaw Pact to the abolishing of apartheid in South Africa, the final decades of the century pulled tangibly in the direction of political freedom with a distinctly Western tinge.

1986

Accident at the Soviet
Union's Chernobyl
nuclear power plant

>

Space Shuttle
Challenger explodes
on takeoff from
Cape Canaveral

Ferdinand Marcos flees
the Philippines

At the same time, the rise of Islamic fundamentalism countered the notion that the world agreed with America's foreign policy in every instance. In a single year—it could hardly be imagined—the more deadly of two attacks on American soil came from an American citizen intent on punishing the government through its proxy in Oklahoma City.

The Reagan years receding into memory, dramatic rifts in American society opened and reopened. The most popular president since John Kennedy was succeeded by a pale follow-up with none of Reagan's charisma, and though President George H.W. Bush would actually preside over some of the highest ultimate achievements of Reagan's policies—democratic change in Eastern Europe being the most evident of these—the more aloof Bush failed to win the hearts of Americans, and lost reelection to a virtually unknown southern Democrat with a natural gift for political warmth. Under Reagan, national tragedies like the explosion of the space shuttle *Challenger* were soothed by his presence; under Bush, the lack of a telegenic presence and sense for public gestures turned a 92 percent approval rating at the beginning of the Gulf War into an incumbent loss of the presidency. Without Reagan's paternal presence it seemed simpler to let divisions, particularly political divisions, widen instead of heal.

It didn't seem like the beginnings of a golden age of cars, but that's precisely what the industry faced when it stopped reeling from the legislated emissions hangover of the 1970s and near-death experiences of the early 1980s. Within a decade, the power and performance of vehicles like the Chevrolet Corvette, Dodge Viper, and Ford Mustang would rival and surpass that of the fastest muscle cars of the 1960s—with the added bonus of better reliability thanks to Japanese competition and extensive use of computers.

All the recent history of the automobile is framed by the effect of those 1970s laws on cars, on the way they are designed, engineered, built, and driven. By the time the mid-1980s rolled into sight, Detroit had accepted the rules that the federal government had placed on emissions and safety and had begun to adapt. One of the ways the companies were able to adapt was through computerization. As computing power rose and chip sizes and prices shrank, it became ever more common for cars to depend on them for major processes. Modern emissions controls wouldn't be possible without the precise spark timing and fuel metering that an underhood computer can offer—nevermind the luxuries more often seen as norms, like CD players and automatic climate control. Like the world around it, in the midst of the rise of the Internet and the mass popularization of e-mail, the car industry was seeing a technological revolution that was making it cheaper, simpler, and less labor-intensive to design and manufacture cars.

At the same time, the car industry had found some clever ways around the rules written by the government to rein in gas guzzlers. While the Corporate Average Fuel Economy (CAFE) rules had forced passenger cars to downsize and improve, these same draconic rules didn't apply as strictly to trucks. Detroit led the way, but soon all the world's automakers

Oliver North testifies
before Congress about
his involvement in the
Iran-Contra affair

Pop art dandy
Andy Warhol dies

1988

Pan Am Flight
103 explodes over
Scotland; 270 die

Vice President George
H.W. Bush is elected
president over
Michael Dukakis.

realized that building pickups and SUVs and selling them to American customers would give customers what they wanted—roomy, powerful, safe vehicles—with less of an engineering burden. Unwittingly, the government had fueled the rise of the SUV as it tried to cut fuel consumption in cars, and it wouldn't become apparent what had happened until the early 1990s with the rise of popular SUVs like the Ford Explorer, Jeep Grand Cherokee, and Nissan Pathfinder.

Yet in the midst of it all, manufacturers found a way to have fun once more. Chevrolet had finally figured out what a valuable presence the Corvette had in buyer's hearts and wallets, and soon ZR-1 versions were pumping out more than 300 horsepower and shifting the perception of the company. Even more dramatic was the Chrysler Corporation's new Viper sports car, a hunkering piece powered by a brutal 8.0-liter V-10 engine. Driven by Chrysler's product guru Bob Lutz, the Viper and a new generation of cab-forward sedans and coupes would revitalize the perennial number-three company in Detroit and boost the image of Motown in revival.

In Ann Arbor, the magazine adapted to the pulse of its new culture. Instead of the manic 24-hour rhythm of Manhattan, the annual migration of students in and out of the town became the background to the magazine's booming success. In Ann Arbor most of the ten years following the departure of David E. Davis, Jr. were consumed with raising *Car and Driver* magazine to its top spot in circulation among the monthly car magazines.

Until November of 1985, the magazine operated on cruise control. It began a new tradition, the 10 Best competition. But in the conglomerated publishing business of today, even money-makers have little control over their fate. Such was the case in 1985 when CBS purchased *Car and Driver* from Ziff-Davis and,

in short order, David E. Davis, Jr., left the magazine to start his own crosstown rival.

"Six months ago, a dark cloud passed over *Car and Driver*," wrote Don Sherman, newly elevated to the editor's desk. "Within just a few weeks, our editor-publisher, David E. Davis, Jr., four staff members, and three contributing editors were swept from our midst. In the aftermath, Rich Ceppos became executive editor and new faces came into the mix. When David E. announced his intention to leave this publication, CBS responded in less of a panic than he expected. There was no Dan Rather announcement on the *CBS Evening News*, and top executives of the company did not rush to Ann Arbor in the corporate jet. There were, of course, negotiations, but they ended unsuccessfully; and when the dust had settled, David E.'s resignation was accepted."

Sherman gave Davis not only credit for steering the magazine to the top of its profession, but also for having the foresight to put it where it could perform even better. "All of us admire David E. and have appreciated his mighty hand on the controls. Sifting back through the 108 issues and nine years of his administration, it's clear that he made innumerable contributions to the health and well-being of this publication, plus a handful of crucial changes in path. In 1978, David E. packed us up in our One Park Avenue Manhattan refuge and plunked us down on Hogback Road in Ann Arbor, Michigan. Overnight our lives and our magazine changed for the better. Instead of fighting our way tooth and nail through the hostile New York City environment to write about cars, it was a simple matter to walk out of the building, insert a key in an unvandalized car, and drive away like normal citizens," Sherman observed. David E.'s next accomplishment was assembling the current staff of magazine makers. The method to his madness was to recruit pros who know how to have fun at their work. The process is never ending, but we have enjoyed remarkable stability, thanks to the mortar that David E. used to cement our bunch together. And it is a remarkably good team. Whether it's a knowledgeable person to answer a telephone inquiry, a spokesman for the *Today Show*, or a managing editor who knows how to get our product into your hands on time and with proper punctuation, we've got you covered."

As for his tenure, Sherman predicted more of the same. "I know that *Car and Driver* will be just as irreverent, will stir up fresh controversy, and will scout the paths to great automotive adventures in the future. I'm sure of this because *Car and Driver* has a soul that at times seems like a living, breathing entity, and one that hasn't missed a beat or a breath in the 30 years of this magazine's existence."

Sherman's tenure saw *Car and Driver* test everything from a Honda lawnmower to the outrageous Porsche 959 supercar. But despite the high-water marks in performance and writing in the magazine under his leadership, Sherman would leave *Car and Driver* in 1988 as the magazine again changed hands. CBS jettisoned the magazine as well as *Road & Track* as it rapidly deflated its magazine empire—and a new editor would take charge as Diamandis Communications took ownership. Sherman announced his departure in the February 1988 issue briefly and memorably: "I'm sad to report that my editorial license has been suspended. Next month, this page will be devoted to something completely different. Meanwhile, I leave you with the immortal words of Bartles and Jaymes: 'Thank you for your support.'"

The new editor would be William Jeanes, former *Car and Driver* feature editor and advertising executive. A graduate of Millsaps College in Mississippi and a former Navy officer, Jeanes

had been hired by Davis in the 1970s into the advertising realm to write copy for Goodyear and Chevrolet. Then in 1985, Jeanes was among the columnists to join Davis in his new venture, *Automobile* magazine.

In early 1988 Jeanes began his tenure by meeting with former editors in New York: Leon Mandel, Bob Brown (who had left *Car and Driver* in 1975 to become a senior editor at *Sports Illustrated*) and Steve Smith, who had preceded Mandel as editor and was in advertising. With the advice of former *Car and Driver* editors and those still on staff—including Yates, Bedard, Csere, and Ceppos—Jeanes embarked on a six-year tenure in Ann Arbor that saw the new golden age of cars come into its own. There was a new Nissan 300ZX, the Mazda Miata made its debut, as did the Chevy Corvette ZR-1. Under Jeanes *Car and Driver* would rescue a Trabant from East Germany, fling a Mini from the end of a British-built trebuchet, witness the passing of Enzo Ferrari and settle the whole Clarence Thomas/Anita Hill thing by boarding bumper cars and playing a sort of mildly drunken racquetball instead of just flipping a coin. Cars like the Miata and SHO were emerging from an industry battered by new regulations. The fact that enthusiasts could get excited once more about cars as inexpensive as the Miata meant that the experience of being the editor of *Car and Driver* would be even richer.

Maybe that's why Jeanes so looked forward to his return: "My homecoming could not be more joyous for me. I rejoin the *Car and Driver* staff after 12 years, one month, and one day. In the interval, I enjoyed more success than I probably deserved in advertising. Four years ago, I returned to my first love: writing. With the help of a lot of friends and a little hard work, I did well and led a good and rewarding life. Only the best job in the world could have coaxed me away from that. "

1990

Iraq invades Kuwait

>

"The Simpsons"
animates the Fox lineup.
"Seinfeld" begins its
run on NBC

NASA launches the
Hubble Space Telescope

1991

South Africa repeals
apartheid laws

Nirvana releases
"Nevermind " and
ignites the Seattle
grunge music scene

What's so funny about cars? You have to ask? Did you ever stare the front end of a 1958 Buick in the grille? Have you ever considered the function of "cruiserline ventiports"? What about "stabilizer fins," like the ones on a 1959 DeSoto?

Modern cars are funny, too. How about that slow-'em-down wing across the rear end of a Lamborghini Countach? Now that's funny. A Chevette with a bra and ground effects is funny too. Come to think of it, all Chevettes are funny. Funny isn't "Fiat stands for 'Fix It Again, Tony,'" especially if you have to pay Tony on a biweekly basis. Funny isn't "looks like an Oldsmobile sucking a lemon," though it was in the late 1950s. Funny isn't Ralph Nader.

To find out what funny is, we went to the experts— professional comedians. If you don't laugh, they don't eat. Well, maybe they don't eat as well. So laugh already....

Henny Youngman
My wife called me. She said there was water in the carburetor. I asked her where she left the car. She said in the middle of the lake.

Joan Rivers
From her book, *The Life and Hard Times of Heidi Abromowitz* (New York, Delacorte Press, 1984):
She was 24 before she realized you could use a car to drive in and that front seats weren't optional. Her bedroom was decorated l ike the inside of a home. You had to climb over the front seat to get to her bed. She told me that the only way she could get really comfortable was to lie on her back with her feet out the window.

Steven Wright
One time the police stopped me for speeding. They said, "Don't you know the speed limit is 55 miles an hour?" I said, "I know, but I wasn't going to be out that long."

Robert Klein
Here's the ultimate in cheek. Have you heard the commercial where the announcer says in a very righteous way, "Ninety-nine out of 100 people tested preferred the Dodge 600ES to the Mercedes-Benz?" I'd very much like to meet these 99 people. I'd like to give them a Rorschach test in a locked, padded room with a Pinkerton guard armed with a Marlin Perkins tranquilizer dart gun. How do they obtain these test results? They've got to use North Korean police methods and electric cattle prods....
Test administrator: "Which do you prefer, sir? The Dodge or the Mercedes-Benz?"
Testee: "You've got to be kidding! Of course, the Mercedes."
Test administrator: "Prod, please."
Testee: "The Dodge! The Dodge!"
Test administrator: "Chalk up another one for the Dodge...."

Rodney Dangerfield
I have the same trouble with cars as I do with women. On a cold winter morning, when I want her to turn over, she never does.

George Carlin
From the album *Carlin on Campus* (Los Angeles, Eardrum Records, 1984):
Have you ever noticed when you're driving that anyone who's driving slower than you is an idiot? And anyone driving faster than you is a maniac! You say, "Look at this idiot here. Will you look at this idiot? Just creepin' along...Whoa, look at that maniac go!" I mean, it's a wonder we ever get anywhere at all, with all the idiots and maniacs there are.

Steve Martin

I would like to remind you of something the great Maharishi Guru taught me over 15 years ago. The Maharishi was a close personal friend of mine, and I studied with him for 15 long, long, boring years. I didn't really learn that much.... The day I was leaving, the Maharishi said something to me I've never forgotten. Whenever there's a crowd of people like this, I always like to pass it on because I'll bet a day hasn't gone by that I haven't thought of this particular thing.... The Maharishi said, "Always...Wait, it was 'Never'...No..." Always take a litter bag in your car; it doesn't take up much room. If it gets full, you can always toss it out."

Gallagher

Vans are handy. When you need something, you just slam on the brakes and it hits you in the back of the head.

David Steinberg

You know what the definition of "mixed feelings" is? Seeing your mother-in-law drive over a cliff in your new Ferrari. (Actually, although Steinberg related this joke to us, he says it's very old and takes absolutely no credit for it. Or blame.)

Eddie Murphy

My car talks. You leave your lights on, the car say: "Lights are on." I take a girl out, I leave the lights on on purpose, you know. I get out the car, car say: "Lights are on." The girl says, "Did your car say something?" I say, "Yeah, it did." I bought it from my neighborhood, though, man. It got a different rhythm to it. You leave your lights on, the car say: "Say, man, you left your lights on! I said your light is on, man!...What the fuck, you blind and deaf?! Turn off your fuckin' lights!" Got in the car the other day, put the key in, and "Ding... Somebody stole your battery! I say we go get the motherfucker!!"

April 1986
Ford Taurus

A milestone machine that lives up to its billing. Now there can be no more excuses. The Taurus is finally in production, and it either lives up to its promise or it doesn't. Ford revealed this car to the press so early in the development process that it seemed like an old friend long before the production lines were cranked up to full speed. That's the soft spot in the early review process. Mass production, like marriage, always changes something. Some pieces of the giant mechanical jigsaw puzzle suddenly won't fit anymore, because a stamping machine in some far-off factory has gone out of tolerance—or who knows what might happen? Anything can go wonky. For this reason, we tried in our previews of this car to keep a tight rein on hyperbole. That was tough, because cars as promising as the Taurus come along only once in a while. Now that I've finally driven a production Taurus, I'm more than ready to tackle the question we've been posing for the past several months. Is this Ford really a breakthrough, a car with European breeding, German luxury-car moves, a strong dose of value, and all the goodness that can be packed into a cut-rate Audi 5000? The answer is "yes."

April 1986
Yugo GV

It's obvious to me that the Yugo GV is inferior to every other car sold in America. Therefore, the real question is whether its $3,990 base price is low enough to offset its multitude of shortcomings. The easiest way to determine this is to compare the Yugo with a known quantity like the Chevette, which sells for about $5,650. First of all, I think a $1,000 discount is appropriate because of the Yugo's unproven reliability and service network. Another $500 should be subtracted for its high noise level, and the same amount for its limited interior space. Its pronounced torque steer would produce at least $300 worth of irritation over several years of use, as would its imprecise shifting. The brake dive, the crude climate-control system, the used-towel upholstery, the feeble roadholding, and the limited mileage range each qualify for a $200 penalty. On the plus side, the Yugo deserves a $100 bonus for distinctiveness. These calculations suggest that the right price for the Yugo is not $3,990, but only about $2,150. In view of that, if I had only four grand to spend on a car; I'd rather buy a two-year-old Chevette.

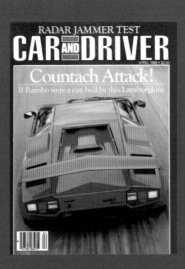

January 1987
Cars That Changed the World

- 1886 Benz Patent Motorwagen: "And the other machines like it, constitute the genesis of the automobile. Before, man had dreamed. Now he could drive."
- 1907 Cadillac: Interchangeable parts made this a breakthrough vehicle and laid claim to the "standard of the world."
- 1914 Model T: The car that drove America and put the country on wheels.
- 1927 LaSalle: Harley Earl gives up his customizing business in Hollywood and pens the first "styled" car for the mass market.
- 1940 Jeep: More than 600,000 were built during World War II by Willys and Ford, and carried the Allies to victory.
- 1949 VW Beetle: The long-lived anti-establishment car sold for 30 years.
- 1958 Edsel: "It gave America a new metaphor for failure." One of the most notorious marketing failures of modern times.
- 1960 Morris Mini-Minor: The origins of today's econobox were penned by Alec Issigonis.
- 1970 Datsun 240Z: Permanently changed the way Americans thought of Japanese cars, with its great looks and snappy performance.
- 1981 Audi Quattro: Made the world "take a long, hard look" at the benefits of four-wheel drive not long before the SUV craze swallowed America.

—*Rich Ceppos*

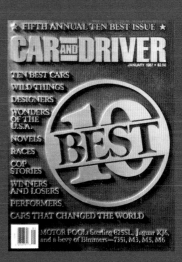

BELOW: A 1949 Beetle.
OPPOSITE: A Ford Model T.

July 1987
One Very Close Call

By Csaba Csere

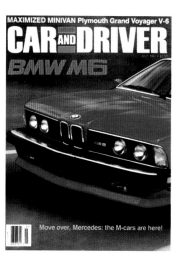

Until recently I believed that I was virtually indestructible when behind the wheel of a car. Not that I suffered from some kind of superman complex: I didn't feel the same way about motorcycling, scuba diving, rock climbing, or any number of other activities. But deep in my soul, I knew that my driving skills were good enough to get me out of any threatening situation.

232

That rosy delusion was shattered last December 4 when my wife, Mary, and I were leaving for New York in *Car and Driver*'s long-term Audi 5000. It was snowing lightly, but there was no accumulation, and in the 30-minute drive from our home to downtown Detroit we had not encountered so much as a hint of icy or otherwise slippery pavement. Traffic was flowing at normal speeds. Since we weren't in any rush, I was matching its pace.

On the two-lane bypass to Canada, we were traveling at about 45 mph when we crested a small hill and saw a tractor-trailer stopped in our lane a good 200 yards ahead. I eased on the brakes, but nothing happened. I verified that my foot was on the brake pedal, and still nothing happened. I declutched and nothing happened. I pressed for all I was worth and nothing happened. What was worse, there was nowhere to go. The right lane was stopped up with cars working their way around the truck, and the narrow left shoulder was bordered by a concrete divider. I was doing everything I could do, but we just kept on gliding toward the truck as if on a cushion of air. In fact, we were on a sheet of ice. The Audi's anti-lock brakes kept us from skidding sideways, but not even the miracle of electronics can create traction where none exists.

We hit the back of the semitrailer dead-on at about

40 mph. Despite being fully belted in, I broke my nose when my face struck the steering wheel. Mary wasn't so fortunate. Although she didn't hit anything inside the car, the restraining forces produced by her shoulder belt crushed one of her vertebrae, collapsed one of her lungs, and caused a few minor bone fractures as well. Had we not been wearing seatbelts, neither of us would have stood a chance.

My recovery was quick and easy, but Mary's is taking some time. So far she has endured the installation of two stainless-steel rods in her back and three and a half months in a body cast. She faces six more months in a back brace and another operation to remove the rods. She isn't expected to be back to normal—or virtually normal—until next spring. Even so, she's lucky. She came close to being paralyzed.

Not a day has gone by since the accident without my thinking about what I might have done differently. Even in hindsight, though, it's clear that hitting the truck sideways or in one corner would probably have been fatal. Changing lanes and rear-ending one of the cars to our right would probably have resulted in less serious injuries, but such a move would have required suppressing my instinct to avoid hitting solid objects.

It would have hurt other people, too. Still, when I think about what Mary has been through, I wish I had taken that course.

I also wish that my driving comeuppance had happened when I was alone, and at a time when my driving made me more deserving of it. There have certainly been plenty of times when I have tempted fate at the wheel. There will be fewer such times in the future. If I can almost kill my wife when driving carefully and conservatively on the freeway, in the best car in the world for the conditions, then a serious car accident can happen to me, or anybody, at any time.

That somber spirit of caution is always with me now when I drive. I don't mean to say that I've given up fast cars and hard driving. I enjoy them too much to forsake them. But I appreciate the joys of driving now in a fashion more in keeping with my newly discovered mortality. I'm convinced that extra caution could not have prevented our accident, but it

Ten Best Road Signs

• Ah, the call of the open road: adventure, danger, excitement, interesting reading . . . that is, if you're careful never to take a road sign for granted. Wit, charm, humor, irony, good ol' country wisdom, empty-headed buffoonery—they're all there in foot-high letters for everyone on wheels to see.

You readers didn't miss a one. Whittling your rich offering of entertaining roadside notices down to just ten proved impossible: we've thrown in a bonus photo at no extra cost. Although Escondido, California, hasn't really named two avenues in our honor, we thank Mr. Bandosz for his attempt to put *C/D* permanently on the map.

Our congratulations to the winners, but those of you whose photos missed the cut shouldn't give up hope. We received so many sensational entries that we're contemplating an all-road-sign special issue. After all, a sign is a terrible thing to waste.
—*Rich Ceppos*

R. Abner Perney, Salina, Kansas

Jim Nephew, Coralville, Iowa

Andy Opsal, Thousand Oaks, California

Paul E. Mossberg, West Orange, New Jersey

Wayne Steele, Lower Hutt, New Zealand

Phillip Powell, Atlanta, Georgia

Warren Y. Smith, Kingsport, Tennessee

Robert E. Poliachik, Damascus, Maryland

Hudson Bandosz, Escondido, California

Russell Iannuzzelli, Silver Spring, Maryland

Sandi Shannon, Visalia, California

234

January 1988
10 Best Quotations

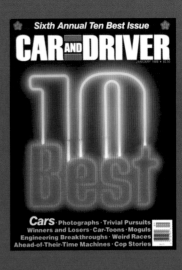

Sixth Annual Ten Best Issue

CAR AND DRIVER

JANUARY 1988

10 Best

Cars · Photographs · Trivial Pursuits
Winners and Losers · Car-Toons · Moguls
Engineering Breakthroughs · Weird Races
Ahead-of-Their-Time Machines · Cop Stories

"History is more or less bunk. The only history that is worth a tinker's damn is the history we make today."
—*Henry Ford I*

"It isn't that we build such bad cars, it's that they're such bad customers."
—*Charles F. Kettering, Director of Research at General Motors from 1920 to 1947*

"I build my cars to go, not to stop."
—*Attributed to Ettore Bugatti*

"General Motors is not in the business of making cars; it's in the business of making money."
—*Alfred P. Sloan, Jr., President of General Motors, then Chairman, 1923 to 1956*

"What's good for General Motors is good for the country."
—*Commonly attributed to Charles Wilson, President of General Motors from 1941 to 1953. However, what "Engine Charlie" really said was rather different. In 1953, in hearings before the Senate committee that ultimately approved his nomination as Secretary of Defense, Wilson was asked how he would deal with a decision that forced him to choose between the interests of the U.S. and those of General Motors. He replied: "I cannot conceive of one because for years I thought that what was good for our country was good for General Motors, and vice versa."*

"Those of us who move will die. Those who don't are already dead."
—*Jean Behra, Grand Prix ace of the 1950s.*

"If you're under control, you're not driving hard enough."
—*Parnelli Jones*

"Never complain, never explain."
—*Henry Ford II, when caught in compromising circumstances on an L.A. freeway.*

"If you can find a better car, buy it."
—*Lee Iacocca*

"Wow, this stuff is as good as gold!"
—*John DeLorean, on the closed-circuit FBI-TV network.*

Henry Ford I

April 1988
Secrets of My Success

By Brock Yates

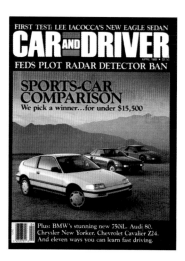

As I write these words, it is more than likely that several dozen other mildly desperate men scattered around the nation are engaged in similar endeavors. Being automotive journalists of one sort or another, and facing the obligation to write monthly columns such as this, they sit hunched over their typewriters and word processors, each struggling to think an original thought.

After all, some of these guys—just like me—have been regularly scratching out opinions, anecdotes, pontifications, and recollections about cars for more than two decades. The rub is that much of the subject matter has been steadily putrefying for years, ever since the late, great Uncle Tom McCahill and Ken Purdy packed it in. In fact, our sort has been picking at the bones of automotive lore ever since the big-time car books—*Car and Driver, Road & Track, Motor Trend* and *Hot Rod*—burst upon the scene in the 1940s and 1950s and began chewing up columns like a giant Waring blender, leaving little unsaid or unrecorded. The result is that much of what is published on the subject today is nothing more than artful repackagings of that which has already been said, ad nauseam.

Being a veteran at this sleight of hand, I offer herewith, as a public service, a short primer on writing a car column. I hope that it will not only prove helpful to the novitiates of this profession but also serve to streamline the reading habits of the enthusiast, who will henceforth recognize instantly when a favorite columnist is about to embark on yet another trip down a well-traveled road.

It has been said that in the history of the novel there have been but seven basic plots, and I have lately reached a similar conclusion regarding the automotive column. After extensive research and rumination I have categorized the genre according to seven basic themes that can be employed over and over, like the names of Italian volcanoes and Middle Eastern monetary units in crossword puzzles, or cliché-ridden graphics in automotive TV commercials. They are, in order of preference and general overuse, as follows:

The Car-Love Column: When the well runs dry, the practiced columnist can always dredge up some warm and cozy words about an ancient crock that passed through his life at one time or another. This can be a rusted pickup truck (preferably from Texas or Oklahoma, where the pickup religion is a kind of motorized Islam), or Pop's old Buick, or one's first hot rod, or the classic sedan in the backyard that was sold for a pittance, or, but only if the desperation is overwhelming, a simple listing of all the cars one has owned in one's lifetime, which can be nearly as riveting as the recital of one's laundry list. Perhaps the most successful purveyor of this theme is a columnist for a hard-core enthusiast's journal who has for years, week in and week out, chronicled his ownership of a Lotus Elite in Alaska.

The How-Was-It-Out-There? Column: It is crucial to the psyche of any automotive journalist that he be convinced of his utter virtuosity behind the wheel. It is but a trick of the Fates, in fact, that he is not commonly mentioned in the same breath

November 1988
Enzo Ferrari 1898–1988

Enzo Ferrari died on Sunday, August 14, 1988. He died at his home in Maranello, Italy. The following day, he was buried nearby, outside Modena. Ferrari was 90. For months, his impending death of kidney disease had been a sad topic among lovers of spirited automobiles throughout Italy and the world. In the 41 years since Ferrari's cars began racing, the red machines have propelled seven Formula 1 piloti—Alberto Ascari, Juan Manuel Fangio, Mike Hawthorn, Phil Hill, John Surtees, Niki Lauda, and Jody Scheckter—to nine World Driving Championships, with Ascari and Lauda winning two apiece. Between the championship's inception in 1950 and Ferrari's death, his cars won 93 of the 434 Grands Prix in which they competed. The F1 team won eight Worlds Constructors' Championships. Between 1953 and 1967, 11 World Championship of Makes sports-car titles went home with Ferrari. The howling cars from Maranello finished first in the 24 Hours of Le Mans on nine occasions. Racing marked the highest and most of the lowest points of Ferrari's life. Except for the death of his son, Dino, Ferrari suffered the most when the drivers of his cars died

in crashes. Poorly educated but bright and witty, the former journalist wrote a series of autobiographies, one title *My Terrible Joys*, was about the emotions he felt in building magnificent machines in which men won, lost, or died. Ferrari could be mean and conniving, pitting his minions against each another to produce an advantage for his cars. But in doing so, he made great things happen. For that we will remember him.

—*Larry Griffin*

with Mario Andretti and Alain Prost. The skilled columnist, therefore, is always prepared to whack out a potboiler about high adventure on the racetrack. Such a column generally involves low-rent competition, as in Showroom Stock racing, though on occasion a higher form of involvement is recounted in the first person—along with a lengthy, self-serving explanation of why the point of view is situated at the back of the pack.

The Epic-Journey Column: The subject-parched auto scribe can always report on a trip. Coast-to-coast jaunts are forever green, laced as they are with insights from gas-station attendants, short-order waitresses, truckers, et al. A junket to Europe as the guest of an automaker can provide even more grist, giving the journalist an excuse to exhibit his epicurean tastes for vintage wine and Continental cuisine, as well as his well-traveled knowledge of charming inns and trattorias. It is difficult to comprehend the output of verbiage, much less the input of rich food and drink, that has resulted from such enterprising investigative legwork.

The Soapbox Column: Every automotive columnist has a repertoire of prejudices that, when his CRT goes blank, he can haul out and pass off as serious editorializing. My personal favorites are the bozos who run our domestic automobile business, the Washington bureaucrats, and the patent idiocy of speed-limit enforcement. Constant readers know my moves, just as good hitters know what kind of pitch the veteran reliever will toss in a tight situation.

The Nutball-Gadgets-and-Technological-Secrets Column: In the course of his travels the average automotive-journalist columnist encounters legions of promoters, inventors, mad scientists, workshop geniuses, visionaries, discredited auto moguls, malcontents, and outright charlatans, all huckstering weird devices intended to revolutionize the world of cars. Some of these gadgets are legitimate; most are worthless. Either way, they are column fodder, especially for the writer who deals in the more technical aspects of the subject. Here's a tip for the reader: if a column is set in the hinterlands of New Jersey or Orange County, you can bet you're about to be introduced to an eccentric but lovable engineer who is working in his backyard shop on a tiny turbo kit that plugs into the cigarette lighter.

The Unforgettable-Character Column: This can be a variation of the Car-Love Column (lovable old cars often involve lovable old characters) or the Nutball-Gadgets Column (which involve nutball people as well as nutball devices). Better yet, if the columnist writes about a celebrity—Lee Iacocca, Paul Newman, and John Z. DeLorean are some of the regulars—readers can be bludgeoned with the word that the writer hangs out with folks who count. Folks who otherwise wouldn't go near him. Or her.

The List Column: Magic stuff, the list. One can tote up the best and the worst, the famous and the infamous, the hated and the loved, and the ins and the outs again and again, because nobody ever tires of reading lists. Such efforts are all but inevitable at the end of the year, when recent triumphs and tragedies in the car biz can be categorized.

Come to think of it, one could even write a car column listing the seven basic themes of car columns. Which in turn just might inspire me next month to write about this beat-up Wartburg sedan that I used to race all over the country, much to the dismay of the loons and dimbulbs of the safety establishment, who got particularly peevish when I accidentally squashed this wonderful old inventor who wore his sneakers on the wrong feet....

November 1988
Top-Speed Blowout

Most people will tell you that if one of your tires blows out at high speed, you're doomed. The car will go out of control and either wad itself into a ball or scatter into a million pieces. Either way, both it and you will end up in final resting places. Before participating in the *Sport Auto* high-speed test, I was one of those people. Fortunately, I'm living proof that a high-speed blowout doesn't always mean certain disaster. All of the top speeds reported in this story were measured on the six-lane Autobahn 5, just north of Karlsruhe, West Germany. A *Sport Auto* driver and I tested the Callaway Corvette at 4 a.m. on a Sunday morning to avoid interference from traffic, especially trucks, which need a special permit for Sunday autobahn appearances. Stefan Roser was in the Callaway's driver's seat. Roser is the head tester at *Sport Auto*, a part-time racer, and a damn good driver. He knew this stretch of unlimited-speed autobahn well, so he drove. Securely belted into the right seat, I manned a stopwatch to measure our progress past the kilometer posts. Despite a surprising amount of traffic, Stefan had to back out of full throttle only once

during our ten-mile southbound run. The Callaway wasn't wonderfully stable at top speed, but it stayed in its lane as the kilometer posts flew by less than 12 seconds apart. That translated into more than 190 mph, with the headlights up. We turned around for our return trip (to compensate for any wind) and blasted off again. After about five flat-out miles—with the speedometer indicating 195 mph—the car suddenly began to vibrate heavily. I looked over at Stefan, and he said just one word: "Tire." The left front tire had blown apart, and we were going fast enough to fly. To its eternal credit, the Corvette plowed straight on, drifting only slightly to the left. Stefan eased off the gas and concentrated on keeping the Callaway from getting sideways. He didn't touch the brakes; if he had, he might have upset the car's stability. It seemed as if I could have written a book in the time it took the car to slow to 130 mph. At that point, Stefan gingerly started applying the brakes. By 80 mph we seemed to be going so slowly that I was ready to get out and walk. As we slowed further, Stefan pulled over onto the right shoulder and brought us to a dignified stop. We stepped out. The car rested on its left front wheel. The front spoiler had been ground away, and some of the bodywork had been destroyed by the disintegrating tire. The battery was dangling by its cables in a pool of acid. The only rubber left on the wheel was an inch-wide strip on the inside bead. We later found the carcass in one large piece about a mile back down the autobahn. The rear tires were fine, but the right front tire showed signs of stress on its inner rib. Happily, the Corvette was in one piece. And so were we. Should you ever experience a blowout at speed, do what Stefan Roser did. Don't panic. Ease off the gas and don't even think about braking. Your only priority is to keep the car going in a straight line. As your speed dissipates and you develop a feel for the car's stability you can try braking very gently, but be ready to back off if the car pulls to one side. Thanks in part to Stefan's expert driving, I survived an ultra-high-speed blowout. But I don't ever want to risk the odds again.

—Csaba Csere

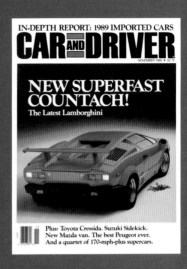

239

March 1989
Mazda MX-5 Miata

If you were reading this magazine 30 years ago, you were reading *Sports Cars Illustrated*; that was our name then, a clear reflection of the motoring enthusiasms of the day. Sports cars were more than just two-seaters. They were a way of life, with social protocol, weekend competitions, heroic tales of roadside repair, and animated nattering about the marque you owned and the one you hoped to own next—just as soon as you got the money together. Sports cars were much more than cars; they were the nucleus of a movement, a reason to get out of bed on Saturday morning. If the *Sports Cars Illustrated* reader of that time could have described his dream car—the absolute best thing he could imagine—it would have been a lot like the Mazda MX-5 Miata. But it wouldn't have been as perfect as the Mazda: no one would have dared dream for a two-seater so deft in its execution, so lacking in sports-car nuisances. There's a reason why this discussion is starting with a 1959 viewpoint. It's because the Miata is very much a traditional sports car. It doesn't issue forth as a styling statement from some overwrought design department, as the Fiero did. It's not

a marriage of mechanical convenience either, whereby some econobox front-drive powertrain is stuffed behind the seats to make—wowee!—a mid-engined car; Fiero-MR2-X1/9 thinking is conspicuous by its absence in the Miata. Instead, Mazda went back to the roots of the movement, back to the spirit that found magic in MG, Triumph, Austin-Healey, Lotus, Jaguar, and Alfa-Romeo. Within the company, from the moment of conception until the present, the Miata project was always referred to as "the lightweight sports car." That description was an ever-present reminder of the mission: make it small, make it simple, make it light, and make it feel good to humans. A brisk drive on Mazda's Miyoshi proving grounds in a pre-production Miata says, "Mission accomplished, Sir." This car is completely unexpected, given today's enthusiasm for sporting two-plus-two coupes instead of real sports cars. Unexpected, but delightful. You don't even need authentic memories of traditional sports cars to enjoy this piece. But if you already have a few, the Miata will remind you just how far modern carmaking has progressed.

Top speed: 116 mph (manuf. ratings)
116 hp, 100 lb-ft of torque
Price: $13,000 (est.)

—*Patrick Bedard*

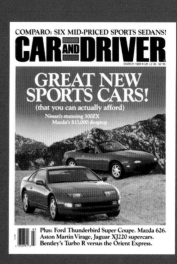

BOTTOM, RIGHT: The three drunkateers (left to right), Art St. Antoine, Cliff Weathers and Rich Ceppos.

May 1989
D.W.I.

By Csaba Csere

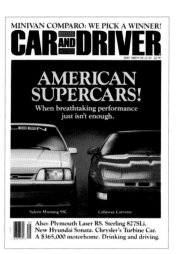

We learn that it's possible to drink and drive. But it's still the worst idea we can think of.

Rich Ceppos: They tell me I had a great time at the *Car and Driver* drink-a-thon, but I don't remember. I don't recall slapping everyone high-fives, or falling down, or breaking my eyeglasses, or telling Deputy Giffin to perform foul acts on himself, or wrestling with Art, or kicking Nicholas in the chin (don't ask). What a guy! What a party! What a scientific investigation!

Make no mistake, this was a trying experience for me. I am not Morgo the Party Animal. I do not get loaded and bite the heads off of chickens. I have been failing-down drunk a few times in my life, and I'll admit to having driven home on a couple of occasions when I shouldn't have. But these days I back off at the first sign of a buzz. I dreaded the whole event, paranoid that the alcohol devil would unshackle some monster locked deep in my psyche. I feared I would say things that would make my coworkers hate me and my boss hand me a pink slip.

I'm pleased to report that none of that happened. But I sure got drunk. After my first round—a double vodka with a splash of OJ, yech!—I was as high as I ever get at a dinner party. But Csaba wouldn't let me go home. I was as amazed as anyone that I could still stand up—let alone drive a car—after three rounds of doubles. Or was that four rounds? Somewhere in there Deputy Giffin pronounced me legally drunk.

Several things strike me about imbibing and driving. I had no trouble passing our tests until my blood alcohol level was astronomical. That I could navigate the test courses at all suggests something badly amiss with our tests. Apparently, focusing one's concentration for a few seconds is still possible when drunk, especially when the task is simple.

And simple it was. Compared with the complexity of driving in the real world, our proving-grounds tests were a day at the beach. On the road you must make split-second decisions—correct decisions—every mile. At the proving grounds, my mind was free of such weighty responsibilities. Nor did I need to rely on my ability to take in the big picture. In fact, I barely needed to look where I was going. I remember arrowing down the approach to the lane change seeing six traffic signals instead of three: I decided I'd simply swerve toward the pair of lights that stayed green. Hey, no sweat! Barkeep, another round! Then I drove off the track.

For me, the most illuminating insights came the evening following the test. We had quit drinking by 4:00 p.m., and I was delivered home by dinnertime. I don't know what my blood alcohol level was at that point, but compared with where it had been I felt like I had both feet on the ground again. I knew what was going on around me. I was sobering up. Or so I thought. My wife reports all sorts of erratic behavior. I had a hard time with simple motor skills, like sliding a slice of pizza out of the box without leaving the cheese behind. I remember watching TV that evening holding one eye closed so I wouldn't see double.

These harmless antics were anything but. I was still wasted, but my judgment of my own condition was so clouded I might have attempted to drive. Now that would have been deathly funny.

That false sense of reassuming control is the one insidious thing I didn't expect. Your judgment seems to come back. You start to feel better. You're confident that you're sober enough to get behind the wheel. Then you drive off the road—only you're not at the Chrysler proving grounds, you're in someone's front yard. Or into another car. Head-on. Friends, I urge you to beware.

243

Art St. Antoine: I have been known to enjoy a drink on occasion. But never having had my inebriation measured with a breath tester or any other such device, I didn't have any idea how much alcohol it took to become "legally drunk."

I therefore embarked on our test with some apprehension. I'd heard that the last time the magazine conducted this experiment, two of the three volunteer drunkards couldn't even reach 0.10 BAL—Michigan's legal limit. Could I reach the limit? My God, I wondered, how drunk is 0.10? I thought I'd been plenty drunk before, but maybe I was only racking up a 0.06 or a 0.08? Maybe to get to 0.10 you had to drink ten Jack Daniels in an hour and then knock back a couple of beers and then eat a slice or two of brandy cake. Maybe at 0.10 you'd be staggering around drooling and yelling like a lunatic. Maybe this whole drunk-test idea was going to be a real nightmare.

I needn't have worried. Judging by the amount of drinks it took to get me to 0.10, I've been over the limit on a number of occasions. Sometimes way over.

Anyone who drinks has probably been over the limit many times. And that's the scary part.

Ten minutes after my first two shots of JD, which I imbibed at 12:20 p.m., my notebook read: "Feeling a bit warm. Where the hell is the ice?"

Ten minutes after that, I was very conscious of having had something to drink. "I can feel my mind getting a bit cloudy, losing some sharpness," I wrote.

About 30 minutes later, after my second round of drinks, I noted that "My lip muscles are getting numb—it's harder to speak crisply." I had also now shifted into the party mood. I was no longer concerned about reaching the dreaded 0.10 figure; in fact, I was beginning to enjoy myself. My notes reflect that

mood change. At 1:49 p.m., I wrote, "I'm losing my buzz. We need to pick up the pace here." I also remember laughing a lot.

By 3:33 p.m., having consumed a good portion of my bottle of Jack Daniels, I was undeniably drunk. I knew it, and the breath tester proved it. By the end of the test I pegged the meter at 0.17 BAL—almost twice the legal limit in Michigan.

Despite my condition I didn't do too badly on the test courses. But the results don't tell the whole story. I remember being very aware of the fact that I was being scrutinized at every turn. I was determined to do well, and so I concentrated on not making mistakes. On a short test course that I had run many times, that wasn't too difficult.

What concerns me more was how I felt as I neared and then busted through the legal limit. I lost my ability to be rational and make sound judgments. I became pushy, even belligerent. And I became careless, having much too good of a time without any concern about the consequences. At one point I jumped into a nearby car and started doing full-power doughnuts on the skidpad.

On the test track, that was nothing more than an amusing stunt. But I shudder to think what would have happened if I'd been let loose on a public road.

Cliff Weathers: When I was in college, my friends and I thought beer was food. There were parties to go to almost every night and we got woolly and drank liquid bread for supper. I was even stupid enough to drive when my soberness was questionable. Most other drunks were all over the road, but I was harmless, I reasoned, obeying the limit and staying within the lines. I believed that until a friend heatedly pointed out otherwise. One night she walked the last mile home in a high-crime area rather than ride with me. I changed my ways soon after.

244

Since then, I've wondered just how bad my driving was when I imbibed. That's why I readily volunteered to be a guinea pig for the sake of science.

Let me first explain that my driving skills aren't nearly what Art's or Rich's are. I'm no pro, just Joe Commuter. I'm also the type of drinker who often tries (and succeeds) to act semi-sober after six or seven drinks. Even during the test, people were telling me, "You sure don't act drunk. You seem perfectly sober."

Their comments scared me. I wondered how many bartenders or party hosts would be able to spot someone in my condition. Not many, I figured.

After two drinks I noticed only a mild euphoria. Other than missing one of the lane changes, I didn't believe the alcohol influenced my driving.

At 2:22 p.m., after my fourth drink and third time behind the wheel, I jotted in my notes that I was getting more aggressive. I was trying to attack the autocross. Avoiding the cones was suddenly second priority to having a good time. I noted that I drove okay only because I had become accustomed to the autocross, and this offset my increasing inebriation.

At 3:00 p.m., after six drinks, I was more concerned that no one thought of getting me a lime for my gin than I was about the test. I started having doubts about my sobriety, and I couldn't stop laughing at Rich and his high-fives and other drunken antics.

Behind the wheel, I once again tried to steam through the autocross. For some odd reason, I was able to concentrate well on the course. I was satisfied with my runs, but I think luck got me through.

After eight drinks someone again told me that I didn't seem drunk. I laughed because, at that point, neither Rich nor I could

read an analog watch. I was supposed to write something about my latest ordeal at the wheel, but it was a blur. I wasn't even sure if I drove. Someone told me I did. I had become quite confused.

At 4:45 p.m. I finished my last driving segment. I remembered this one, but couldn't find my notebook. I'm surprised I even finished the autocross. My reflexes were poor, and I started to get tunnel vision. I trashed a lot of cones and wanted to quit before I went through the course a second time.

I'm told that when I finished I finally blew over 0.10 into the breath tester. I know that I was drunk long before.

In my last notebook entries I remark that the course was not a good gauge of how I drove while intoxicated. The course became easy because it was static—no surprises like cars cutting me off or pedestrians jaywalking in my path. There was none of the spontaneity of everyday driving. In real-world conditions I would have shown a marked drop in driving skills earlier on. Of that I'm certain.

Then I thought about my college party-animal days and a chill went through me. You know, I could've easily killed someone out there.

More than ever, we're convinced that drinking and driving definitely don't mix. If you have more than one drink per hour and a half prior to driving, your abilities behind the wheel will be impaired. If you drink enough to raise your BAL over 0.05, you are definitely a hazard to yourself and to everyone else on the road. And if you should be so foolish as to drive with a BAL of 0.10 or more, don't delude yourself into thinking that you've fallen victim to a harsh and capricious law if the police arrest you. Be thankful that you're still alive. And clean up your act. The next time you might not be so lucky.

Passages

By William Jeanes

Once upon a time a small boy, left to the loneliness of a fatherless home, found that he loved cars. Long before he would drive a real car, he had a white pedal car, decked out in fire-chief livery, with a bell that he could ring by pulling a string. The string was perpetually broken, but that didn't take away the fun.

On a December evening in 1941, the boy saw worried faces gathered around his grandparents' Stewart-Warner console radio. Instead of smiling at the ether-borne antics of Jack Benny and Fred Allen, they listened as a newsman brought news of Pearl Harbor. The boy sat on the floor and played with a red metal toy car, a replica of a Cord convertible. The Cord Car, as the toy was known, had once gone to faraway Fort Oglethorpe, Georgia, to keep the boy entertained as his aunt gave birth to his first cousin. Aunt and Uncle, he a doctor in the army, had taken the new cousin to Honolulu, which explained the worry.

The war came and the boy's mother went to work in Chattanooga, more than 200 miles to the east. There a courtship began, one that would result in the boy having a man to teach him, by word and example, how to cope with a world that daily grew more complex and confusing.

Newly graduated from Fort Benning, this infantry second lieutenant brought no little excitement into the boy's small-town life. The excitement included rides in the lieutenant's black 1941 Ford two-door sedan. The Ford had a rough, rumbly sound that the boy liked to hear.

All in the family, including the Ford, survived the war. The lieutenant, now a veteran of General MacArthur's staff, returned from the Philippines and Japan laden with unbearably fascinating swords, pistols, and picture books. The marriage in 1945 changed the boy's surroundings forever, and for the better. In the afternoons, after school, he would wait at his grandparents' house on Sixth Street for his new father to pick him up and begin the 22-mile drive home to Pickwick Dam, Tennessee. With minimal pleading, the boy would be allowed to sit on his father's lap and steer the Ford along the two-lane. This was fun.

As in so many postwar American homes, the advent of a new car could set the neighborhood talking for a week. The new family's first new car, a 1948 Chevrolet Styleline four-door, was not of the stuff that caused visions of sugarplums. But it served a purpose.

Again resident in the town of Corinth, Mississippi, in a renovated house that had a long driveway, the boy's father taught him to use the Chevy's clutch and column-mount gearshift, and let him spend unsupervised hours backing the car up and down the driveway.

"If William ran up one mile doing that, he ran up a thousand," the father would say years later. He took pride in having taught well the art of backing a car without turning your head, using only the road ahead as reference.

In 1949, when the boy was 11, the former lieutenant took a job that was to last for the next 40 years. This brought with it a move to the state capital, where the boy began the seventh grade in a strange school, among strangers. The family's car of record became a black 1950 Packard sedan. It would be followed by other Packards and joined by a used 1946 Ford two-door sedan.

On the gravel streets and roads of what would now be called exurbia but what the boy's new friends called the boondocks, he learned to drive properly in the Ford. Driving an automobile came to be second nature, up to and including learning lessons in oversteer that only a gravel road can teach. He was by now 13.

By 14, the boy was allowed to drive the two miles to the end of the bus route and pick up Sarah, the girl who kept house for his parents.

At 14 and a half, in the Mississippi of 1953, if one's parents would abet, a boy could have a learner's permit that legalized his appearance on public roads when accompanied by an adult. The boy's father, who had sanctioned previous, illegal, unaccompanied trips, thought the permit a fine idea, as did the boy. The mother wasn't so sure, but reason prevailed. He got the permit and, a half-year later, his license.

As the boy grew up, his father's business provided trucks to learn about, from fast, clappy pickups to thundering airhorned diesel tractor-trailer rigs. In these same years, unaccountably, the boy's father and mother developed a fondness for convertibles. Two Pontiacs, a red one and later a red-and-black one, played roles in the boy's high school and college years.

A time came when the boy became a young man and joined the navy. On a chill, gray February afternoon in 1960, the ex-lieutenant and the ensign-to-be shook hands on the steps of the antebellum farmhouse that now served as home. Neither cried, but the miss was a narrow one.

During and after the navy came the sports cars. And any number of foreign cars—as they were called—that the boy's father had never liked and was determined never to like. And never did.

The convertible attraction, however, resurfaced in 1990. In the middle of his 75th year, the father bought a Cadillac Allante. "It's for your mother," he told his son. The son wasn't altogether sure. He also questioned whether his father would find the suspension too stiff. As it turned out, he didn't; he loved it. This was the subject of the last conversation between father and son about cars.

Late in his 75th year, Harrell Freeman Jeanes died suddenly and unexpectedly, leaving a wife, a sister, two sons, and a wealth of friends. The elder of the two sons would not have the good fortune to be where he is had his father not said "yes" when he begged to be allowed to steer a 1941 Ford.

March 1992
Dodge Viper RT/10

The windows don't roll up. Matter of fact, there are no windows. Or outside door handles. Not much protection against the weather, either—the "top" is simply a section of canvas that stretches from the windshield header to the "sport bar." There is no hard top. But what there is in this Dodge Viper RT/10 is a ten-cylinder, 488-cubic-inch powerplant producing 400 horse-power and a *Car and Driver*-measured 13.2-second quarter-mile time that makes it quicker than the altogether outrageous Chevrolet Corvette ZR-1. And with the wind ripping new configurations in your eyebrows and the engine in full honk, you're not going to care one whit about absent windows or door handles. Because this Viper is one of the most exciting rides since Ben Hur discovered the chariot.

> Top speed: 159 mph
> 0-60 4.6 seconds
> 400 hp, 450 lb-ft of torque
> Price: $54,640 (est.)

—Kevin Smith

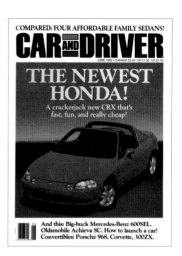

June 1992

The Many Faces of Peter Gregg

By Ed Hinton

His mother was on her way home for his seventh birthday party when she decided to kill herself. She stepped in front of a subway train. Some birthday, for a rich little boy in Manhattan in 1947. Some life, from there to Mickler's Landing in 1980. Some character, even today, the ripples from Peter Gregg's existence are still moving.

Mickler's Landing is an unmarked place. You have to ask. There is no landing. Just an acutely lonely gap in the seaside opulence of Ponte Vedra Beach, south of Jacksonville. Just a quarter-mile of dunes, some two stories high, their sea oats waving sadly. Among the dunes run little ravines strewn with old campfire beds and half-buried blankets—the leavings of the assignations of youth.

Up the beach, a boy and girl in their late teens are walking, the girl taller than the boy. When they see someone in the dunes, their steps quicken, as if to pass on by.

"Excuse me," you call. "Is this the place they call Mickler's Landing?"

"Mickler's Cutoff, the surfers call it now," says the boy, approaching. To his face comes a little smile of amusement as he looks the fortyish intruder over. "Why? You meetin' somebody here, man?"

"No," you say. "Just looking around. "This is where Peter Gregg killed himself. You ever hear of Peter Gregg?"

"Peter Gregg? Was he a surfer?" "No," you say, somehow amused.

"One thing he wasn't was a surfer."

Indifferent, the boy and girl break into a jog toward old Highway A1A, leaving you alone in the windswept sea oats, and you can almost sense Peter Gregg himself answering the kid:

"A surfer? What an idiotic notion."

"What skill, wit, wealth, or daring is required of a surfer? Surfers are a pestilence on this beach. Generally, they are neither wealthy nor brilliant and therefore not worthwhile. How dare anyone speculate, even wildly, that I would deteriorate to such a state?"

That is how he might have reacted in one mood, in the mode his first wife, Jennifer, calls simply, "the bad Peter." But on the day he died, a dozen years ago among these dunes, cradling a brand-new .38 revolver that he barely knew how to load and fire, "the good Peter" in tragic ebb might have envied the surfers their simple sport and uncomplicated copulation. Yet even his envy would have been condescending, with a sort of "ignorance is bliss" attitude toward "the poor" a class that, to Peter Gregg, included everyone who was not rich.

He was the kind of man whose day could dawn in Daytona, darken in New York, and dawn again in Paris. He once made *Cosmopolitan*'s most eligible bachelor list, but at a dear price: he'd managed to screw himself—literally and figuratively—out of a lovely marriage to Jennifer, an heiress to the Johnson & Johnson fortune, and he'd panicked when she ran out of patience. For most of his life he was alternately bored and obsessed, depressed and euphoric.

251

He was a manic depressive who once spent an afternoon arranging his lithium pills in intricate geometric patterns on his desk, then turned to his business right hand Bob Snodgrass, and said, "I'm stronger than any drug," and with an arm swept all the pills into a wastebasket. He was a Harvard graduate (English literature), a former naval intelligence officer, a millionaire on his own, something of an intellectual, thoroughly a snob, a patron of the arts, a superb organizer, a tyrant, and an intriguing conversationalist with a switchblade tongue.

But he was best known as a racing driver, which was how he wanted it. In his time, he was the best in North America at sports-car racing, especially in endurance events. In 1976, after his third consecutive victory in the 24 Hours of Daytona, Gregg was asked by a German journalist to explain the common denominator of winning two straight in Porsches codriving with Hurley Haywood, and then a third in a BMW with Brian Redman.

"It's because I'm right with Jesus," Gregg said with a serene sigh and smile that threw the media. He was an avowed atheist, but you never knew where his mood swings would take him.

He won five IMSA Camel GT season championships in the 1970s and reciprocated for each title with at least one controversy—from suing IMSA in federal court over one of his design innovations, to suggesting that Sebring promoters "should give free dope and contraceptives" to each paying spectator. He was not as well known for nerve and talent as for obsessive preparation, pure outrageousness, and snobbery toward the competition, thus his nickname at the tracks: Peter Perfect. He was an excellent driver, but it was

as a team owner and manager that he was superb and unforgiving. Had he decided to continue living, it probably would have been as another Roger Penske—but considerably more colorful—applying his organizational talents to an Indy-car team.

He owned the most prestigious Porsche dealerships in North America—Brumos of Jacksonville and Atlanta—and a Mercedes-Benz dealership. Porsche owners from across the continent would write to Jacksonville requesting license-plate brackets bearing the Brumos logo. Gregg once tossed away a BMW franchise in a business tantrum.

In his time, he was a monumental enigma to American sports-car enthusiasts. He was doubly maddening, exponentially fascinating, because he seemed to lay his brilliance and his madness out for all the world to see, and still no one could quite figure him. A dozen years later it turns out that, like even the toughest riddles, he is fairly simply explained. And he is worth revisiting.

A sort of Peter Gregg revival began among sports-car lovers last year when Snodgrass, still president of Brumos after all these years, and Haywood, with Porsche factory backing, brought the old Gregg number (59) and Brumos traditional 911s to the IMSA Supercar series.

At the tracks, "People would come up to me with tears in their eyes and say, 'This is wonderful to have this back,'" says Haywood, who was Gregg's protegé, longtime codriver, and close friend. "Everyone had a Peter Gregg story to tell."

At the tracks, or around the dealership, "Peter's name comes up in conversation literally every single day," says Haywood. "Peter never thought that anybody liked him. He'd

A series of white, number 59
Porsches made Peter Gregg and
Brumos Racing famous.

say, 'Oh, everybody hates me,' but if he could hear all the people, and all their remarks, and all the things they remember him by, I think he would be really happy."

"What made Peter happy was—who knows?" says Haywood. "Winning races made Peter happy. Being Mr. Big Shot made Peter happy. But did it make him happy deep inside? I think it made him happy just on the outside... regardless of what he was doing, there was always this underlying feeling of unhappiness."

Virtually all of those who knew him sense that Peter Gregg now knows that people found him fascinating, and is content. He seems to abide: those who worked and drove for him still sense his presence, even talk out loud to him: "People around here chat to him every day," says Haywood. Snodgrass, who drives an old Gregg Porsche in vintage-car races, often feels "an eerie sense that Peter is in the car with me—and I'm not the type to get that sort of feeling."

By the signs of their partying, it doesn't appear that the surfers on Mickler's Landing feel anything ghostly, any residual unhappiness in the dunes. Maybe, here, that afternoon in 1980, sat Peter Gregg resolved, resigned to himself at last, at least in his ravaged psyche. Here, at least, sat Peter Gregg with his mind made up, writing fast on a legal pad.

"Dec. 15th-2:30 p.m.

Debbie. First I love you and this isn't related to you. I don't want to live with my lifelong illness of driving everything away, with making myself and others miserable.

Please don't feel you are partly responsible—you're not. Try to have a happy life. I'm no good for you in the long run.

Jason & Simon. Forgive me. I just don't enjoy life anymore. I must have the right to end it.

Jennifer. You helped me more than anyone. You shielded me from despair for years. Thank you.

Bob S. You've been so wonderful to me. I want you, Myrtis and Siggy to own auto business with Debbie. Debbie, please honor my request about Bob getting to own car dealership.

I don't feel crazy. I have done all I want to do. That's it."

And now the wind is harder, colder through the sea oats, and Mickler's Landing is deserted...and it is nearing Christmas time, 1980...

Deborah Marrs Gregg, 25, is his bride of nine days. They met by chance, four months earlier at a Japanese restaurant in Jacksonville. She is bubbly, bright, pretty, but essentially middle class by background and therefore draws raised eyebrows from his old moneyed friends.

His "lifelong illness" may in part refer to his manic-depressive disease. But more likely (and more in the Peter Gregg idiom), he is simply weary of being an ass—a condition which he has elevated to an art form, has seemed to enjoy, but in fact has suffered terribly from. In recent months, his mood swings have become more and more drastic, from cruel to whimpering and back again. He has begun ordering Brumos employees to line up shoulder-to-shoulder in the service department for military-like review. As he passes down the row, he tells each employee, "Take one step forward." Each employee must state his name, position, and salary. Say it's $18,000 a year. Gregg might say, "I don't think you're worth $18,000. Your salary is now $15,000.

Step back." Each decision is recorded and implemented.

He suffers double vision as an after-effect of a road crash in France the previous summer. On his way to the Le Mans track, he left the road and crashed in a street Porsche to avoid a farmer who backed out in front of him. Casual observers believe the head trauma "set him off." Closer friends realize the real trauma of the accident is that crashing on a public road has sorely embarrassed the man who considers himself most of all a racing driver and considers the German executives of Porsche, ultimately, his family.

He feels finished as a racer. The vision problem provides a superficial excuse, but Haywood knows better. Gregg, once nearly invincible on American tracks, is now vulnerable to an onslaught of younger European drivers—Hans Stuck, Bob Wollek, Klaus Ludwig—and his former protegé Haywood. Not only can they beat him, but they are adjusting to the ground-swell trend of sports-car racing toward prototype cars, which are little more than Formula 1 cars with fiberglass shells and bubble cockpits laid over them. Gregg has long been terrified of open-wheel, open-cockpit, and/or prototype cars. The sedan era, and Peter Gregg's reign, he fears, are over.

Years later, Haywood will note: "He felt that because he wouldn't be competitive, people wouldn't want to bother talking with him. He figured people wanted to talk to him because he was a race driver, not because he was a nice guy and had interesting things to say."

During the five years since his divorce from Jennifer, Gregg has dashed through a number of flings "through a lot of really, really neat girls," Haywood knows, having had some of them cry on his shoulder and having told them, "just bear with him; the condition will change tomorrow." But in recent months, close friends say, Gregg has proposed to a number of women, including one in Atlanta whom he has never seen, only talked to on the telephone. "Any woman with her shit together would know," says Haywood, "that this [binge of marriage proposals] is totally crazy." But Deborah Marrs, whom he met by challenging her to a street race after dinner, has decided to marry Peter Gregg.

She is not sure why....

Jason and Simon are his two sons from his first marriage. In December of 1980 they are 18 and 16, respectively. Though their father asks their forgiveness in his suicide note, he does not mention them in his will. He figures their mother's fortune will more than take care of them. In a classic example of Peter Gregg's difficulty in relating to other people, he has not considered the importance, the simple loving act, of leaving his sons something that was his.

Toward Jennifer, he has been increasingly belligerent in recent months. She suspects that he is conducting some sort of final break with her, psychologically, because he is marrying somebody else. He acknowledges that "you helped me more than anyone," yet all these years he has kept enormous secrets from her. On December 15, 1980, Jennifer does not know that the man she has known since 1960 is a manic-depressive, or that his mother committed suicide.

Bob Snodgrass knows both secrets, and others. He is Peter Gregg's greatest single confidant. Ramrod of Gregg's businesses since 1972, Snodgrass is in many ways Gregg's Sancho Panza, loyal and supportive almost to a fault. Lately, Gregg has seemed compelled to put Snodgrass's loyalty through harder and harder tests.

Recently he has called Snodgrass into his office and asked, "Are you my friend, Bob?"

"Yes, Peter. I'm your friend."

"Are you sure?"

"Yes. I am your friend, unequivocally."

"Do you know that I am not your friend?"

"Well, I can believe that."

"Well, if you're my friend and I'm not your friend, are you still my friend?"

"Yes, Peter. I'll be your friend no matter what."

And only moments before marrying Deborah Marrs, as Gregg and Snodgrass stood in the church vestibule, Gregg has sprung another test:

"Bob, are you happy that I'm getting married?"

"Peter, if it makes you happy, it makes me happy."

"Well, Bob, you should know that if the Good Lord reached out of the sky and killed me with a lightning bolt right now, 51 percent of everything I own is yours. But when I stand up there at the altar, the second I say, 'I do,' nothing would be yours if I died. Now are you happy that I'm getting married?"

"If it makes you happy, it makes me happy."

"Bob, when I'm standing there saying 'I do,' I want you to think of the millions of dollars falling through your fingers at that moment."

Gregg has changed his will so that Deborah will get everything. But now in the dunes of Mickler's Landing, as he is about to die, Peter Gregg tries to recant: "I want you, Myrtis [Myrtis Howard, Brumos's loyal and trusted comptroller] and Siggy Siegmund Mayerlen, former chief mechanic for Pedro Rodriguez and now Brumos's service manager] to own auto business with Debbie... Debbie, please honor my request about Bob getting to own car dealership."

But because a suicide-note request does not constitute a will, Deborah Marrs Gregg, overnight tough businesswoman, will not hand over any of her inheritance to Gregg's old inner circle. Resentment will run deep for many years to come. This is almost like Peter Gregg's final game playing—his inability to leave this earth without leaving controversy to ripple perpetually off his existence.

With the final three sentences of the note, Peter Gregg brings his guard back up, brings himself back into character with the Peter Perfect perceived by the public and its proxies, the media: "I don't feel crazy. I have done all I want to do. That's it."

A Peter Gregg calculating coldly that there was no more reason to live would end as the abrupt, arrogant, outrageous Peter Perfect. The public never saw him weep into his hands.

Among the media, "Everybody always wanted to talk to Peter, because nobody knew what the hell he was going to say," says Haywood. "He wanted to be the center of controversy, regardless of whether it was what he ate for breakfast or what he'd done to his car for the race."

A dozen years in retrospect, there was madness to his method; there was anguish behind virtually every media shenanigan he pulled.

In the summer of 1975, after Jennifer left him, he suddenly announced during an interview that, in a drastic turnabout of philosophy, he intended to go to Europe and drive Formula 1 cars. "I think I'll drive for Ferrari." He was pressed about his sincerity. He claimed he meant it, and that

Gregg, at right, with perennial
codriver Hurley Haywood, himself
a road-racing legend.

he had an inside track: "I know Dr. [Enzo] Ferrari very well."
Previously he had expressed nothing but fear and loathing for
Formula 1, but "I don't feel the same way about all things
all the time," he said. "Suddenly life is different. I've got to
find a new wife, and I've set an October deadline for finding
one...I think I'll run an ad in *The New York Times*." Pressed
again about sincerity, he reconfirmed it.

Weeks later, upon encountering the reporter who wrote
the story, Gregg said, "You printed that, you idiot!"

It seemed to confirm the theory that Peter Gregg had
the subtlest sense of humor in motor racing—that he would
jest at great length with a very straight face. In fact, it
supported the suspicion that after a drastic mood swing
occurred, he would recant Mood A by claiming during Mood
B that he was in jest the first time.

At the same time he announced his "plans" for Ferrari,
there was more and stronger evidence that the manic side
of Gregg's personality was winning out over the depressive
side during the trauma of losing Jennifer.

"After I decided we would split up, he decided he
was going to 'fix' the Porsche company," Jennifer recalls.

Snodgrass recalls that Gregg boarded a plane for
Germany with a Ford Motor Company executive in tow—
Gregg's personal choice to become Porsche's new chairman
of the board in his inspired restructuring. They walked into
Ferdinand Porsche's office "and got thrown out," Snodgrass
recalls, "with Dr. Porsche saying, 'No, no, no, we're not
going to change chairman.'"

Also in 1975, Gregg sued IMSA for outlawing a custom
tail configuration he'd designed for his Porsche Carrera racing
cars. The federal judge could understand Gregg's complaint
that American makes—such as John Greenwood's notorious
"Batmobile" Corvettes—were being allowed drastic
departures from stock design, though German cars were
being held to stricter standards. But the judge couldn't buy
the complaint on which Gregg's lawsuit was founded—that
IMSA was depriving him of his livelihood, racing. It roundly
seemed outrageous that the millionaire Mr. Gregg would
whimper about making a living.

But Gregg indeed may have been feeling relatively
impoverished at the time.

"Jennifer has an enormous amount of money," says
Haywood, who ought to know a fortune when he sees it—his
grandfather held the patent on the washing-machine agitator
and invented pneumatic tools. "Peter and Jennifer had a very
happy marriage. They had two great kids, they had a home,
and Jennifer afforded Peter the means to get into the
automobile business."

"Peter felt very secure with Jennifer's financial
background and stability. It allowed him to be outrageous in
some of the things he would do, the bottom line was, 'What
can happen to me? Regardless of what I say or do, I still have
this enormous base of power.' Money was very important
to Peter, because money allowed him to be powerful."

"When Jennifer divorced Peter," Haywood continues,
"suddenly he felt very vulnerable. He had plenty of money
but he didn't have that enormous wealth...and now he had to
become responsible."

Prior to 1975, Bavarian Motor Works was known mainly
in North America as a company that produced good
two-cylinder motorcycles, and which had come up with a
deceptively boxy little car that was quick and nimble, the

257

2002. The racing seasons of 1975 and 1976 would be the watershed that launched the BMW marque toward becoming the status symbol it is today. BMW made a splash in 1975 by fielding a team of drivers that included the German prodigy Hans Stuck, the Swedish Formula 1 star Ronnie Peterson, the British mainstay Brian Redman, and the articulate American Sam Posey. It wasn't enough: by 1976, BMW decided it had to have Peter Gregg on its side in North American road racing.

Gregg, adrift, was easily wooed. Rejected by Jennifer, rejected by Porsche in his bizarre reorganization plan, rejected by a federal judge and therefore beaten by IMSA, Gregg searched for new attachments. Once signed by BMW, he became freshly outrageous.

His first race for BMW was the 24 Hours of Daytona. Prior to the start, while being interviewed over the speedway PA system, Gregg asked the youthful revelers in the infield to "smoke one for me," and he didn't mean a Camel. After the race, he made the announcement that he'd won three Daytonas in a row "because I'm right with Jesus."

Prior to the next race, the Sebring 12 hour, Gregg was expressing love for "the circus," the Sebring infield so similar to Le Mans in revelry.

"My motto is they should give free dope and contraceptives to everyone who pays the price of admission," he said. Was he serious? And on the record? "Certainly," he said. "That's my motto: Free dope and contraceptives with the price of admission."

The quotes were published nationally. By the following week, Gregg was on the carpet with Goodyear brass, who were appalled at the remarks. The paradox was that "he would have been insulted if Goodyear hadn't called him," says Haywood. "Because Goodyear thought what he said was important enough to make a comment, he took it as a pat on the back, an implication that 'We think you're so great that we're concerned about what you say, that it might be mistaken by the young people.'"

Peter Gregg was misunderstood by all people, which seemed to be how he wanted it, except for some who found little fragments of the truth. The person who holds the most fragments is his brother, Jonathan, a former architect, now a painter and owner of an art studio in Vermont

Jonathan was six months old and their mother was suffering from postnatal blues (now called postpartum syndrome) when she died. "She was coming home to Peter's seventh birthday party," says Jonathan. "No one can say for sure whether it was suicide, but the authorities told us that in cases of women with postnatal blues stepping in front of subway trains, the statistics were pretty strong that it wasn't accidental. You can't have a mother commit suicide and not grow up with that specter in your consciousness. I assume he grew up with the idea of suicide, the same way I did."

Three children—Peter, the eldest, Susan, and little Jonathan—were left in the care of their father, Robert E. Gregg, who'd made his money manufacturing furnaces and crematoriums, and who "was a very demanding, very critical person," says Jonathan. The 'Peter Perfect,' that would have come from our father." Robert E. Gregg would die of a heart attack in 1969 and later, the atheist Peter Gregg would paint "R.E.G." on his race cars in a gesture of atonement for their stormy relationship, believing his father could see it from heaven. Susan would die of cancer nine months before Peter's suicide. He would not visit her while she was dying, would not attend her funeral, and would not discuss the matter with any of his friends.

To substitute for their mother, "we had a different house-keeper every year" says Jonathan. "We had one from France, one from Germany, one from Sweden, one from Italy, one from England. My father would change housekeepers every year by nationality, so he could have a different type of food. But to us, they were surrogate mothers. So it meant we got abandoned every year."

At puberty, Peter Gregg moved away from the family and went off to prep school in Massachusetts, at Deerfield Academy, at age thirteen. After that, he spent little time at home. At Harvard, he made friends with kids who had fast cars. Jonathan doubts that racing had machismo appeal to Peter, as much as "it was just something he happened to be very good at."

The car enthusiasm took him to Sebring in 1960, when the race was in its international prime and was something of a spring ritual for the well-to-do youth of Europe and North America. There, he met Jennifer Johnson, of the Johnson & Johnson family, who was a student at the Boston Museum School. Back in Boston, they fell in love and married.

After his navy stint, their shared love of cars brought them to Jacksonville, a place they probably never would have lived otherwise. Hubert Brundage, the original Volkswagen importer for the Southeastern United States, had just died and left available a Porsche dealership, Brundage Motors—"Brumos" for short. With a bit of Jennifer's money, the

Greggs bought the franchise. More interested in racing than selling cars, he at first operated Brumos at a loss.

Then came 1973, the great divide of Peter Gregg's existence. First, Brumos went from money-losing confusion to efficient and profitable business within a year after Gregg hired Snodgrass to run the dealership. Then came the races. Gregg and Haywood won the 24 Hours of Daytona and the 12 Hours of Sebring to open the season. Gregg went from competent club racer to acknowledged professional. And he gained some celebrity, which began his downfall.

"While Peter was married to Jennifer, he was a womanizer," Haywood, who was a confidant of both, recalls of the glory years. "A lot of times he would be fairly open about it, but not with Jennifer."

"He was pretty polite about it to me," says Jennifer. "It wasn't like he rubbed my nose in it." But "finally it came up to a situation where he got caught," says Haywood. "And that was that. Coupled with that was that Jennifer wanted to be Jennifer, her own person. She's very talented in a lot of different areas, and Peter would never give her the kind of leeway she needed to accomplish what she wanted to. As soon as Peter snapped his fingers, Jennifer had to be there doing what Peter wanted to do. And she finally just got sick and tired of it."

"Gregg," Haywood believes, "thought, 'Oh, I can do anything I want and Jennifer will always be there.'"

And so her leaving him was such a shock that "the minute he got divorced from Jennifer, he tried to replace that," says Haywood. "But nobody he met was a replacement for Jennifer. And the longer he went, the crazier his specifications for a replacement became." He went from woman to woman, but

Deborah Gregg inherited the
Gregg estate after a marriage
of less than two weeks.

often dropped them abruptly. "He was just off and on again all
the time. I mean, it was crazy. And finally he met Deborah. And
Deborah agreed to get married."

Gregg's inner circle was worried not so much about
Deborah as a person as the haste on Gregg's part, especially
considering his recent track record. Jonathan arrived in
Jacksonville from New England for the wedding, but "I guess
I spent most of the time trying to talk him out of it," says
Jonathan. "The night before, we talked until four in the
morning and I thought we had it on hold. At eight the next
morning they came back and said it was on. I was really sad.
If Peter had expressed a great deal of joy, tenderness, and
happiness, I'd have said, 'Fine.' I was mirroring his own
doubts. Since he had such misgivings, I was saying, 'Nothing
says you have to do this.'"

But Gregg confessed to Snodgrass a fear that "I'd be a
laughingstock" if he didn't go through with the wedding.

So on December 6, 1980, he made Deborah Marrs his
lawful wedded wife. On December 14, he telephoned
Haywood, to whom he hadn't spoken in six months—he'd
blamed Haywood (irrationally) for the loss of a 250-mile race
in which they'd codriven the previous summer—and invited
Haywood to lunch.

"If I'd been trained in psychology, I probably would have
realized what he was planning to do," says Haywood. "He
talked about all that we'd been through, from the time we
met through all the races we'd driven together."

At one point, Gregg asked Haywood, "Do you think
I made a mistake getting married?"

Haywood replied, "Yes."

Gregg dropped the subject, and asked if Haywood would

like to attend a Jacksonville University basketball game with him that night. Haywood said he had a previous commitment. "Then," as Haywood recalls it, "his sons came over and he asked them if they'd like to go to the game with him, but they couldn't go either. So apparently he just rolled up in a blanket on a sofa, thinking, 'Nobody likes me.'"

The next morning he went to a hardware store, bought a gun and ammunition, and drove to Mickler's Landing. He sat down in the dunes and wrote a note, apparently misreading his watch. Examiners determined that he died earlier than the 2:30 p.m. he wrote at the beginning. His handwriting is less and less consistent toward the end, indicating, to Snodgrass, "that he knew what he was about to do and he was scared."

"This wasn't a cry for help," says Deborah. "If he'd grazed his temple, or shot himself in the foot, maybe we'd have recognized a cry for help. But he just did it."

About 12 miles up the beach from Mickler's Landing, Deborah Howe, now married to former racing mechanic Rex Howe and mother of a toddler son, Hunter, has built herself a seaside villa. Built it with Peter Gregg's money, her detractors say.

"Tough shit," she replies. Where once was a bubbly, youthful girl now stands a woman toughened by a decade of hardball business. "It's not Peter Gregg's money anymore. Unfortunately, between what he left me with and how my businesses improved, there was a major difference."

At the time of the suicide, her inheritance was estimated at nine million, but "that was from the people who loved to think big thoughts," she claims. "It wasn't nine million in 1981." But she has parlayed the inheritance into more. She

held the Gregg business kingdom together until 1990, when she sold Brumos to Snodgrass and Winn-Dixie supermarket chain chairman Dano Davis. Her current wealth, she feels, is something she earned.

And emotionally, "I paid a price for what I got. It's something I would never wish on anyone."

She doesn't claim to understand the workings of Peter Gregg's mind: "It takes a lot longer than four and a half months to get to know someone."

After Gregg's death, rumors emerged around racing that he might have been bisexual and might secretly have suffered disappointment in a homosexual relationship—perhaps even with Haywood.

"I hear all these damn things all the time," says Haywood, "and it pisses me off. It's simply not true, as far as I know. What Peter did with anybody else is anybody's guess, but I think I would have sensed that something was going on, and I never did."

Snodgrass believes that, essentially, the suicide was a final statement to Jennifer, a sort of apology. Haywood says that "Whether or not he divorced Jennifer, and whether or not he was still a famous race driver, I think the end result still would have been the same. I think Peter would have been miserable regardless—he was just set up to be that way."

Even Jennifer, the woman Gregg said helped him more than anyone, says, "I didn't know his mother had committed suicide until he did it." Neither had she recognized the manic-depressive illness: "At the time, I thought—and everyone else thought—that he was just being a pain in the ass."

1993

2005

Car and Driver Today

Predicting the future with any reliability is folly—even Jeane Dixon couldn't say when she wouldn't be around to do it. But the future of *Car and Driver* magazine seems secure as it enters its second half century. With a circulation of 1.3 million copies a month, the largest car magazine in the world continues to prosper with a mix of technically precise and entertaining car writing by the best-known names in the business. It's on the Internet, on television, on the radio, and in the popular culture—a cameo player on *Friends* and *This is Spinal Tap* and one of the magazines with a strong following in Hollywood, as well as the mainstay of doctor's offices and high school hot rodders alike.

1993

The Branch Davidian compound in Waco, Texas, burns; 72 die, including leader David Koresh

Clint Eastwood's "The Unforgiven" wins Oscars for Best Picture and Best Director

1994

President Clinton accused of sexual harassment by Paula Jones

For the past decade, *Car and Driver* has been helmed by Csaba Csere, who in June 2005 will become the longest serving editor ever at the magazine. In 1993, not long after William Jefferson Clinton took the oath of office as President of the United States, editor William Jeanes gave up his editorship to become the publisher of the magazine as well as publisher of *Road & Track*. Jeanes wrote:

"Leaving the job of editor-in-chief of *Car and Driver* is as difficult as anything I've ever done, but I have made that departure. Customarily, in the peculiar world of automotive magazines, the head man leaves because he gets tired of his bosses or they tire of him. My leaving is different. Even before making the transition to another job, I had arranged an orderly succession, still another rarity. To that end, I gave Csaba Csere the title of editor, leaving myself the title of editor-in-chief—which I've held but rarely used since I came here in 1987. Csaba and I had intended this arrangement to last until the end of 1993, but circumstances intervened, as they so often do.

"*Car and Driver* has taken me from Tokyo to Morocco, from Russia to Bandera, Texas, and places between. I have known corporate moguls and shade-tree mechanics, racers and rascals, bastards and bimbos, the rich and the poor, the famous and the unknown, the loyal and the disloyal, the worthwhile and the worthless. All those places and people enriched me.

"Through all this wonderment, I've watched our magazine become the largest automotive publication in the world, with a circulation of more than one million. Why? Because no staff does so much so well as the one that each month creates *Car and Driver*. I represented only a tiny percentage of its number, so you need not worry about a drop in quality.

"Now, after five years, four months, and seven days, the second-longest serving editor in the 38-year history of *Car and Driver* takes his leave, with a small tear and a big smile."

Csere's tenure has seen the golden era of cars that began in 1985 continue with no signs of stopping. Computers and CAFE rules may have triggered the revolution that brought out cars like the Corvette ZR-1, NSX, and Miata, but it has been competition that's kept it running. Performance has never been stronger; horsepower numbers have doubled and tripled and as in the case of the upcoming 1001-hp Bugatti Veyron, have quintupled over the averages of the cars of the 1980s.

But the best cars ever—the cars being built today—aren't at all out of the reach of mortals. Csere noted as much when asked to recall the best cars of the early 1990s as the magazine celebrated its 40th anniversary. "In 1990, after years of peeks and previews, Chevrolet finally introduced the Corvette ZR-1, the fastest and best Vette ever. A strong-running ZR-1—they varied considerably—could flirt with 180 mph, yet unlike other cars possessed of similar elemental force, it could be used for everyday commuting. Unfortunately, the ZR-1 cost nearly twice as much as regular Corvettes without commensurate visual distinction. Come September, it will join the L88 and ZL-1 in the pantheon of great former Corvettes.

267

"The Acura NSX appeared at about the same time as the ZR-1, to similar acclaim and also to similarly tepid market acceptance. The surgically precise steering, the V-6 that revs like a Honda sportbike engine, and the most formula-car-like shifter on the road all captivate me every time I drive an NSX, but the upper crust remains reluctant to embrace an exotic from the maker of Accords. Their loss will be our gain on the used-car lots.

"The Nissan Sentra SE-R was a bargain of a different sort. As one of the legion of enthusiasts whose automotive passions were ignited by the original BMW 2002, I've always been an easy mark for any small, practical sedan with a chip on its shoulder. The SE-R fit the formula perfectly. It was fast, nimble, cheap, and eager to run—qualities that gave me a smile every time I drove it, just as my 2002 used to.

"Prices have skyrocketed in the two decades since I owned that little Bavarian wonder, but the BMW M3 delivers comparable value and all-around excellence—albeit on a much higher plane. Compact and practical, it can outrun all but the fastest two-seaters, yet its supple ride is livable even on Michigan's wrinkled and rutted roads. I would gladly drive one every day.

"Today, Chrysler is a cutting-edge car company, but a few short years ago the company was famous for boring sedans, Lee Iacocca, and tediously regular financial emergencies. The LH sedans shattered those perceptions with radical but friendly styling, roomy cab-forward architecture, and European road feel. They made big American sedans respectable for baby-boomers to drive. Most important of all, the LHs proved that product is king in the auto business. May it remain so forever."

Csere's term in office nearly coincided with that of President Bill Clinton's, not unironically. Clinton's term, and those of President George W. Bush after him, saw the car industry fulfilling some of the promise of the legislation that nearly killed it. While it toiled away, it seemed that the country itself was being rendered by political division, the threat of terror at home and abroad, and a deepening of the gulf between America's closest allies and the nations it had pulled from the depths of World War II.

Despite the presidencies of Clinton and Bush, who both had reputations as rift-healers and aisle-crossers, the nation's political divide only grew more intense. Clinton's election swung the pendulum in one direction, while the Republican takeover of the House of Representatives in 1994 pushed it in the other. Clinton's impeachment radically multiplied the hostility in Washington, while Bush's narrower than narrow victory in the 2000 election ended with even the Supreme Court's abilities to judge law impartially called into question.

Americans took to two camps: those in so-called "red states," unabashed in their patriotism, took up driving big SUVs like HUMMER H2s and voting squarely for conservative leaders, while "blue-staters" looked to old *Car and Driver* nemesis Ralph Nader and Howard Dean to rescue their Democratic party from sliding too close to the Republicans. They moved in droves toward a hybrid nation based on global law and did it in new hybrid vehicles.

Unspeakable tragedy lost its power to unite the country in this era. In 1993 a Waco compound was burned. In the same year the World Trade Center complex was bombed. American soldiers died in Somalia in ambush, thousands of Balkan people were murdered, and perhaps 800,000 Rwandans died in a genocide—and in each case, U.S. officials and policies were ineffective in the extreme. Even on September 11, 2001, when the great gulf between radical Islamic terrorists and sharply conservative U.S. leadership collided in midair over New York, Pennsylvania, and the Pentagon, a brief

268

President Clinton wins
reelection over Senator
Bob Dole

1997

Control of Hong Kong
goes from Britain to
China

Princess Diana is killed
with lover Dodi Fayed in
a Paris car crash

<

1998

"Titanic" is the top-grossing film of all time, earning $580 million in the U.S. alone

Viagra is approved by the FDA

1999

Dylan Klebold and Eric Harris open fire at Columbine High School, killing 13 students and themselves

communion in national grief quickly soured and sides withdrew to their positions. Some 2,992 people died as four airliners were turned into terrorist bombs by Al-Qaeda: terrorism had come to U.S. soil and political bickering won the headlines of the day.

Tragedy struck *Car and Driver* as well. For the first time in the magazine's history a staff member died while testing a vehicle. Don Schroeder, a 35-year old Syracuse native, an engineer with degrees in mechanical engineering and applied science from Lehigh University, and a Detroit enthusiast who shared a grand old home in the city's Boston-Edison district with his partner, died in a single-car accident in the RENNTech Mercedes-Benz he was testing on a lonely back stretch of the 7.7-mile oval track at Ft. Stockton, Texas.

In memorial services and in the pages of the magazine, Csere let the rest of the world know what those who knew Schroeder best were feeling, an utter sense of loss. "All of us at *Car and Driver* can scarcely accept that we will never again see Don's cheerful face. No longer will we hear him defending GM styling for taking a risk on the whale-like 1991 Chevrolet Caprice, or recalling his escapades before he came to the magazine behind the wheel of his 1984 twin-stick Dodge Colt GTS Turbo. We'll never again hear him earnestly promoting the urban recovery of the city of Detroit, where he had purchased—some said bravely—a grand old home years ago. We'll never hear him spewing verbal fireworks in political arguments with one of the more conservative members of the staff—such as myself. Although we all intellectually accept that he's gone, in our hearts many of us imagine that he's just off on a long trip somewhere and he'll come strolling through our front door any day now."

Schroeder had died pursuing the best top speed of the vehicle in question. The consummate professional, and an exceptional

driver by any measure, Schroeder was the first fatality in the magazine's testing history. "Neither our safety record, nor the genuine benefits of testing, seem to count for much in the aftermath of Don's death," Csere lamented.

Schroeder's passing sent a wave of remorse through the Detroit community. As the millennium progressed, speed still was at the top of Detroit's wish list. But buyers' tastes were shifting in a new direction. They still wanted speed, as witnessed by the sales of big HEMI-powered Chryslers and the popularity of the reborn Mustang GT. They also began to reject a decade's worth of infatuation with SUVs and turned to a new type of vehicle meant to conserve fuel and reduce emissions—the hybrid.

In the 1990s the sport-utility vehicle ruled the American market. Configured to give buyers the station-wagon capacity they wanted but avoiding big-car fuel-economy rules, SUVs were the emblem of America's car economy in the decade. From less than a few percent of the U.S. market in the post-CAFE 1970s, the SUV eventually represented one in four new vehicles purchased in America. The federal legislation (CAFE) that had set car fuel economy standards had given automakers a loophole—trucks could get lower gas mileage by law—and automakers drove sport-utility vehicles and pickup trucks through the loophole. Unbound by the same fleet economy rules for trucks, the Big Three in particular depended on truck-based products to generate profits and keep the showrooms full. It seemed to work until gas prices, which had dipped to historic lows in 1999, rose to near-historic heights in advance of the U.S. toppling of Saddam Hussein in 2003.

With gas prices on a three-year rollercoaster and liberals aligning themselves with greens to denounce Detroit's poor record on fuel economy, the anti-SUV craze ignited. Talking heads like Arianna Huffington took on Detroit with TV ads claiming that SUVs

271

were fueled by terrorism. *Car and Driver* writers stood on the other end of reason, demanding proof that gas crises could be avoided and asking for proof that SUVs and trucks were any more guilty of oil abuse than other luxuries like homes, boats, jets or the like.

As Csere observed, "If we as Americans develop a national consensus to reduce our oil consumption for whatever reason—political, environmental, financial—we should establish a policy that provides an economic incentive to discourage all usage of oil-derived products. There are many economically sound ways of discouraging energy uses while preserving the freedom of our citizens to decide whether to allocate their energy dollars to fueling an SUV, keeping a large house comfortable, or driving—or flying—across the country. Even if we ignore these arguments, surrender to our fury over the terrorist attacks, and adopt the Detroit Project's knee-jerk prescriptions by trading our SUVs for Ford Focuses and Toyota Priuses, what would happen? Our demand for gasoline, and thereby crude oil, would fall, causing supplies to contract and some oil wells to be capped. But they wouldn't be in the Middle East. Oil from that part of the world is dirt-cheap because it gushes forth as soon as you drill a hole in the sand. Production, or lifting costs, as it is known in the industry, is less than $2 per barrel. North American oil, on the other hand, costs more like $10 per barrel to lift because of more intensive pumping and myriad environmental regulations. So, as in the past, when oil production is contracted, the first wells to close would be in North America. That would mean an even larger percentage of America's oil would come from the Middle East."

What will the future bring for cars? The crystal ball is somewhat clearer in the automotive industry. For the past decade, cars have been aiming for the future: with hybrids, with fuel cells, and with a renewed sense of history.

Since Csere chose his favorites in 1995, even those newer cars have been superseded by models even faster and better built. The new 500-horsepower Viper easily outguns the old Corvette ZR-1, while the latest 300-hp BMW M3 flies by its own ancestor. Nissan's large family four-door Altima has nearly 300 horsepower, too, and the interior room of Chrysler's LH cars. And the latest off-the-showroom-floor Mustang GT hits the same power levels, eclipsing the acceleration of all but the hottest special-edition Mustangs of the 1960s.

But there's new enthusiasm around hybrids and fuel-cell vehicles. Some say they could provide a future less dependent, or even independent, on foreign energy. Hybrids are today's best response to the needs of performance and fuel economy. Pioneered by the Japanese, they use batteries and gas engines to provide power equal to today's cars but with fuel consumption 20 to 30 percent lower. The hybrid concept took some time to build, but already, in its second generation, the Toyota Prius has attracted the celebrity fans and mass-market appeal that hybrids will need to move them into the mainstream.

Fuel cells are the next frontier. And though they may be a decade or more in the offing, they promise an even brighter future. Capturing the electricity generated by the atomic combination of hydrogen gas and oxygen, fuel cells entered experimental stages, and, like the turbines before them, were fraught with problems. Analysts and engineers see fuel cells as a Holy Grail—a way to generate cheap energy with only water vapor emitted, and a way to free America from OPEC's whims.

Even if oil prices hit $80 a barrel as OPEC has threatened, car enthusiasts won't be forced into hiding. Whatever the future of cars—hybrids, fuel cells, or old-fashioned gasoline—it's sure that Americans will read about it in *Car and Driver* first.

272

2005 Toyota Prius.

2003 Space Shuttle Columbia explodes on reentry to earth, killing entire crew

2004 A massive tsunami strikes Indonesia, Sri Lanka, Thailand, and other Asian nations

>

August 1993
Plymouth Prowler

Concept cars can be bellwethers, demonstrating audacity and creative energy that runs deeper than any given sweep of sheetmetal or coat of eye-popping paint. Whether or not the Prowler is produced may be inconsequential. The fact that the Eaton and Lutz team is even considering building it implies that Chrysler is back in the serious automobile business and ready to take major risks. That's the answer to the single salient question about Prowler.

—*Brock Yates*

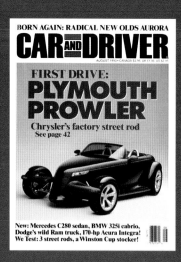

BORN AGAIN: RADICAL NEW OLDS AURORA

CAR AND DRIVER

AUGUST 1993 • CANADA $3.95 UK £1.95 US $2.95

FIRST DRIVE:
PLYMOUTH PROWLER
Chrysler's factory street rod
See page 42

New: Mercedes C280 sedan, BMW 325i cabrio,
Dodge's wild Ram truck, 170-hp Acura Integra!
We Test: 3 street rods, a Winston Cup stocker!

October 1993
Buick Roadmaster

Car and Driver channels the Monty Python crowd and goes into drag to drag-test the new Roadmaster Limited. "True or false: a certain new Supreme Court Justice was once a *Car and Driver* road warrior."

—Frank Markus

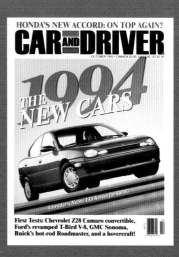

RESTAURAN

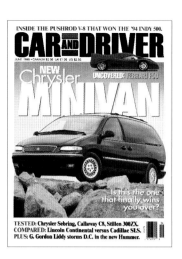

June 1995
How I Became a Death Defying Danger Angel

By Marty Padgett

The most convincing testimony as to the driving skills of the daredevil flock that has evolved into the Joie Chitwood Chevy Thunder Show is that in more than 50 years of crash-and-burn mayhem only two drivers associated with the Chitwoods—one a guy called Lucky—have been killed in the line of duty.

The stunt that killed Lucky Teeter at the Indianapolis State Fair during World War II was called "The Aerial Rocket Car Leap." Lucky had dreamed it up a decade earlier. It's a ramp-to-ramp leap in a car, and when his vehicle fell short of the second ramp, that was it for Lucky.

After Lucky went to his reward, a young stuntman in his troupe named Joie Chitwood bought his equipment and started his own show. And when Joie died in 1988, he left behind his name and his show to his sons Joie Jr. and Tim.

The rocket leap is now the specialty of 39-year-old Tim Chitwood. For 29 years, Tim has made a living spinning cars around on a dime and turning them into metal roughage. For this, the show's grand finale, he drives a Chevy Camaro full-throttle into the mouth of a steel tube just 8 feet in diameter and 20 feet long. Barreling upward through it, he launches the Camaro through a shower of fireworks and over a row of four or five junkers before he lands some 65 feet away.

Another stunt is "Hell Driving," featuring Tim and "Wild Bill" Dominick, a beefy 39-year-old guy who speaks in real short sentences. You would too if all your concentration went into driving a Camaro inches away from another identical new Camaro, weaving bumpers a hair's breadth apart at speeds up to 70 mph. In his nine years of stunt driving with the Chitwood show Wild Bill has had no serious injuries despite finding himself

in nearly a thousand accidents. (AAA says your chances of being in one are about one in four.)

Then there are "Crash Rollovers," the specialty of John Mason. Each year, Mason, an affable man with a moustache and a thick Boston accent, rolls somewhere between 130 to 200 cars doing this stunt. In a junked-out car that has been meticulously stripped of any harmful glass, seats, and knobs, Mason bears down at 30 mph onto a four-foot-tall ramp canted at 15 degrees, launches his car 40 feet, and proceeds to roll the car four or five times on average. Mason modestly gives it a middling grade for difficulty.

The "Leap For Life" stars Jeff Lattimore, a wiry guy who spends his off-season around Connecticut. In his stunt, he stands atop an eight-foot stool while a car charges at him. The car snaps the stool in half, and Jeff leaps to the ground unharmed. This would seem to be as unnerving as, say, jumping from hundred-foot-high perches onto pillows. Which he also does. Last year, Lattimore and Mason leapt from high up in the Providence Civic Center into a huge air-filled cushion 110 feet below—God's own airbag—hitting it dead center. Which they weren't.

The "Human Battering Ram" dates to the 1930s. In the current version, the performer lies face-down on the hood of a car, swaddled in Nomex from his cranium to his toes. He is pointed down the straightaway at a barrier made of horizontal wooden slats that are dressed in paper and doused with

280

gasoline. On the downbeat, the driver zooms at 50 mph toward the wall, which simultaneously bursts into flames. The stuntman pulls in his arms to his sides and, unrestrained by any safety harnesses, crashes through the firestorm. Supposedly unscathed.

Piece of cake, you say? That's what one Florida journalist said while playing replacement daredevil. Unfortunately, he looked up at the last second and got a neck full of rough-cut pine. Mason says, "I asked him, 'You okay?' He was just, 'Hack, hack, phlat, hack, wheeze.'" Another gent gave a dual thumbs-up signal at a colossally wrong moment. "Broke both of 'em clean back," Mason nods.

I shudder politely as Chitwood, Mason, and Lattimore lay out the dangerous way they make their daily bread. Because in a few hours that will be me riding on the hood of a ratty 1978 Olds wagon headed for the fire.

The price of admission to the North Carolina State Fair—at least on Wednesdays—used to be five empty Pepsi cans. Tim Chitwood expects a big crowd for the evening show tonight because it's Wednesday, and even though the Pepsi-can deal was abandoned a few years ago, folks still turn up in droves.

Wednesday, I'm told, will be the perfect day to perform my guest stunt at the Chitwood Chevy Thunder Show. Since I'm the new guy with no experience, I don't get to do any of the trick Hell Driving, the two-car lane-swap that seems to have its origins in a fast-forward Keystone Kops stunt, nor will I participate in Crash Rollovers.

Instead, on a summery evening on the fairgrounds' dirt oval, I will be splayed headfirst across the hood of a 1978 Oldsmobile wagon, like some pal of Marlene Cooke's, and plunged through a wall of burning wood headfirst. As I will soon find out, the

interaction between the fire and my skull will deliver the same thrill, approximately, as breaking down a locked door with my forehead. The really funny part is that Duke University, not 20 miles away, testified in awarding me a bachelor's degree, that I wouldn't be dumb enough to try this.

It occurred to me that on this night I would be competing for the fairgoer's money against the likes of the World's Largest Pig and the World's Smallest Woman, a Whitman's Sampler of weird. Two shows a day, 5 p.m. and again at 8:30 p.m. on the nose, ending an hour later with an explosive bang—my head, perhaps.

The Human Battering Ram stunt I'll perform harks to the earliest days of Joie Chitwood's four-wheeled bedlam. A seven-time qualifier at Indy and a fifth-place finisher three times—in 1946, 1949, and 1950—Chitwood created "the Bat," as it's called, and refined it and other daredevil stunts to such a high form of offbeat art that by 1944, in Williams Grove, Pennsylvania, he was able to sell tickets for his own whole show of stunt driving.

And while the Chitwood name has been synonymous with stunt driving ever since, it also has the longest affiliation with one sponsor in the history of thrill shows. Since 1955, it's been nothing but Chevys.

Before then, Joie used whatever vehicles he possessed. Then in 1949, he was hired as Clark Gable's stunt double for the racing yarn *To Please a Lady*. Ford offered some cars for use during filming, and then stuck with the team until 1953. Questions over the cars' ownership ended the Ford deal in 1953, and then Chitwood switched to Plymouths for a year. The following year, he switched suppliers again. He'd avoided Chevys because they didn't have V-8 engines. In 1955 he ran across his good friend Ed Cole, the chief engineer of Chevy's first eight-cylinder, at Indianapolis. Cole leaked word of

his upcoming V-8, the Chitwood show got them, and it has been all Chevy ever since.

Before Joie Sr. died seven years ago—of natural causes—his two sons had taken over the daily operations of dual shows. In the 1970s and '80s, Joie Jr. and Tim ran a pair of shows, one per coast. Then Joie Jr. suffered a series of serious injuries: his back broken twice, a broken neck, and a separated shoulder. One broken back came during the filming of a 1978 TV movie called *Big Bob Johnson and His Fantastic Speed Circus*, in which Joie Jr. attempted a 110-foot-long leap from a ramp to the ground and landed too hard. He didn't know his back had been fractured until he broke it again while making a commercial for Stanley Tools in 1985. Joie Jr. decided to retire from everyday performing in 1991. At the same time, the brothers decided to merge the shows into one, with Tim at the helm.

By the way, the odd spelling of Joie comes from a misinformed Missouri newspaperman and a printer's error. Father Joie's first name was George. As an unknown—he was being billed as a Cherokee Indian—Chitwood was written up by a reporter who read what he thought was the performer's name on the side of his car—Chitwood, from St. Joe, Missouri. He

wrote "Joe," and a hapless printer added an errant 'i.' It stuck.

Tim officially started in the family business in 1974 when he reached legal adulthood at 18. (He was performing forward spins and precision driving in the late 1960s—until Pennsylvania child-welfare authorities took his dad aside and suggested that because Tim was just 12 years old, he might be in violation of child-labor laws.) He started precision driving and soon earned the title of the World's Number One Ranked Auto Stunt Man. Tim also holds the world distance record for driving an American-made auto on two wheels, for 5.9 uninterrupted miles. He set the record in Richmond, Virginia, in a Chevette in September 1981. He's worked as a stunt driver for TV shows like *CHiPs*, *Miami Vice*, and *Rescue 911*, and his movie credits include *The Firm*, *The Last Action Hero*, *The Cowboy Way* (along with brother Joie Jr., who comes out of the Chitwoods' Tampa office to perform on occasion), and the upcoming three-quel *Batman Forever*.

Under Tim's guidance, the Chitwood show appears from May through October at about 60 fairgrounds, including smaller "punkin" fairs. The shortest stops are overnighters, with a brief lineup of stunts. The longest stop is at the Eastern States Expo in Springfield, Massachusetts. There the show performs 18 of its repertoire of 21 stunts in each of 40 shows over a 17-day stretch.

During the season, Tim marshals a roster of equipment that is comprehensively Chevy. Three Camaro coupes power the Hell Driving sequences. Tim does his reverse spins in a stock Corvette and his two-wheel driving in a Geo Tracker with a welded rear axle (the welding locks the axle so that the earth-borne wheel can continue to power the vehicle). The rest of the fleet includes a pair of Monte Carlos, an S-10 Blazer, a Suburban, and a fleet of extended-cab and dualie trucks.

The team also buys a not-so-fresh set of junkyard-ready bombers for each fair, and subjects each one to a unique form of mercy killing—by rolling it, launching it airborne, and stuffing it into another parked junker, or running it hard through the Bat. They dispatch two or three a day on average, depending on the stunts they choose for the evening's show—John Mason's rollovers use up one; the T-bone crash, in which an unbelted Wild Bill Dominick drives a clunker into the air and lands hard into the hood of a parked heap, usually snuffs a couple more.

It's Wild Bill's job to pick each junker clean of objects that could become embedded in the drivers. "One time we forgot to take the folding seat out of a station wagon," he chuckles softly, "and the driver took it in the head." Bill also dumps all but two gallons of fuel—just enough to do the stunts.

Dominick's other duty is driving the vehicle through the wall of fire in the Bat, and the ratty Olds he's dismembering now is the car I'll ride through the fire. "I don't decelerate until I see you're okay," he says. "Keep your thumbs down at the seams of your pants, and when you get about three inches in front of the wall, put your head down."

I scribble frantically to keep up. How fast do we go anyway, Bill? "It's about 50," he says as he pounds the inner edge of the front fenders on the coffee-brown Olds, denting them to make rudimentary grab handles. "The faster you go through, the less you feel it."

I climb onto the hood. I find that I'm a perfect fit for a 1978 Custom Cruiser wagon. My hands slide into place, and I locate a dull ridge on each side of the hood. My feet are hooked over the frame where the windshield would normally meet the dash structure, and I worry that my left foot might kick the steering wheel, but otherwise it works—my spread arms reach perfectly to the fender's edge. Mason joins the lesson and offers his expertise. He doesn't bump elbows with Costner for top billing, but John Mason has years's worth of experience doing stunt work for TV and movies, on *Spenser: For Hire*, in the David Carradine micro-epic *Distant Justice*, and in *Against the Law*. For seven years before he was promoted (promotion in the Chitwood camp means you get to walk on the car while Tim drives on two wheels), Mason did the Bat.

He and Jeff Lattimore, the guy I'm lying in for, instruct me on the finer points of sending my head unscathed through a set of eighth-inch pine boards. And afterward, in the finer points of soothing a neckache with repeated doses of Goldschlager.

"It don't ever stick to you," Mason says of the litter of broken, burning boards that I must pass through. "It's just gasoline by the time you get to the boards." The technique is simple, he goes on. "Just head-butt the car."

Just head-butt the car. It becomes my mantra.

Mason makes it sound simple. All I have to do, he says, is jump in the car when Dominick pulls around, stand in the passenger footwell, and then lie down on the hood. Grab the fenders, give Bill the go-ahead, and seconds later it'll all be over. I do have one choice: I can keep holding on through the wall, or I can let gravity have its way with me, with only my feet hooked on the dash for peace of mind.

Mason halts the instructions for a moment to inspect my helmet for a leak at the visor. "I have to tape it down every so often," he says. "Every once in a while I'll come in with singed eyebrows." The little hairs on the back of my neck snap to attention because my eyebrows cannot. "That's when it's time for new tape."

"Sometimes you feel it," adds Lattimore. "Sometimes you don't. You always get a headache." Asking around, I find that everyone gets bruised and nicked during a show, mostly during the crash stunts. But no serious harm, usually. The show, while under the Chitwood name, has only suffered one fatality. In the days before most of the gas was drained before a stunt, Snooks Wentzel, the number-one driver at the time, got into a rollover and suffered fatal burns in 1951.

It's an hour to go before showtime, and the sun has already beat a hasty retreat behind Dorton Arena by the time we finish and circle around Tim for a team meeting, to check on the performers' whereabouts and to schedule Tim's golf game for the next morning.

Before I know, we're on. At the top of the hour, the stadium's PA system scratches through an LP of the national anthem. The Chitwood Danger Angels line up and then instantly break out of formation, leap into the Chevys, and erupt into a spray of dirt on the main straightaway. Engines shriek. Fireworks crackle. The announcer steps up the volume a notch and begins an auctioneer's chatter. The crowd is about 500 strong, pretty thick even for a Wednesday, and it roars its approval from the bank of bleachers.

"These guys just like loud things," observes photographer Kelley as he grabs a lens and heads for the back seat of the Geo Tracker, to ride along with Tim as he drives the track on two wheels. Once he hits the increasing-angle ramp, Tim corrects the steering constantly to maintain an uneven keel, sawing left and right irregularly but never too dramatically. He makes his way around one lap and looks bored. Sure enough, a quarter of the way through the second lap, the Geo thumps down softly back onto two wheels. Kelley scrambles out of the back.

"Perfect," he says with awe.

Before we can dissect Tim's performance, Mason roars onto the main straightaway in a beat-up, nondescript Fairmont wagon, headed for a low ramp. He wears no seatbelt. His approach is near-perfect, and the car lifts clean into the air, like a low-level Piper Cub-one with ice on its wings, because it slowly rotates in mid-air and crashes down on a corner. It rolls over easy. Earlier Mason had told me he liked smaller cars, especially Subarus, which he could get to roll four, maybe four and a half times usually. The Fairmont begins to lose steam after three, when flames momentarily leap from beneath the hood. The fire muffles itself out in a second, and he steps out uninjured.

"Carb must have blown up," he says offhandedly. "Some of 'em, you don't know what's gonna happen."

Like, blow up in your face? I grow more nervous as I zip my Nomex suit about my neck, slip a fireproof balaclava over my face, and pull a loose helmet over it. Gloves, don't forget the gloves.

I watch as Lattimore does his Leap of Life. He climbs a ladder next to an eight-foot-tall stool. Another driver takes the ladder away, and Lattimore balances woozily. Only for a moment, though, because Bill Dominick is approaching with a full head of steam from the right. Jeff looks down the track, sees the oncoming car, jumps a moment before the impact and—SNAP!—the stool careens from beneath him, the car whizzes by in a cloud of dirty exhaust, and he falls safely to the ground. "Good luck!" he shouts at me from afar, as he helps to drag the wooden barrier on the track for the Human Battering Ram.

That's me.

Later I'll learn that the local lumberyard cut tonight's boards

way too thick. A good quarter-inch thick, twice as much as most nights. It's better that I don't know, because already my breathing is shallow and my fingers cold and numb.

I slither onto the fender of the car as the announcer goes through a bit of patter about me. Mild applause and amusement, given the fact that "Dookies" (as Duke students are none-too-affectionately known) occupy the same spot on the local social ladder as navel lint.

My feet drop into the passenger seat, and I find firm footing on the floor. I'm standing half-in, half-out of the musty brown Olds, and I get a funny image of myself waving to the audience and wearing a goofy grin. My hands are now sweating. My chauffeur, Wild Bill Dominick, gives me a victory lap down the front lane as we proceed to the far end of the track.

It's time. I lean down and grab the dented-in handles. "Good luck!" Dominick shouts as he winds the Olds around the bend. My chest is thumping hard.

I take a look at the stands and spot a pocket of friends right in front. Great, a sarcastic audience. I put my head down way too early. I don't wanna see it coming, but I catch a glimpse of Lattimore waving a torch like a villager headed for Dr. Frankenstein's castle. Inside the seashell acoustics of my helmet I hear the wall ignite into flames with a WHOOMP!

Dominick nails the throttle. I can feel the carburetors gasping for air right beneath my lungs, like aliens waiting to spring out fully formed. The wall comes up fast, but not fast enough. Imagine knowing in the eighth grade that one day you'd crash through a wall of flames on top of a car in front of thousands (well, hundreds) of howling spectators...

THWAAAACK!

And it's over. Bill grabs my ankle. "You okay? You okay?" he shouts. I grin weakly. He can't see my nod and shakes again. I shout a "Yes."

My knees are shaking. My arms are regaining feeling after a momentarily frightening 15-second numbness. I find a thin bruise running up the center of my chest from the hood's chrome ornamentation, and a dime-sized chunk of flesh missing from my right calf. No singed hair, thank goodness, but the beginnings of the archetypal Excedrin headache.

I stumble off to low applause. All I remember is a lot of fire. "A lot of fire," Kelley whistles low. He assures me it's on film and that I don't have to do it again. I dive into my pool of friends and babble incoherently for a couple of minutes about the thrill and the danger of it all. They eye me suspiciously.

Later, I recall that I wrote something in my notebook. I recover four words from it, written in a shaky but intelligible hand: "Head trauma. Very cool."

The show slips away along with the warm air and my desire to remain sober much longer. Another half-hour lost to the 80 percent of my brain I don't use.

A fraternity brother, Kyle, who stood up immediately afterward and shouted, "Do it again!" now asks if I'm going to stick around the fair. They've got four Ferris wheels, he says. Ferris wheel? It doesn't really register.

Another pal, Rebecca, flashes her infamous blue eyes and gives me a hug. "You made it," she grins.

Brother Jason, whom I have to shake hands with carefully since he and I try to crush each other's hands whenever we meet, just laughs to himself. "He's not ready for a Ferris wheel. "He needs a drink."

June 1995
A Hardnose Road-Tests a Hummer

By G. Gordon Liddy

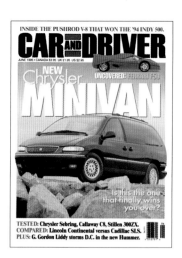

Because I currently live out my misspent life on the radio, I had casually mentioned on the air that *Car and Driver* was arriving momentarily and that the magazine had asked me to evaluate the gasoline-engined version of AM General's HMMWV ("Humvee" or "Hummer" to the rest of us), this one destined not for the military but for the carriage trade.

Now, as I approached the behemoth for a closer look, I found for the first time what proved to be true for the next two days that I had this bruiser in custody: a Humvee in mufti draws crowds. The *Car and Driver* guys—executive editor John Phillips and photographer Aaron Kiley—were grinning as they handed me the keys. One of them said, "Lord Vader, your car awaits you." I don't know whether they remembered, but a quarter of a century ago *The Washington Post* had dubbed me "the Darth Vader of the Nixon Administration."

This particular Hummer certainly qualifies as a Darth Vader, glistening in its black wet-look paint, like the Imron used by proud owner/drivers of the menacing big-rig Peterbilts, Kenworths, and Freightliners that suddenly appear in your rear seat with a blast of the air horn when you momentarily stop paying attention in the fast lane. But the big rigs do not blow their horns at the Humvee.

So there it sat, the civilian Hummer, the self-appointed king of wheeled off-road vehicles, dominating the parking lot of radio station WJFK in metropolitan Washington, D.C. My task, among others, was to see whether the machine was as "bad" on the road as its reputation off the road. Alas, in the urban jungle, this baby proved to be a pussycat, not a tiger.

It wasn't the absence of a gun turret, although I did notice this immediately. Nor was it the surprisingly comfortable Isringhausen seats. Nor even the "don't ask, don't tell" quality of the vehicle's "Hummer" nickname, which was emblazoned across the liftgate. No, the tip-off that the legendary Humvee has been emasculated by the forces of political correctness was the first thing the driver sees after climbing in: the underside of the sun visor is placarded with admonitions to "Wear Seat Belts" and "Don't Drink and Drive." Marvelous. Somewhere, I am certain, there's a sign inside that reads "Wash Hands After Going to the Bathroom."

Then there's the engine. This vehicle weighs 6,766 pounds. What did AM General choose to propel over three-and-a-quarter tons? A 350-cubic-inch small-block Chevy. Although that engine is configured for maximum torque (300 pound-feet at 2,400 rpm) and is more or less politically correct, it is overwhelmed, pushing this machine from 0 to 60 mph with all of the acceleration available to a beached whale: 18.1 seconds. Eighty mph comes up in 46.8 seconds—it only feels like a week—which also brings you to within 3 mph of the Hummer's top speed.

If you slow for traffic on the infamous Washington Beltway (at 55 mph, you'll be rammed from the rear by traffic flowing 30 mph faster, although in the Hummer you won't feel the impact), then you'll be two exits behind your running mates by the time this machine gets back up to speed. All the while, the straining small-block sounds as if it were lubed with sand imported from Daytona Beach.

November 1996
Porsche Boxster

If there has been a contest going on among BMW, Mercedes-Benz, and Porsche to see which German automaker could build the best-performing small roadster, Porsche should be passing out cigars right now. The new mid-engined Boxster is all Porsche, a simply marvelous sports car and the most dynamic and exciting of all the new generation of two-seat roadsters. Where the BMW Z3 is soft and affordable and the Mercedes SLK so civilized it's hedonistic, the Boxster is pure, taut, and sparkling with desirability. It is also the first truly new Porsche road car in 19 years. Nothing about its mid-engined layout, its MacPherson-strut suspension, or its water-cooled boxer engine is revolutionary, but all these pieces are new to the Boxster and share nothing with the 33-year-old 911 model or the 968 or 928 cars. This is one of those rare new-from-the-ground-up designs. The Boxster—available here in January—represents a return to the company's original philosophies, wrapped in an entirely contemporary design. No other roadster offers the same dazzling blend of performance, handling, ride, and refinement. Yes, it is dynamically superior to the classic 911, though it is not quite as quick. How things have changed for Porsche. Just five years ago, the company was well on its way toward developing a four-door sedan, the 989, a $90,000 luxury car with sporting connotations. At the time, the Boxster did not exist. But at the end of 1991, there was a palace revolt in the board room and a resulting 180-degree shift in direction. The 989 was dropped, and Porsche went back to basics. The engineers wondered about a front-engined replacement for the 944/968 but eventually decided real Porsches use a boxer engine, located somewhere behind the driver. The Boxster is dazzling evidence that they were right.

—Peter Robinson

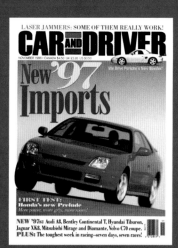

290

Brakes? Another problem. Wear steel-soled motorcycle boots and drag your feet. Decelerating from 70 mph to a dead stop requires 253 feet—the worst figure *Car and Driver* has reported since its last Hummer test, in July 1992. And speaking of feet, mine weren't happy during my daily 60-mile round-trip commute. The heater (whose controls have been lifted from my 1994 Chevrolet Suburban but should have been based on the simpler and and more effective controls in my '95 Chevy C/K pickup) is of the fry-one-leg-and-freeze-the-other variety. It recalls vehicular memories, but only to those of us who have been around for a while. My mother always told me that if I couldn't say something good about someone, I shouldn't say anything at all. And the United States Army taught me that I shouldn't report a problem without suggesting a solution.

So let me first say good things about the Hummer. The finish is first-rate, exactly as it should be for a vehicle costing $71,760 that seeks to hang out in country club parking lots competing with Range Rovers. Moreover, if you get stuck in traffic, the Hummer has huge steel hooks fore and aft, with which you can be plucked skyward by a cargo helicopter and loaded easily aboard a ship. In addition, no one wants to mess with you when you're driving a Hummer. Buy a red one and they figure you're with the fire department. Blue paint hints of a police department. And black? Well, a black Hummer is something from the DEA's SWAT team, no question about it. Loom up in their rear-view mirrors and watch them give way.

You can get girls with the Hummer, too. The problem is, once you've got one on board, what can you do with her? The Hummer is so wide (86.5 inches, making it 10 inches wider than a Chevy Caprice), the driver is in Washington, D.C. and the passenger is in Baltimore. Seriously, if you stretch out your right arm and your

newfound girlfriend signals a left turn, you just might be able to grasp hands over the immense drivetrain tunnel that separates the front seats. The huge lids covering the drivetrain, fore and aft, serve as a giant bundling board. Mothers nationwide can relax.

As for solutions, a better engine for the civilian Hummer already reposes under the hood of my Suburban: a 454-cubic-inch big-block. If that engine engenders fuel-economy fears, well, the Hummer's current small-block can't do any better than seven to nine miles per gallon—and that was predominantly freeway driving. (Given the vehicle's wildly pessimistic fuel gauge, we thus had a Beltway cruising range of only 135 miles.) Given my experience with big-block Suburbans, the larger engine, doing the same job without working up such a sweat, would do as well on fuel economy and probably better. And it would add a dose of testosterone in the bargain. The Hummer also needs bigger brake rotors, a set of flashy Brembos would be nice, if only for the image. And someone at AM General is going to have to cut through the bureaucratic red tape and dispense with all the politically correct placards in the cockpit, letting those of us who know which end of the tube the round comes out of enjoy the heavy iron.

This evil monster came into my possession shortly after the White House had been shot up, front and rear, and had been kamikazied by a Cessna. So we figured the President and her consort would be a bit edgy. We thus circumnavigated the Chief Executive's mansion several times, imagining Bill and Hillary peering through the curtains and muttering, "Oh God, what now?" as they rang frantically for the Secret Service.

See, you thought I was rehabilitated. In your dreams, baby. For once, *The Washington Post* was correct. When AM General gets the civilian version of the Hummer right, then Lord Vader wants one. In black, of course. Oh, how I love the dark side.

February 1997
Chevrolet Corvette

If, as they say, God is in the details, then this is the first holy Corvette. Chevrolet has presented new Corvettes that have stimulated our cranial synapses with exotic new technology, elevated our pulses with bump-and-grind styling, and sent our adrenal glands into overload with tire-scorching performance, but this new 1997 model is the first Corvette that presses all of our livable and useful buttons with its relentless attention to detail and meticulous engineering. Corvettes, of course, have always delivered tremendous performance for the buck. But purists have tended to dismiss this value by reciting the litany of quality and refinement shortcomings that accompanied it. With the C5, that list is suddenly very short indeed.

—*Csaba Csere*

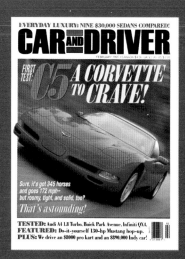

June 1999
Cadillac de Ville Popemobile
Zero to 60 in an eternity
(Hey, who's in a hurry?)

And Jesus showed us the way to the popemobile. No, not that Jesus. This Jesus—it's pronounced "hay-soos"—is the deeply tanned, smiling golf pro at the club de golf, which amounts to a few dozen acres of Mexico City's most prized real estate, full of bent grass and wealthy citizens wearing Ben Hogan caps and smoking big cigars. If you've ever driven in Mexico City traffic, even behind the wheel of one of the zillions of wheezing little Volkswagen Beetles that seem to account for at least half the cars in this overloaded city, you can appreciate the difficulty General Motors de México faced when we asked the folks there to find a nice spot where we could test-drive the Cadillac popemobile, which was commissioned for Pope John Paul II's visit last January. They turned to Jesus and the club de golf, where the blacktopped cart trails are just big enough for a de Ville that has been stretched 34 inches beyond its already horizon-challenging 209.8 inches. So we spent the better part of

an afternoon terrorizing golfers, but what were they gonna do—curse the popemobile? Some even removed their Ben Hogan caps when we passed by, which we saluted with an appropriate papal wave. Jesus thought it was cute. Jesus the golf pro. The Cadillac popemobile was built solely for the pope's appearance before some 100,000 worshipers at the Estadio Azteca, a sports stadium. Millions more Mexicans came to see him during a less exclusive appearance at the local Formula 1 racetrack, leading to speculation that Indianapolis Motor Speedway honcho Tony George may invite the pope to the Formula 1 race at Indianapolis in 2000, in hopes of drawing a big crowd. GM de México's little design studio sketched out the popemobile in record time. "We had just three weeks," said Humberto Ortiz, creative designer, who at one time built school buses. It was an honor, said de Ville brand manager Patrick Kemp. "This is a continuation of Cadillac's long history of providing vehicles for world leaders." After all, Kemp said, "Cadillac provides 90 percent of Americans' diplomatic vehicles at embassies and consulates worldwide." Why, of course it does. Ortiz and his team designed the car to the Vatican's specifications, then sent the plans to aftermarket suppliers Eureka Coach of Norwalk, Ohio, and Roush Industries

of Livonia, Michigan, for conversion. (Admirably, Roush fought the temptation to install one of its NASCAR Winston Cup engines in place of the 275-horsepower Northstar V-8.) They whacked off the Caddy's roof, then added 34 inches to the rear door area. The driver's-side rear door folds down into a step-up-to-the-throne-like chair that looms above the back seat. The entire platform that chair sits on rises and lowers a distance of one foot, thanks to a hydraulic lift run by a one-horsepower compressor in the trunk. The throne/chair has a U-shaped, fold-up handrail that is probably not a National Highway Traffic Safety Administration-endorsed option, but if the pope isn't safe, who is? You've probably noticed that the pope's favorite color is white. And most everything inside is covered in white leather. The Vatican logo is stitched into the seat and affixed to the doors. Yellow flags fly from the front fenders: You get your choice of rigid, always-erect flags, or conventional cloth flags that flutter with the breeze. Despite the fact that the pope will soon release his own compact disc—we are not making that up—the Cadillac popemobile had no compact disc player! (That's worth an exclamation point, isn't it?) But that may be rectified before the de Ville is delivered to the Vatican, where it will join the papal fleet, which includes a half-dozen four-ton armored vehicles, apparently for use in countries where His Holiness is more likely to run into lunatics. Like, in Italy. On the road, or on the golf-cart trail, you have a commanding view from the elevated rear seat, though you're vulnerable to any number of insect, or errant golf ball hits. Small price to pay as you practice your little cupped-hand, then arm-extended papal waves. Behind the wheel, you are immediately aware that this is one large and heavy Cadillac. The Northstar was up to the weighty task, and we were well on our way to a respectable 0-to-60-mph time when we had to brake suddenly for a golf cart driven by a presumed agnostic who very nearly became a believer as a 20-foot topless Cadillac barreled toward him. Fore! No one at General Motors seems to know exactly how many pesos it cost to design the popemobile in Mexico, have it built in the Midwest, then flown to Mexico City—all in just six weeks, and all for a very short trip around the inside of a soccer stadium—but it seems pleased with the publicity the vehicle generated. "The Cadillac market in Mexico is growing every day," Ortiz said. We can testify to this: It makes a dang nice golf cart.

—*Steve Cole Smith*

OPPOSITE: Noted author Smith assumes the pontifical stance. The chair he's seating on is raised and lowered via a dashboard switch.
BELOW, LEFT: Pope John Paul II during his visit to Mexico.
BELOW: Rear door opens to reveal trick chair. The steps are manually operated.

Another Roadside Attraction: See Mother's Bloomers

By Patrick Bedard

For a good time in Texas, call 1-800-452-9292. A nice lady on the other end of the line will tell you where the wildflowers are blooming their little hearts out so you can drive over and ooh at Mother Nature's latest screen saver. Texas doesn't have an exclusive on Mother's spring show, of course, but the state has been tending its roadside flowers since the 1930s, and now it's inviting tourists to come get an eyeful; mid-March through May is peak season.

Dare I hijack a page from this journal of full-throttle motoring passions to talk about ditches full of flowers? If next month finds me sent down to the minors, playing on a *Better Homes and Gardens* farm team, you'll know the gasoline rushing through my veins was found to have dropped below Mr. Csere's minimum octane requirement. But spring is here and the screaming yellow coreopsis are nodding their heads in agreement with all of my thoughts and I'm caught up in nature's annual coming-out party.

Hell, I'm even going to say nice things about the government departments that tend the roads. These wildflower shows get a lot of human help. I called the Departments of Transportation in five states, and every one has an enthusiastic flower guy heading a posy program. Texas puts out 60,000 pounds of wildflower seeds each year, Florida about 20,000. All these departments do their best to midwife their native wildflowers, helping them reseed themselves.

These programs have a practical side. Native plants root eagerly, serving as a first line of defense against soil erosion. And the mowers have a good excuse to skip the blooming months, thereby easing the budget. Flowers are proven effective against road rage, too, so we won't be needing President Clinton's plan for 100,000 cops with tranquilizer darts on the interstate highway system.

Mostly, though, the programs exist because "the public likes the look," says Don Ferrington, Louisiana's Johnny Appleseed for coreopsis. Doing projects of civic beauty is the mark of a great culture. Much has been written about marble monuments from Greek and Roman times, and we keep trucking granite into our own Washington, D.C. But the best tribute to a democratic society is surely the civic beauty that comes right out to the ordinary people. Imagine a 200-mile corridor lushly carpeted with pink and rose-red Drummond phlox. That's the festival of color that rushes in through your windshield as you drive I-75 between Tampa and the Georgia border this time of year. It cannot match the Parthenon for staying power, but as a timely reminder that not all of our tax dollars are wasted, it surely does more for the nation's good than another pillared building named after some pork-barrel politician.

Wildflowers remind us of something else, too. No matter how clever we are, humans are still in a joint venture with Mother Nature. And she has the veto. Ferrington says

Louisiana started by planting a variety of pretty flowers, but many gave up or were crowded out within a few years, leaving mostly the ones Mother Nature assigned to that area in the first place. The native garden-variety coreopsis is "very competitive," he says. Look for brilliant yellow blooms with brown centers.

Generally, Mother seems to like coreopsis best; the lance-leaved variant with its all-yellow daisy-like blooms has spread over North America from its native territory east of the Rockies. If the yellow bloom has a daub of maroon in the center, that's tickseed coreopsis. Swamp coreopsis has pink petals around yellow centers. Coreopsis is the state wildflower of Florida and Mississippi.

Not surprisingly, the "state wildflower" does especially well in its own state. The yellow rose of Texas gets great PR, but the blue-bonnet has the title and it likes Texas best, shooting up its spike of densely packed indigo blooms over most of Lone Star territory. Oklahoma is home of big red daisies with lemon-tipped petals, a gaillardia variation called Indian blanket. Kansas is the Sunflower State. California shares its state flower, the golden poppy, with other southwestern states; look for brilliant orange cups atop bluish-green foliage.

Roadsides, of course, aren't the only places wildflowers can grow. Maybe you're tired of mowing the front yard. One of the largest seed sources for state road crews is Wildseed Farms (800-848-0078; www.wildseedfarms.com), which also fills small orders for greenthumbers.

Although I've steered this page way off the pavement, let me reassure you that *Car and Driver* remains the testiest of all the car magazines, and nothing escapes our judgmental procedures. I know you've been wondering: What's the best roadside wildflower? My 100-point editor's rating goes to (drum roll, please) Phlox drummondii. From a distance, you see candy reds, pinks, and whites growing low, hugging Earth's contours. Up close, perfectly proportioned five-petal blooms cluster together, punching up the color, multiplying it like joyous little massively parallel processors. What spirit! There's more. This wild phlox "escaped from cultivation," says the Audubon Society Field Guide to North American Wildflowers, and now happily roams over the southeast U.S. from Florida to Texas.

Hurrah for liberated phlox, too energetic, too spunky, to remain in confinement behind the gardeners' fences. We humans escape confinement our own way on our wheels. And now we kindred spirits, we fellow escapees, all crowd to the same getaway routes, steering along the pavement, the phlox crowding up close on the shoulders, waving in the breeze of each passing car. I always wave back.

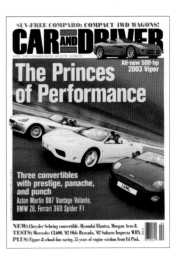

April 2001
A Pilgrimage to Maranello

By John Pearley Huffman

Italy is more than shaped like a boot. More than the world's best kitchen.
More than the creative center of the universe's fashion and design industries.
More than chock-full of fabulous, olive-skinned babes. More important
than its art, drama, and intellectual contributions, Italy has Ferrari. It's nearly
enough to make one overlook fascism.

Unlike the Vatican, Ferrari's factory in Maranello isn't a separate city-state, but it's approached with similar reverence and has more security. And whereas remembering the names of all the saints is tough, there's yet to be a less-than-memorable Ferrari: glorious creations forged from metal, genius, gall, and racing legend. Even if you've never driven one, names like Lusso, GTO, Daytona, and Testarossa shudder your spine and shackle your heart. Each prowls the world's streets and racetracks inspiring epiphany.

Until his death in 1988, "Il Commendatore," Enzo Ferrari, ruled his namesake company, like the pope, with presumed infallibility; but now it's almost wholly owned by Fiat. Has this changed the soul of the world's greatest automotive-sex-machine builder? That question was our excuse to drain the travel budget. We've done a zillion "Inside Ferrari" articles, but good story ideas are rare, and we enjoy the trip.

Our Alitalia jumbo settled at Rome's Da Vinci airport, and we found our guide: Ferrari test driver Luigi Magarelli. Luigi, of Mediterranean charm, Formula 1-level driving skills, and Italian legal-system intimacy, proved invaluable during our visit. We were off on our "pilgrimage to Maranello."

The roads to Maranello cross the verdant Tuscan hills and are the same ones traveled in the legendary Mille Miglia. Imagine Stirling Moss and Denis Jenkinson racing down these country lanes at 160 mph in a Mercedes 300SLR! Although the race is gone, the beauty of the countryside remains, and the peasants are quick with legendary hospitality. We couldn't resist stopping at local merchants for delightful food and the abstract expressionist handicrafts.

At Da Vinci airport, we were surprised that it seemed much smaller than we had remembered it. No matter, our hearts surged in our chests when we saw a new 550 Maranello and a classic 365GTB Daytona awaiting us curbside. We'd have the unique opportunity to compare the two eras of the great marque! Our Samsonite luggage apparently offended Italian aesthetic sensibilities and was never seen again.

There was little room for it in the cars anyhow.

Can any sight excite an enthusiast more than the shipping dock at Ferrari? There are acres of Ferraris ready for final inspection and anxiously awaiting export. All travel aboard Ferrari's own fleet of specially fitted ships from the docks at Maranello, which are unique in the inland province of Modena. Some will go to America, some to the Middle East, a few to Africa or Australia. Wherever they go, they will be cherished.

299

Editor's Note: Just out of grad school in 1989 and looking for a job, John Pearley Huffman put together "A Pilgrimage to Maranello" as part of a magazine parody and sent it, along with his résumé, to 80 publications. He got four job offers, took one at *Car Craft*, and since 1993 has been a freelance writer.

Finally, we arrived at the main gate of Ferrari's Maranello factory, familiar from "Il Commendatore"'s Goodyear tire commercial in the late '80s. We felt instantly at home—despite the presence of this large and particularly ferocious guard dog.

Inside the factory, craftsmen skillfully use hands trained in ancient coachbuilding techniques to mold the latest space-age polymers and bonding compounds into Ferraris. The introduction of Japanese-style just-in-time inventory controls has resulted in the neatly organized shop depicted here.

H ere our guide, Luigi Magarelli, enjoys a plate of fine pasta and a bottle of vividly flavored table vino at the legendary Il Cavallino Ristorante (named for the Ferrari prancing-horse emblem) across from the factory. We enjoyed many such repasts with Magarelli, where he regaled us with stories of romantic conquest and automotive derring-do. Upon returning stateside, though, it was discovered that Magarelli had seduced this writer's wife.

A visit to the great man's personal office, preserved just as it was when he ran the company, is similar to entering a basilica. Among the art is the gorgeous fresco on, of all places, the ceiling! The painting depicts the mythic moment God told Enzo to leave Alfa and build His own cars.

Unfortunately, the trip ended with this introduction to Italian authorities.

Fortunately, with Magarelli's help and Italy's complex extradition laws, the charges have not followed us home.

Ultimately, a visit to Ferrari's factory enhances the legend, and we left with warm arrivedercis in our ears and the hope in our hearts that we'll once again return. Is next month too soon? Not for us.

July 2003
Ferrari Enzo
**An F1 car, a tough old man
in sunglasses, and 75 years of
glory stuffed into one
easy-to-swallow capsule**
THE VERDICT
Highs: Perfect steering, perfect brakes, perfect handling,
perfect power. (Did we mention that it's just about perfect?)
Lows: The oil costs $60 a quart, the brake pads $6,000,
and its nose is easily bruised.
The Verdict: If this isn't your dream car, you're having the
wrong dreams.

—Aaron Robinson

Credits